Public Financing
in American Elections

PUBLIC FINANCING
in AMERICAN ELECTIONS

EDITED BY Costas Panagopoulos

TEMPLE UNIVERSITY PRESS   PHILADELPHIA

TEMPLE UNIVERSITY PRESS
Philadelphia, Pennsylvania 19122
www.temple.edu/tempress

Library of Congress Cataloging-in-Publication Data

Public financing in American elections / edited by Costas Panagopoulos.
   p. cm.
 Includes bibliographical references and index.
 ISBN 978-1-4399-0692-7 (cloth : alk. paper) — ISBN 978-1-4399-0693-4
(pbk. : alk. paper) — ISBN 978-1-4399-0694-1 (e-book)
 1. Campaign funds—United States. 2. Elections—United States. I. Panagopoulos, Costas.
JK1991.P82 2011
 324.7'8—dc22

                                                              2010046508

♾ The paper used in this publication meets the requirements of the American National
Standard for Information Sciences—Permanence of Paper for Printed Library Materials,
ANSI Z39.48-1992

Dedicated to my brother, Tim—

With love and gratitude for your generosity
and for all you do to enable me to do what I do

Contents

Preface   *ix*

Introduction · COSTAS PANAGOPOULOS   *1*

PART I The Lay of the Land:
Public Financing in the American States

1 Back to the Future? The Quest for Public Financing
  of Congressional Campaigns · R. SAM GARRETT   *11*

2 Small Donors, Large Donors, and the Internet:
  Rethinking Public Financing for Presidential Elections
  after Obama · MICHAEL MALBIN   *36*

3 Public Financing in the States and Municipalities
  · ROBERT M. STERN   *62*

4 Public Attitudes toward Publicly Financed Elections,
  1972–2008 · STEPHEN R. WEISSMAN AND RUTH A. HASSAN
  (WITH ASSISTANCE FROM JACK SANTUCCI)   *124*

PART II The Consequences of Public Financing

5 Campaign Finance Reform Reconsidered: New York City's
  Public Finance Program at Twenty · JEFFREY KRAUS   *147*

6 Leveling the Playing Field: Publicly Financed Campaigns
and Electoral Competition · COSTAS PANAGOPOULOS   *176*

7 Public Financing and Candidate Participation in Gubernatorial
Elections · CONOR DOWLING   *184*

8 Public Money, Candidate Time, and Electoral Outcomes
in State Legislative Elections · MICHAEL G. MILLER   *205*

9 Does Public Financing of State Election Campaigns Increase
Voter Turnout? · JEFFREY MILYO, DAVID M. PRIMO, AND
MATTHEW L. JACOBSMEIER   *225*

10 Public Financing, Attitudes toward Government and Politics,
and Efficacy · MICHAEL G. MILLER AND COSTAS PANAGOPOULOS   *238*

Conclusion: The Future of Public Financing
in American Elections · COSTAS PANAGOPOULOS   *249*

Contributors   *251*

Index   *253*

Preface

In 1992, while I was an undergraduate at Harvard College, I ran for the Massachusetts House of Representatives to represent my home district in Middlesex County. I challenged an incumbent who had held the seat for the prior ten years. Through the valiant efforts of a deeply dedicated volunteer campaign staff, we managed to raise and spend about $20,000 over the course of the campaign. My opponent, on the other hand, spent over $80,000, outspending me by about a margin of four-to-one.

I ended up losing the election by a few percentage points of the vote. Over the years, I have often wondered if access to more resources could have changed the outcome of that election. Additional campaign funds would have enabled us to communicate more with voters via radio and newspaper advertising, direct mail, and phone calls. Perhaps we could have bought more lawn signs and bumper stickers or had adequate funds to procure professional campaign services. And maybe, on election day, these could have made a difference.

This was a long time ago, and I rarely indulge in these speculations of late. But in every election cycle there are overmatched candidates fighting uphill battles against better-financed opponents. I would argue a majority of candidates are in this camp, most often challengers seeking to unseat incumbents. One wonders how different election outcomes—and maybe even democracy *writ large*—would be in America if policies were in place to level the playing fields of available resources for candidates in races across the board and across the country.

Public financing programs for campaigns aim to bring us closer to that reality. Over the past few decades, there has been marked proliferation of these programs in states and localities nationwide, and there are efforts afoot to expand public financing to federal elections.

A leading example of a pioneering program of public financing of campaigns was established in New York City in 1988. In February 2008, the Center for Electoral Politics and Democracy at Fordham University, which I founded and direct, co-organized and hosted a day-long conference to commemorate the twenty-year anniversary of the New York City program. The event was attended by luminaries and scholars; politicians, including former New York City mayor Ed Koch, former U.S. senator Bob Kerrey, and former U.S. representative Chris Shays; and advocates, and it was an occasion to reflect on public financing in U.S. campaigns. Exchanges at the event and the stimulating debates that ensued set the stage for the creation of this volume. It is compiled to help demystify the landscape of public financing of campaigns in America and to evaluate their impact and effectiveness along several dimensions.

I am deeply grateful to the many top-rate scholars whose contributions fill the pages that follow. I also thank colleagues and administrators at Fordham for their strong support for the conference and for the Center for Electoral Politics and Democracy. I am indebted to the staff at Temple University Press, including Gary Kramer and Joan Vidal, and to Micah Kleit and Nancy Lombardi in particular, for embracing this project and for invaluable assistance that allowed the production process to progress seamlessly. As always, I am sublimely grateful for the inspiration fueled by my family's unending love and support that makes this work possible.

Costas Panagopoulos, Ph.D.
New York City

Introduction

COSTAS PANAGOPOULOS

I n any democratic polity, vigilance is necessary to ensure that the electoral process is unsullied and legitimate. In the United States, concern about the role and influence of money in the electoral arena has made campaign finance a focal point for assessing the vigor and vitality of the democratic process. The focus of many reforms designed to avoid corruption—or the appearance of corruption—revolves around campaign finance issues. In recent decades, one category of policy initiatives, public financing of elections, has become an increasingly popular approach in jurisdictions across the nation as a means of diminishing the potential for the corruptive influence of money in elections. This volume examines public financing in American elections.

Money alone does not ensure electoral victory, but candidates for offices at all levels of government pursue fund-raising tenaciously. Fund-raising is typically an essential first step; without funds, campaigns cannot be competitive. Staffs, advertising, office space, and other expenditures are essential to nearly all campaigns, and the costs increase correspondingly over the duration of the campaign.

As campaign costs escalate, candidates increasingly prioritize campaign financing. The money must come from somewhere, and the most effective advocates for any campaign tend to be the candidates themselves. So candidates must use valuable time that might otherwise be spent holding press conferences, meeting with constituent groups, or boning up on issues to "dial for dollars" and otherwise massage donors (often wealthy or influential power brokers) for contributions.

There is concern about the effect that this process has on American democracy. Critics argue that the growing emphasis on fund-raising renders donors more important than voters and ordinary citizens and that this compromises the legislative process and ideals of representation in the United States. Political action committees (PACs), 527s, and other organizations, many of which are nationally based but may contribute to or advocate for a campaign based on the candidate's position on a single issue, are often especially frustrating for local voters who may feel shoved out of the way for an interest group based across the country. Citizen disillusionment with politics generally and the role of money in elections specifically is rampant.

For their part, the candidates are generally just as bemused at how the game is played. Given the choice, most politicians would much rather immerse themselves in the other aspects of campaigning—*any* other aspect of campaigning—than the repetitive and awkward money grab. Recently, there have been several high-profile examples of how powerful the very specter of fund-raising can be in determining who will even participate in certain elections. When appointing Secretary of State Hillary Clinton's successor in the U.S. Senate, New York Governor David Patterson bypassed several high-profile aspirants in favor of a little-known congresswoman from upstate, Representative Kirsten Gillibrand, in part because of her demonstrated fund-raising prowess (Powell and Hernandez 2009). And when California's Lieutenant Governor John Garamendi was asked about his decision to seek a seat in Congress rather than follow the more conventional path to the governorship, he put it this way: "I thought, how am I going to spend two valuable years of my life? Am I going spend two years dialing for dollars, or am I going to spend four months out ringing doorbells and campaigning person to person and the other 20 months working on issues?" (McKinley 2009).

As public frustration with current campaign finance practices has soared, reformers have turned to a variety of initiatives to ameliorate conditions. Sweeping changes to the federal campaign finance laws were adopted in 2002, for example. The legislation championed by Senators John McCain (R-AZ) and Russ Feingold (D-WI) and signed into law by President George W. Bush raised the dollar-amount ceilings on certain types of donations, but outlawed other types altogether. For example, corporations and unions were no longer permitted to directly finance television commercials that mention a federal candidate.

Public Financing of Elections

One class of reforms—public financing of campaigns—has been adopted in several states and municipalities across the nation. The mechanisms and conditions vary, but the general operating principle of public finance in the

United States is that a candidate agrees to certain conditions (i.e., to not raise or spend more than a certain amount of money) in order to receive money from the corresponding jurisdiction's public coffers. As of 2008, nearly half of the fifty states offered some form of public funding in at least one election. Most states provide matching funds to candidates or parties; others utilize various mechanisms of partial public financing, in which candidates receive subsidies that constitute a percentage of campaign costs. Full funding, wherein the candidates' funds are almost totally composed of public money, has become more common; in 2008, it was offered in at least some elections in six states and also in two major metropolitan elections.

Behind all these different public finance programs, however, lies the same goal: to return elected officials to their electors—the constituency. Advocates of public election financing believe these initiatives will improve democracy and electoral politics. If the public program's spending limits prevent excessive fund-raising (or in some cases, prevent fund-raising altogether), the argument goes, the winner of the election will not owe his or her seat to special-interest donors but rather to the community. Reducing the role of private contributions also frees up the candidate to participate in other aspects of the campaign, such as spending time with the voters and learning about the issues that are important to them.

Public finance advocates also argue that these programs enhance citizens' attitudes toward government and the political process. They assert a more active role for voters, who effectively assume an ownership stake in the publicly funded campaigns. Voters thus have a higher degree of interest in the election, which is theoretically sustained by the high level of accessibility to publicly funded candidates. Come election day, voter turnout should be higher, since a relatively higher percentage of the public has invested in the candidates and the candidates have repaid that investment by focusing on the problems and priorities of the public. Unfortunately, these claims have been difficult to evaluate because of the dearth of scholarly research on the impact of public finance.

Public Financing in Presidential Elections

Interestingly, while public programs continue to grow in states and municipalities across the United States, many are predicting the demise of public financing in presidential elections. In recent years, presidential candidates have shown increasing reluctance to submit to the spending limits attached to eligibility for the public program. In 1996, Steve Forbes became the first high-profile contender for a major party presidential nomination to refuse public funds for the primary election; four years later, George W. Bush became the first major party nominee to do so. In 2004, Bush again opted out, joined by Democrat front-runners John Kerry and Howard Dean. The 2008 campaign saw all the front-runners refuse public funds for the primary season.[1] Senator Barack Obama took the eschewal of public finance to the final step, became the first major party nominee to refuse public money for the general election. Consequently, his opponent, the publicly funded Senator McCain, found himself massively outspent, outmanned, and outbroadcast (Cummings 2008).

In the wake of his loss, Senator McCain has publicly ruminated about the future of presidential public finance. An outspoken advocate of campaign finance reform, McCain recently declared, "No Republican in his or her right mind is going to agree to public financing. I mean, that's dead. That is over. The last candidate for president of the United States from a major party that will take public financing was me" (Curl and Dinan 2009).

On this point, there are signs of growing consensus. Newspaper editorial boards, long a bastion of support for public finance, roundly criticized Senator Obama for reneging on his pledge to accept public financing for the general election. Nevertheless, a majority of them eventually endorsed his candidacy for president over that of Senator McCain. And the national electorate, whom the public program was designed to protect, seemed quite willing to overlook Obama's transgression. A historic number of Americans rained money on the campaign, mostly in modest amounts. As the candidate himself put it, "We have created a parallel public finance system" (Tapper 2008). While Senator Obama's war chest expanded, participation in the real public finance program through the tax checkoff plummeted to a historic low. The 2008 presidential election was by far the most expensive in history, and yet the winner's victory was decisive. Thus, despite Americans' insistence to pollsters that they are fed up with the role money plays in elections, the real story seems a bit more complicated.

The Need for Scholarly Analysis

Even as a growing number of jurisdictions adopt public finance programs and the future of the presidential public program continues to be debated, comprehensive scholarly investigations about the impact of these reforms remain scarce. Lawmakers and activists considering similar policy options often debate the value of public financing reforms with only minimal and inconclusive empirical evidence. The growth in experimentation with public financing programs provides an unprecedented opportunity to embark on scholarly reflection and analysis about the range of reform options and their political effects. This is the primary goal of this book.

This volume brings together detailed description and rigorous analysis of public financing programs. The selections reflect the insights of leading scholars at the forefront of academic campaign finance research and provide the most up-to-date thinking about public finance reforms. The authors explore the variation in public financing reforms and proposals at the local, state, and federal levels to provide a comprehensive understanding of public financing initiatives in the United States and their impact. They also present focused analyses of several of the public programs currently in existence, offering the benefit of data and conclusions arrived at scientifically. Simply put, this volume aims to remove much of the guesswork from the discussion about public finance.

Of course, the conclusions arrived at in these chapters do not unanimously support one side of the debate over another. Rather, they lay the foundation from which a solid consideration of public finance may be made. Such a foundation is of critical importance and immense use to pundits, campaign operatives, political scientists, legislators, and anyone else desiring to approach the convoluted realm of public finance armed with the best available research from the field's keenest scholars.

Plan for the Book

The volume is divided into two parts. Part I is primarily descriptive and presents an overview of public financing programs across the country. In Chapter 1, R. Sam Garrett, a researcher at the Congressional Research Service, focuses on initiatives at the federal level and examines the historical and legislative precedents for public financing. Garrett begins with an overview of the current state of federal campaign finance, and then traces the landmark public finance bills of the twentieth century, as well as the arguments for and against public finance that accompanied them. He concludes with a look to the future of the congressional public financing legislation.

In Chapter 2, Michael Malbin, one of the nation's leading campaign finance experts and executive director of the Campaign Finance Institute in Washington, DC, considers the state of public financing at the presidential level. Malbin discusses the shortcomings of the system as it currently exists and offers extensive evidence from recent election cycles. He also deconstructs the goals of presidential-election public financing and discusses the practicality of each. The chapter additionally offers an overview of several major proposals to overhaul the system.

Chapter 3, by Robert M. Stern, a leading authority on the topic and president of the Center for Governmental Studies, offers a comprehensive look at the range of public financing programs in place in states and municipalities across the United States. The author breaks down the principal variations among the programs, such as the source of the money in the public pot and the strings attached to it. The chapter also features an extensive set of tables that show all of the different state and local jurisdictions with public financing programs and the stipulations particular to each.

In Chapter 4, the Campaign Finance Institute's Stephen R. Weissman and Ruth A. Hassan evaluate levels of public support for clean elections programs. The authors analyze available survey data and consider trends over time. They also speak to the apparent discrepancy between support for the concept of public financing and actual participation in these programs.

In Part II, the chapters examine the consequences of public financing on electoral competition, candidate behavior, and citizens' attitudes and political activity. The analyses advanced by the authors reflect rigorous and systematic examination of empirical evidence and represent the most up-to-date assessments of these crucial questions.

In Chapter 5, Jeffrey Kraus discusses the ramifications of the New York City Campaign Finance Act. The chapter first recounts the circumstances that led to the law's passage. Kraus then explains the details of the 1988 legislation and evaluates its effectiveness at meeting each of the stated objectives. Finally, the chapter includes an overview of the changes for the 2009 election cycle and Kraus's analysis of the general success of the act.

In Chapter 6, I present evidence from recent field experimental studies to evaluate the likely effects of public funding programs on electoral competition.

Chapter 7, by Conor Dowling, a postdoctoral fellow at Yale University, examines the impact of public funding on candidate behavior in gubernatorial elections.

Michael G. Miller, a political scientist at the University of Illinois at Springfield, uses original survey data to explore the relationship between public financing and candidate behavior in state legislative races in Chapter 8.

The impact of public financing on citizens' attitudes and behavior is considered in the following two chapters. In Chapter 9, Jeffrey Milyo, David M. Primo, and Matthew L. Jacobsmeier investigate whether or not public financing influences voter turnout. In Chapter 10, Michael Miller and I analyze the impact of public funding on attitudes toward government and elected officials and, more generally, on citizens' levels of political efficacy.

The final chapter presents a brief discussion and conclusions.

In sum, and by way of preview, the chapters in this volume reveal the richness and variation of public funding programs across the United States. The analyses conducted by the authors also suggest there may be limits to what public funding programs can achieve.

NOTE

1. Senator McCain, the eventual Republican nominee and architect of campaign finance reform, finally decided to opt out of the public program only after his campaign conducted a protracted, public calculation of his fund-raising prospects. At various points during the primary cycle, he was out of public system, then applied to the Federal Election Commission for public funds, was granted them but did not collect, and then decided once again to opt out. The McCain campaign's sudden departure from the public program drew the ire of the FEC, which in February 2008 contended that its own approval was required for such a departure to be legal (Mason 2008). The commission, after finally gaining a quorum in June, unanimously voted in August to release Senator McCain from the public program for the primary (Renick Mayer 2008).

REFERENCES

Cummings, Jeanne. 2008. "2008 Campaign Costliest in U.S. History." *Politico*, November 5. Available at http://www.politico.com/news/stories/1108/15283_Page2.html.

Curl, Joseph, and Stephen Dinan. 2009. "McCain: Public Financing Is 'Dead.'" *Washington Times*, March 29.

Editorial Board. 2008a. "A Reformer's Progress." *Wall Street Journal*, June 20, p. A12.

———. 2008b. "Public Funding on the Ropes." *New York Times*, June 20.

Mason, David M. 2008. "Letter to Senator John McCain." Federal Election Commission, February 19. Available at http://www.fec.gov/press/press2008/FECtoMcCain.PDF.

McKinley, Jesse. 2009. "Congressional Race in California Draws a High-Profile Cast." *New York Times*, July 3, p. A10.

Powell, Michael, and Raymond Hernandez. 2009. "Senate Choice: Folksy Centrist Born to Politics." *New York Times*, January 23, p. A1.

Renick Mayer, Lindsay. 2008. "FEC Frees McCain from Primary Public Financing." Center for Responsive Politics, August 21. Available at http://www.opensecrets.org/news/2008/08/fec-frees-mccain-from-primary.html.

Tapper, Jake. 2008. "Obama Prepares Argument to Discard Public Financing Principle." *ABC News* Online, April 8. Available at http://blogs.abcnews.com/politicalpunch/2008/04/obama-prepares.html.

I
The Lay of the Land

*Public Financing
in the American States*

1

⬦ ⬦ ⬦

Back to the Future?

The Quest for Public Financing of Congressional Campaigns

R. SAM GARRETT

In his 1907 message to Congress, President Theodore Roosevelt proposed what he called "a very radical measure," one that he conceded would "take some time" to consider: the public financing of federal campaigns (Roosevelt 1907, 78).[1] The president argued that "the need for collecting large [private] campaign funds would vanish if Congress provided an appropriation for the proper and legitimate expenses of each of the great national parties" sufficient to run campaigns. Roosevelt's proposal, however, was not without strings. He stipulated that, in exchange for public money, "no party receiving funds from the Treasury should accept more than a fixed amount from any individual" in private funds. This first proposal for public funding was limited to presidential campaigns,[2] but its effect could have been easily translated to congressional campaigns because, in Roosevelt's day, political parties were the major forces in electoral politics.

In some ways, Roosevelt's proposal could not be farther from the public financing debates of in recent years. First and foremost, it is unlikely that parties could today be a feasible mechanism for funding thousands of individualized federal campaigns. Indeed, limits on "coordinated" campaign expenditures would prevent parties from communicating with campaigns

This chapter represents the views of the author. It does not necessarily represent the views of the Congressional Research Service, the Library of Congress, or any other institution with which the author is affiliated.

in some circumstances.[3] More generally, the candidate-centered campaign has allegedly led to a decline in the importance of political parties, often in favor of political consultants (Shea and Burton 2001; Garrett 2010a). Although national parties continue to play large fund-raising roles, candidate campaigns are now much more involved in their own financial fates than they would have been in Roosevelt's era (La Raja 2008).

Even the form of Roosevelt's message today seems antiquated. His call for public financing amounted to a relatively brief paragraph among a laundry list of legislative recommendations on topics ranging from the military to public health. What was then a written message to Congress would today be known as the State of the Union address, a prime-time, televised event that generally focuses on a few major themes.

But another look suggests that this first public financing proposal[4] started a conversation that has remained largely consistent for the past century. Public financing still has ardent supporters and fierce opponents. The form and specifics of the debate between those two groups may have changed in the past hundred years, but the core issues remain largely unchanged.

Even in the most active periods of House and Senate support for congressional public financing, the 1970s and 1990s, few observers alleged outright corruption resulting from what one prominent work has labeled the "money chase" of private fund-raising (Magleby and Nelson 1990). Those favoring public financing have generally always contended, however, that *private* financing presents at least the potential for conflicts of interest among lawmakers (or would-be lawmakers). As Roosevelt suggested, concerns of influence peddling are particularly strong when "special interest" money is involved— from corporate and union contributions before modern campaign finance law banned the practices in the early and mid-twentieth century, to political action committee (PAC) money in the 1980s (see, for example, Wertheimer 1986; La Raja 2008). More recently, attention has turned to "bundlers," who critics say provide a new example of circumvention of federal law limiting campaign contributions.[5] Against this backdrop, public financing proponents suggest that only eliminating or significantly curtailing private money in politics can ensure that lawmakers and candidates are not beholden to a relatively few individual donors and PACs. Supporters also view public financing as a means to limit ever-growing campaign spending. Anticorruption efforts and cost containment remain cornerstones of arguments supporting public financing.

Opponents counter that public financing is unnecessary. In particular, they argue that the public simply does not support using taxpayer funds to finance political campaigns (see, for example, McDonald and Samples 2006). They also often suggest that taxpayer funds could be better spent on other needs, that public financing risks wasting money on unqualified or "fringe" candidates, or that viable candidates should be able to attract sufficient support from private contributions. More to the point, opponents say, the need for public financing is not necessarily compelling, or a viable solution is constitutionally unworkable (see, for example, Smith 2001). These perspectives, too, remain hallmarks of the debate.

This chapter explores how the debate over public financing evolved in Congress during the twentieth century and beyond. The following discussion is limited primarily to congressional public financing bills passed by at least one chamber. The first serious public financing proposal, introduced in the mid-1950s, begins the discussion. Congress was particularly focused on public financing during the mid-1970s and again in the early 1990s. Only once, in 1992, have both the House and Senate enacted duplicate public financing legislation for the president's consideration. George H. W. Bush vetoed that measure. Public financing of congressional campaigns received some renewed attention in 2007, during the 110th Congress, but that legislation did not advance beyond a Senate committee hearing. The 111th Congress (2009–2011)—the current Congress as of this writing—also reconsidered proposals to publicly finance House and Senate campaigns.

How Congressional Campaigns Are Financed Today

Before understanding how public financing would change the status quo, it is first essential to understand how campaigns are financed today. Congressional campaigns have never been publicly financed. Instead, they are funded by private contributions from individuals, party committees, and PACs. Most candidates receive support from all three sources. Most candidates also contribute at least some of their own money to their campaigns, although the extent to which they do so varies widely. Each election cycle, a few candidates' campaigns are almost entirely self-financed. Most, however, raise the bulk of their money from other sources. In short, for good or ill, the entire structure of House and Senate campaigns is based on an ingrained system of private financing.

Under the Federal Election Campaign Act (FECA),[6] U.S. citizens and permanent resident aliens ("green card" holders) may contribute to federal campaigns, as may PACs and party campaign committees. The most recent changes to federal contribution limits came with the passage of the 2002 Bipartisan Campaign Reform Act (BCRA), which amended FECA.[7] Also known as McCain-Feingold for its principal Senate sponsors, John McCain (R-AZ) and Russell Feingold (D-WI), BCRA represented the first increase in federal contribution limits since Congress enacted FECA in 1971.[8] BCRA also indexed most federal contribution limits, including the individual limit, for inflation. These changes occurred largely because the $1,000 limit on individual contributions established in FECA was widely viewed as antiquated by the 1990s. Even as the cost of campaigns grew steadily between the 1970s and the early 2000s, federal candidates still had to raise large sums in comparatively small increments under the old limits.

As Table 1.1 shows, for the 2008 cycle, BCRA's inflation-adjustment provisions raised the individual contribution limit to $2,300. As a practical matter, this meant that an individual could give $2,300 *per candidate, per election*, for a total of $4,600 ($2,300 each in the primary and general) to any one federal candidate campaign. If a rare runoff election occurred, another $2,300 could be contributed.[9]

Public financing would represent a dramatic change in the way in which Americans elect politicians. As the preceding discussion suggests, federal campaigns depend heavily on private contributions (and lots of them). As Table 1.2 shows, during the 2008 election cycle, the average winning House candidate raised almost $1.5 million and spent about $1.4 million. Slightly more than half the amount raised (51 percent) was from individual contribu-

TABLE 1.1.   FEDERAL CONTRIBUTION LIMITS, 2008 ELECTION CYCLE

	To Candidate Committees	To National Party Committees	To PACs	Aggregate Limit for Entire Cycle
Individuals	$2,300 per candidate, per election*	$28,500 per calendar year	$5,000 per calendar year	$108,200 ($42,700 to all candidates; $65,500 to parties and PACs)
Party committees	$5,000[†] per candidate, per election	Unlimited	$5,000 per calendar year	Unlimited[§]
PACs[‡]	$5,000 per candidate, per election	$15,000 per calendar year	$5,000 per calendar year	Unlimited

Source: Adapted by the author from Federal Election Commission, "Contribution Limits for 2007–2008," available at http://www.fec.gov/ans/answers_general.shtml#How_much_can_I_contribute; accessed July 5, 2008.

*Individuals may give $2,300 to any one candidate committee during the primary and during the general (and runoff, if applicable) campaigns.

[†]This amount refers to direct contributions, not coordinated party expenditures. Coordinated party expenditures are purchases parties may make on behalf of, and in concert with, candidate campaigns.

[‡]Refers to "multicandidate" PACs, which are the most common type of PAC. Multicandidate PAC status is triggered when these committees make certain aggregate contributions to multiple candidates. For a straightforward discussion of PAC status, see Federal Election Commission (2007, 5).

[§]This excludes a special $39,900 limit for contributions by party committees to Senate campaigns (shared between the party campaign committees and the national committee—e.g., the National Republican Senatorial Committee and the Republican National Committee).

TABLE 1.2.   AVERAGE FUND-RAISING AND SPENDING BY 2008 WINNING
             CONGRESSIONAL CAMPAIGNS

	Average Amount Raised	Average Amount Raised from Individuals	Percent Raised from Individual Contributors	Average Amount Spent
House	$1,472,146	$755,161	51.3	$1,372,591
Senate	$7,297,936	$4,811,856	65.9	$7,539,470

Source: Adapted by the author from Center for Responsive Politics analysis of Federal Election Commission data, available at http://www.opensecrets.org/bigpicture/stats.php?cycle=2008&Type=W&Display=A, accessed September 15, 2010. The author calculated percentages in the "Percent raised from individual contributors" column.

Note: Senate expenditures outpaced receipts. Presumably, funds from the previous cycle explain the "additional" spending.

tors. By contrast, the average winning Senate candidate raised approximately $7.3 million and spent about $7.5 million.[10] Senate candidates raised almost two-thirds of their funds (66 percent) from individuals.

Party committees, PACs, and 527 and 501(c) organizations raised and spent even more.[11] Although some 2008 fund-raising and spending in congressional races was less than comparable amounts in 2006, the overall trend in political money has steadily increased for decades.

As this book was going to press in the fall of 2010, every indication was that 2010 would witness substantial spending. Many experts predicted that "outside" spending would be bolstered by the January 2010 Supreme Court ruling in *Citizens United v. Federal Election Commission*, which permitted corporations and unions to use their treasury funds, for the first time in modern history, to explicitly call for election or defeat of political candidates. The effects of the ruling will take years to definitely sort out, but it almost certainly placed additional pressure on candidates to be financially well armed to fend off criticism not only from opponents but also from outside interests.

What does all this mean for a historical discussion of attempts to enact congressional public financing legislation? First, the financial overview presented in the preceding paragraphs highlights evidence that often appears in ideological debates surrounding public financing. For proponents of public financing, the "money chase" of electoral politics has become all-consuming. And, these observers say, the only way to regain control over political fundraising is to replace or heavily subsidize private money with public money. However, opponents of public financing have not changed their positions either. As the following pages demonstrate, although the specifics of congressional public financing proposals have changed in the past fifty years, ideological differences have remained consistent.

Second, the data reinforce the obvious but nonetheless fundamental point that money is essential in congressional elections. If the private money that

funds campaigns today were to be replaced by public funds, substantial resources would be required. Historically, most public financing legislation
would require those participating in public financing to limit their campaign spending, including spending from the candidate's personal resources.
Some more recent proposals would permit unlimited spending, but private
fund-raising would still be limited. Therefore, campaign spending would not
necessarily be as voluminous under a public financing system as under the
current system of private financing. However, in its landmark *Buckley v. Valeo*
(1976) decision, the U.S. Supreme Court held that limiting candidate spending violated the First Amendment—unless the campaign *voluntarily* limited
its spending in exchange for accepting public financing. In the absence of a
constitutional amendment to the contrary, public financing would uniformly
reduce campaign spending only if all candidates chose to participate.

Therefore, the challenge for public financing supporters becomes creat-
ing a benefits package that is attractive to all candidates and that is constitutionally viable. Constitutional concerns have not always been at the forefront
of the debate, but as we will see, Congress has consistently and sometimes
fiercely debated which provisions public financing legislation should include—and whether public financing should be enacted at all.

An Overview of Congressional
Public Financing Legislation

The House, Senate, or both chambers have passed congressional public financing legislation eight times (excluding conference measures) since 1973.
Table 1.3 summarizes those bills; the remainder of this chapter discusses the
debate surrounding those bills. At the outset, it is important to note that although the legislation that we discuss has advanced farthest in the legislative
process, Congress has also considered dozens or hundreds of other congressional public financing proposals during the past fifty years. In addition, although this discussion emphasizes public financing, the bills at issue often
contained other campaign finance provisions not discussed here.

A First Attempt
at Congressional Public Financing, 1956

Congress first considered legislation to publicly finance its campaigns in the
1950s and 1960s. Specifically, Senator Richard Neuberger (D-OR) introduced
S. 3242 on February 20, 1956. The bill was untitled, but Neuberger called the
legislation the Teddy Roosevelt bill, after the president's 1907 public financing

TABLE 1.3.   CONGRESSIONAL PUBLIC FINANCING BILLS PASSED BY AT LEAST ONE
CHAMBER OF CONGRESS

Legislation	Year of Passage	Congress/ Session	Overview of Major Provisions (congressional public financing only)	Outcome
S.Amdt. 651 to H.R. 11104	1973	93rd 1st session	Mandatory public financing in general-election campaigns Spending limits equal to federal grant	Passed by Senate
S. 3044	1974	93rd 2nd session	Voluntary public financing in primary and general-election campaigns Matching funds in primary campaigns Spending limits equal to federal grant in general-election campaigns	Passed by Senate
S. 137	1990	101st 2nd session	Voluntary public financing (benefits) in general elections Grants in general-election campaigns provided only in response to certain levels of opponent spending independent expenditures Public benefits of broadcast vouchers, reduced advertising rates, and reduced mailing rates provided to participants	Passed by Senate
H.R. 5400	1990	101st 2nd session	Voluntary public financing (benefits) in general elections Subsidies for one free broadcast ad for every two ads purchased, reduced advertising rates, and reduced mailing rates provided to participants	Passed by House
S. 3 (see also conference version below)	1991	102nd 2nd session	Voluntary public financing (benefits) in general elections Grants in general-election campaigns provided only in response to certain levels of opponent spending or independent expenditures Public benefits of broadcast vouchers, reduced advertising rates, and reduced mailing rates provided to participants	Passed by Senate
H.R. 3750 (see also conference version below)	1991	102nd 2nd session	Voluntary public financing (benefits) in general elections Matching funds in general-election campaigns for small contributions Grants in general-election campaigns provided only in response to certain levels of opponent spending or independent expenditures Public benefits of reduced mailing rates provided to participants	Passed by House

(continued on next page)

TABLE 1.3.   *Continued*

Legislation	Year of Passage	Congress/ Session	Overview of Major Provisions (congressional public financing only)	Outcome
S. 3 (conference version)	1992	102nd 2nd session	Voluntary public financing (benefits) in general elections Matching funds in general-election campaigns for small contributions (House candidates only) Grants in general-election campaigns provided only in response to certain levels of opponent spending independent expenditures Public benefits of broadcast vouchers (Senate candidates only), reduced advertising rates (Senate candidates only), and reduced mailing rates provided to participants	Passed by House and Senate; vetoed by President George H. W. Bush
H.R. 3	1993	103rd 1st session	Voluntary public financing (benefits) in general elections Grants in general-election campaigns provided only in response to certain levels of opponent spending or independent expenditures Advertising vouchers based on matching-fund structure	Passed by House
S. 3	1993	103rd 1st session	Voluntary public financing (benefits) in general elections Grants in general-election campaigns provided only in response to certain levels of opponent spending or independent expenditures Reduced advertising and mailing rates	Passed by Senate

Source: Author analysis of bill text and related documents.

proposal (Neuberger 1956, 2855). Indeed, S. 3242 was similar to Roosevelt's proposal—as we shall see, far more so than later congressional public financing bills. There is no record of congressional action on S. 3242 beyond introduction, but the bill offers important lessons for subsequent proposals.

Like Roosevelt's proposal, S. 3242 proposed public funds for political parties rather than individual campaigns. The legislation would have provided federal grants to "major political parties," meaning those whose candidates received at least 10 percent of the popular vote in the preceding election. For all practical purposes, this meant that third parties would be ineligible for funds. Those parties that were eligible would have received 15 or 20 cents (depending on whether it was a congressional or presidential election year) multiplied by the average number of votes cast in recent elections. Neuberger projected that, under his bill, the Democratic and Republican parties would have each received between approximately $5 million and $11 million for every election cycle between 1952 and 1958 (Neuberger 1956, 2856). Participation in public financing would have been voluntary— as is typically the case—but public funds would have been reduced if parties chose to accept more than $100 in private contributions from any individual.

How does this first attempt at congressional public financing compare with later efforts? Although S. 3242 was similar to Roosevelt's proposal, it generally stands in stark contrast to later bills, at least in its technical provisions. First, the bill assumed that parties were the central force in electoral campaigns. As noted previously, this point is debatable today, but congressional campaigns now are far more responsible for their own fund-raising and spending than they were in the 1950s. Second, the Neuberger bill is remarkable today for its simplicity. The entire bill appears on a single page of the *Congressional Record* (Neuberger 1956, 2855), despite the major change it would have represented. Modern public financing bills tend to be far longer and more complex, because of both the changing nature of campaigns and the changing nature of the law. In Neuberger's day, public financing legislation could essentially begin from a blank slate, whereas later efforts typically attempted to amend FECA, the Internal Revenue Code (IRC), or both. Therefore, although Neuberger's proposal was perhaps a greater departure from the status quo than more recent bills, his task was arguably simpler because the legislation did not have to fit into the preexisting and complex framework of campaign finance and tax laws that surround public financing legislation today.

Despite those technical differences with more recent proposals, the brief debate over S. 3242 foreshadowed many of the arguments that would appear in future public financing legislation. Neuberger's introduction of S. 3242 came just weeks after two select (special) Senate committees had been formed to investigate an oil and gas company's alleged attempt to curry favor with another senator in exchange for a $2,500 campaign contribution.[12] Citing that episode and other concerns, Neuberger stated:

> [Private] contributions, in my opinion, have become an unbearable yoke to many of the men who must accept them. They even have become onerous and objectionable to the individuals who parcel out such contributions. Yet everyone has been caught in the ensnarling web of campaign financing. . . . [Large campaign] expenditures have become necessary because of the tremendous cost of reaching people through modern media of communication, particularly through radio and television. . . . I am convinced that neither candidates nor

contributors want this frenzied scramble for campaign financing to continue. (Neuberger 1956, 2854)

Those favoring congressional public financing often echo Neuberger's sentiment. In particular, three points found in Neuberger's quotation would become hallmarks of arguments in favor of congressional public financing: (1) Private contributions are potentially corrupting; (2) the increased need for money is directly related to broadcast communications; and (3) large private contributions are distasteful for candidates and donors alike.

Although little opposition to Neuberger's bill appears in the record of debate, at least one of Neuberger's colleagues raised the question of possible overreaction. Senator Homer Capehart (R-IN), while suggesting that he might have supported S. 3242 in general, warned against "legislat[ing] against honest men" with an overly punitive bill. Capehart continued:

I feel very sorry that because of the contribution of $2,500, it is said there is a need for [S. 3242]. Let each Senator take a good look at himself in a mirror; he knows whether he has a clear conscience. . . . How else is a candidate going to handle his campaign if he does not obtain contributions from his friends, or put up all the money himself? Who says that every contribution is made for some ulterior motive? I say shame on any Senator who makes such a suggestion. (Capehart 1956, 2863)

In the future, these and similar sentiments would become themes often found in opposition to public financing. In short, those opposed to public financing generally contend that public financing advocates too often use isolated cases of abuse to make the claim for broad reform. Whether for those reasons or others, there is no evidence that S. 3242 received any additional consideration beyond Neuberger's introductory statement. Even if the Senate (not to mention the House) shared Neuberger's concerns, they chose not to enact congressional public financing legislation in the 1950s or 1960s.

Despite the lack of movement on the Neuberger bill, public financing continued to attract periodic attention. Throughout the 1960s, various committees inside the legislative and executive branches considered public financing measures or other issues related to campaign fund-raising or spending (see, for example, U.S. Senate Committee on Rules and Administration 1961 and U.S. President's Commission on Campaign Costs 1962). Congress passed a *presidential* public financing bill in 1966, but the measure was repealed the following year (Corrado 2005, 19).[13] Although there was some committee action on other public financing bills during the 1960s, not until the 1970s did congressional public financing legislation make significant legislative progress.

The 1970s: Renewed Attention amid FECA and Watergate

Just as a perceived scandal had provided fodder for the first attempt at congressional public financing in 1956, Watergate gave the issue renewed focus in the mid-1970s. Even before Watergate, in the early 1970s, congressional attention turned to campaign finance as it never had before. In 1971, Congress passed, and President Richard Nixon signed, the Federal Election Campaign Act. FECA replaced the Corrupt Practices Act, which had last been amended in 1925 and was widely regarded as inadequate to address modern campaign finance (Corrado 2005, 20). FECA remains the cornerstone of the nation's campaign finance law.[14]

Also in 1971, Congress again enacted voluntary public financing for presidential campaigns. That system also remains in effect today, although even supporters of the program agree that it needs updating.[15] Nonetheless, even with all these factors that would suggest improved chances for congressional public financing, Congress would not enact such legislation until the 1990s.

The House and Senate made significant progress on legislative public financing bills at two different points in the 93rd Congress (1973–1974). This period marked the first time that either chamber passed congressional public financing legislation. First, in November 1973, the Senate passed an amendment to an unlikely legislative "vehicle," H.R. 11104 (introduced by Representative Albert Ullman, D-OR), which was aimed at increasing the nation's public debt limit. Senator Ted Kennedy (D-MA) sponsored a public financing measure in the form of Senate Amendment 651 (S.Amdt.) to H.R. 11104.[16]

Senate Amendment 651 differed from the 1956 Neuberger legislation in at least three major respects. First, the Kennedy amendment was longer and more complex than Neuberger's bill, reflecting the evolution of campaign finance law that had occurred in the interim (most notably the enactment of FECA). Second, the Neuberger bill would have permitted congressional appropriations to cover public financing, but did not speak in detail about how those appropriations would be funded. By contrast, the Kennedy amendment, like many public financing bills today, amended federal tax law (specifically the Internal Revenue Code, today found in Title 26 of the

United States Code). The connection to tax law has been prominent in public financing proposals since at least the 1971 Revenue Act, in which Congress enacted the current *presidential* public campaign financing system. In the most visible connection to tax law, as a result of the Revenue Act, individual federal tax-return forms contain a "checkoff" question that permits individuals to voluntarily designate a portion of their tax dollars for the presidential public financing program. Kennedy's amendment, and many public financing proposals since, proposed adopting the checkoff mechanism for legislative campaigns rather than providing funding through congressional appropriations. (However, Kennedy's amendment also allowed for congressional appropriations to prevent insolvency in the proposed public financing fund.) Third, S.Amdt. 651 proposed providing funds directly to candidate campaigns rather than routing them only through political parties.

The Senate eventually passed Kennedy's amendment, which envisioned broad public financing of presidential and congressional campaigns.[17] Specifically, the amendment proposed mandatory public financing of general-election campaigns. Funds would have been available to all candidates who met specific qualifying criteria. For congressional candidates, federal funding would have been limited to the greater of 15 cents multiplied by the voting-age population (VAP) of the state or $90,000 for House candidates, or the greater of the formula amount or $175,000 for Senate candidates.[18] Minor-party candidates would have been eligible for lesser amounts. Those thresholds were consistent with spending limits previously passed by the Senate (in S. 372) earlier in 1973, although that bill did not become law. In exchange for receiving public funds, candidates would have had to certify to the U.S. comptroller general that their campaigns would submit to federal audits, that they would make no expenditures in the general election beyond the amount provided by federal funds, and that they would not raise private funds for the general election.[19]

During floor debate, senators considered what goals public financing should accomplish and how, and whether the initiative was truly necessary. As Neuberger had in 1956, Kennedy invoked concerns about corruption. He said when the amendment was introduced:

> I am convinced that most, and probably all, of the very serious problems facing this country today have their roots in the way we finance political campaigns for high Federal office. We would have a different America today if the political power of campaign contributions were measured by their votes and voices instead of their pocketbooks. Beyond any doubt, the year-long revelations of Watergate demon-

strate the insidious influence of private money in American politics. (Kennedy 1973, 38177)

Senator Walter Mondale (D-MN), who noted that the amendment was the product of various senators' proposals, echoed those comments, saying, "The average person who works every day, pays his taxes, and maybe gives 10 bucks to a candidate, cannot find anyone in Government who cares about him or his problems. No wonder he feels cut off from Government. No wonder he does not trust politicians. No wonder he thinks we are all crooks" (Mondale 1973, 38183).

Others, however, were skeptical. Senator James Allen (D-AL), for example, questioned why private contributions in general elections would be permitted, but only if given to parties rather than candidates. Allen contended that the flow of individual contributions through parties "looks like a subsidy added to private contributions" (Allen 1973, 38185). Allen also questioned the cost of public financing—a point that has been a common topic of congressional debates over the issue. Barry Goldwater (R-AZ), among others, also raised constitutional concerns about barring private contributions. Others senators objected to raising the public financing issue by means of the debt-ceiling bill rather than through other procedural avenues. Senator Adlai Stevenson III (D-IL) cautioned after S.Amdt. 651 was passed that Kennedy's amendment was "a pure public financing proposal" because, except in some circumstances, it "permits no private contributions" to publicly financed candidates (Stevenson 1973, 38226). Instead, Stevenson proposed an alternative amendment (which was unsuccessful) that would have created a hybrid system combining elements of private and public financing. The House companion bill did not include a congressional public financing provision.

Many of the same issues raised in the 1973 debate reemerged when Congress turned to congressional public financing during consideration of the 1974 FECA amendments. The FECA amendments eventually became law, but congressional public financing did not. As with S.Amdt. 651 the previous year, in 1974 the Senate passed congressional public financing legislation, but the House did not.

The Senate version of the FECA amendments, S. 3044, was sponsored by Senator Howard Cannon, a Nevada Democrat and chairman of the Senate Committee on Rules and Administration, which typically has jurisdiction over campaign finance matters.[20] The committee held hearings on the bill, including a congressional public financing provision, in February 1974 (U.S. Senate Committee on Rules and Administration 1974). The majority views in the committee report held that public financing was an essential reform. Although the committee recognized "that the issue of public financing has been a controversial one for several years" and that various competing proposals existed, "there is no question that the public appreciates the pervasive evils of our present system for campaign financing. The potentials for abuse are all too clear" (U.S. Senate Committee on Rules and Administration 1974, 4). Nonetheless, although S. 3044 was ultimately successful in the Senate, it was not without controversy, even among some supporters.

The measure came to the Senate floor in April 1974.It was principally concerned with other amendments to FECA, but the version reported to the Senate by the Rules and Administration Committee also included language that would have extended the checkoff-based model of presidential public financing to congressional campaigns. The committee-reported version of S. 3044 proposed full public financing of general-election campaigns and a matching fund system for primary campaigns (in which public funds would have supplemented private fund-raising, as is the case with the presidential public financing system). Much of the bill's language was based on S. 372, a 1973 campaign finance bill that was ultimately unsuccessful. By including primary campaigns, S. 3044 represented another phase in the evolution of congressional public financing proposals. In addition, perhaps because of the previous lack of success moving mandatory public financing legislation, S. 3044 would have made participation voluntary.[21]

The bill's supporters viewed the continued press for public financing, and the proposed expansion to primary campaigns, as a continuation of Congress's efforts to restore faith in government following Watergate. Others, however, argued just the opposite. Although he emphasized the need for political reform generally, Senator Peter Dominick (R-CO) strongly criticized the bill's public financing language:

> I support reform and have consistently voted for it. I am against—irrevocably against—efforts to establish a Federal financing system as proposed in [S. 3044]. Giving taxpayers' money to politicians to run for election can only reduce further whatever confidence Americans retain in their political leadership and institutions. Taking away from the individual the decision as to whom their money will go excludes the individual from a vital part of the political process and reduces the voters' involvement, participation and commitment to candidates and parties. Reducing the dependence of candidates and elected officials upon the rank and file of their party and upon the individual citizen voter will insulate representatives further from individual taxpayers who will be, nonetheless, paying their campaign

bills. . . . To adopt "public financing" would be the ultimate evil legacy of the Watergate era. (Dominick 1974, 10948)

Adlai Stevenson, who had raised objections to elements of S.Amdt. 651, reiterated his concern that S. 3044 would unnecessarily restrict small contributions, saying, "This bill implicitly distrusts the people and their good sense" (Stevenson 1973, 10950).

These objections to public financing (especially Dominick's remarks) emphasized some of the most common arguments against public financing at the time and throughout the history of debate over the issue. As Dominick suggested, opponents often view public financing not as a method of "cleaning up" politics, but as a method of limiting individual liberty. In their view, public financing forces voters to make political contributions indirectly through their tax dollars, and to do so in ways that they might find objectionable. Furthermore, they say, *private* financing is not a means to corruption, but an incentive to keep candidates close to their constituents and their concerns. Critics also often contend that public funds could be better spent elsewhere.

Despite some opposition to the bill, S. 3044 passed the Senate on April 11, 1974.[22] Even some senators with reservations about the bill were persuaded that congressional public financing was a necessary approach to achieving renewed trust in government. For example, despite what Senator Pete Domenici (R-NM) called "glaring deficiencies" in the bill, "to be effective in reforming our election procedures, we must follow a comprehensive approach. . . . [P]ublic financing is required to achieve the fundamental objectives of limited contributions and limited spending, both of which must be strictly enforced and completely disclosed" (Domenici 1974, 10951).

As with S.Amdt. 651 the previous year, the House did not follow the Senate's lead on S. 3044. There were attempts to include congressional public financing provisions in the House version of the bill, but the language was eventually dropped from the 1974 FECA amendments that became law. However, an expansion of the presidential public financing program survived a House-Senate conference committee and became law, as did spending limits on congressional campaigns. The Supreme Court would declare the spending limits unconstitutional in its 1976 *Buckley v. Valeo* decision, which also preserved presidential public financing as long as participation was voluntary.

Although there were attempts to revise congressional public financing throughout the 1970s, including various congressional hearings, no legislation advanced as far as S.Amdt. 651 had in 1973 or S. 3044 in 1974. Jimmy

Carter's support for congressional public financing was also insufficient to substantially move the issue in Congress (Carter 1977, 482). The stalemate would last throughout the 1980s in one form or another. The debate over campaign finance policy also shifted in the 1980s to concerns about PACs and whether their role as vehicles for "special interest" money circumvented federal law (see, for example, Sabato 1984; Matasar 1986). Neither chamber of Congress would pass public financing legislation again for almost twenty years.

The 1990s: Different Proposals, More Legislative Progress

In the late 1980s, attention began to shift back toward congressional public financing, but in a different form than in the 1970s. The primary differences in the public financing legislation that passed the House and Senate in the early 1990s compared with the 1970s were twofold. First, the 1990s marked the first time that the House, rather than just the Senate, passed public financing legislation. By contrast, despite several ambitious House proposals during the 1970s, none of that legislation passed the chamber. Second, and more important, the 1990s legislation that passed the House, Senate, or both shifted the understanding of what constituted "public financing." Whereas the 1970s legislation focused on providing subsidies—public funds—directly to campaigns, the 1990s legislation proposed indirect benefits to campaigns. Specifically, the 1990s legislation would have provided direct funds in some cases, but emphasized advertising vouchers or mail subsidies that would have provided less-direct financial benefits than traditional proposals for grants or matching funds.

The House and Senate had begun considering legislative public financing bills again in earnest during the 100th Congress (1987–1988). In the 101st Congress, the House passed public financing legislation for the first time. However, even though both chambers passed public financing bills during that Congress, efforts to resolve differences between the chambers in a conference committee were unsuccessful.

When the 1990s arrived, the Senate passed its bill first, on August 1, 1990.Sponsored by Oklahoma Democrat David Boren, S. 137 had been debated on the floor throughout late July, after being revised during the preceding spring. The bill was subject to multiple amendments on subjects ranging from political use of union dues to soft money and public financing.

Unlike the legislation that the Senate had passed in the 1970s, S. 137 proposed providing public money directly to campaigns only under limited circumstances. Participating campaigns would have received taxpayer funds only if nonparticipating opponents exceeded a spending cap of no more than $5.5 million. Federal funds also would have been available to respond to spending on independent expenditures—typically broadcast advertisements aired by political parties, PACs, or other groups—that exceeded certain amounts.

Most of S. 137's benefits, however, would not have provided federal funds directly to campaigns. Instead, participants would have received federally funded vouchers for broadcast advertising time. Similarly, the bill would have provided favorable advertising rates to participants through adjustments to a federal provision known as the "lowest unit charge" (sometimes called the "lowest unit rate"), which essentially requires that uniform, comparatively low prices be charged for the same class of broadcast advertising during the same period of a given day.[23] Participants would also have received discounted postal rates.

Support for S. 137 was based on familiar arguments surrounding public financing, as was opposition to the bill. Debate over providing public financing in exchange for limiting campaign spending was particularly prominent, as it had been in the past and continues to be today. As Senator George Mitchell (D-ME), then the Senate majority leader, noted before the Senate began debate on final passage of S. 137:

> [It has been] clear to all that the central difference between the two parties on campaign finance reform was spending limits. Democrats in good faith believe deeply that some limit should be placed on the amount spent in political campaigns in America. Republicans in equally good faith believe deeply that there should be no limit to the amounts spent on political campaigns in America. The debate . . . has served merely to confirm that difference. As we have heard over and over and over again from our colleagues, it is opposition to spending limits which is at the heart of the disagreement over this bill. (Mitchell 1990, 20314)

As Senate passage of S. 137 neared, proponents, including Boren, suggested that the bill deemphasize the previous and controversial topic of providing taxpayer funds directly to candidate campaigns. Those favoring the bill hoped these changes would appease the bill's critics. They apparently did not. Senator Mitch McConnell (R-KY), a critic of public financing legislation, said during floor debate that the bill's supporters "have dredged the 1970's [and] found a lemon of a campaign finance vehicle, tuned it up a little and unveiled it in 1990 as the panacea for real and perceived corruption in the political process. Mr. President, underneath the hood, it is the same old lemon running on taxpayer financing and spending limits" (McConnell 1990, 20303).[24]

The House took up floor debate on its own bill, H.R. 5400, just days after the Senate passed S. 137 in August 1990. That bill was sponsored by Representative Al Swift (D-WA). The House and Senate measures were generally similar, but contained one major difference. The version of H.R. 5400 eventually passed by the House contained no provisions for providing public funds directly to candidate campaigns. As noted previously, S. 137 proposed to do so in response to nonparticipant spending or independent expenditures. Also, H.R. 5400's advertising benefits differed from those of S. 137. Although vouchers proposed in the Senate bill would have covered partial costs of broadcast ads, participating candidates under H.R. 5400 would have received one free ad for every two purchased. The two bills' other public benefits, such as reduced mailing rates, were largely similar.

As with some other bills containing public financing provisions during this period, much of the debate over H.R. 5400 focused on unrelated issues, particularly provisions concerning PACs. When debate did turn to public financing (or benefits) provisions, supporters contended that the legislation included a variety of needed reform measures and emphasized concessions that had removed direct subsidies to candidate campaigns. They also emphasized that the bill provided incentives to limit campaign spending. Opponents, however, countered that public funds nonetheless were subsidizing benefits such as reduced mailing rates. Some opponents also complained that the bill had not been considered in committee.

Although each chamber had passed similar legislation, details relating to public financing provisions and, perhaps more importantly, other campaign finance issues, kept the two chambers far apart. The House and Senate bills were never reconciled in conference committee. Those efforts would nonetheless become the foundation of monumental public financing legislation in the 102nd Congress.

In 1991–1992, both houses of Congress finally agreed on and passed public financing legislation. Although the act was vetoed, the episode marks the most substantial legislative progress a congressional public financing bill has ever attained. The public financing provisions of the Senate bill, S. 3, were substantially similar to S. 137, which the chamber had passed in the previous Congress. As with S. 137, S. 3 would have permitted direct payments to candidate campaigns only in response to certain opponent spending or independent expenditures. The bill's main public benefits provisions included broadcast vouchers and reduced mail rates.

As proponents had done since public financing reemerged in the late 1980s, S. 3's supporters framed the bill not primarily as a public financing measure, but as a means to controlling campaign costs, as the bill's benefits would be available only to those who agreed to limit spending. As David Boren, S. 3's sponsor, explained shortly before the bill passed the Senate:

> This [bill] is not about financing. It is not about taxpayer financing. . . . This bill is about whether or not we are going to stop the money chase in American politics. . . . If you can really say that you think more and more money pouring into American politics has encouraged competition, then of course you should oppose S. 3 and spending limits. But when you look at the facts, I do not see how you can answer the question that way. (Boren 1991, 12340)

Opponents, however, as they had also done in previous Congresses, objected to the bill and raised constitutional questions about whether the legislation unfairly rewarded participants while punishing those who chose not to limit their spending. According to Wyoming Republican Alan Simpson, "Candidates who do not agree to the spending limits [in S. 3] not only do not get any public subsidies if they go over their [spending] limits, their opponents get additional public money as a penalty. . . . [A]s a constitutional matter, there is nothing 'voluntary' about the campaign finance system established by the pending legislation" (Simpson 1991, 12339).

Representative Sam Gejdenson (D-CT) sponsored the House bill, H.R. 3750. In a departure from the House's bill that had passed during the 101st Congress, H.R. 3750 would have provided matching funds for small contributions (up to $200 each, for a $200,000 aggregate). The bill also proposed grants in response to certain opponent spending or independent expenditures. Public benefits were confined to reduced mailing rates. A House working group, the Campaign Finance Reform Task Force, was responsible for much of H.R. 3750's development.

Like other bills considered during the period, much of the debate surrounding H.R. 3750 concerned the bill's proposed restrictions on PACs rather than public financing per se. Also like other bills proposed during the period, H.R. 3750 was framed more as a spending-limit bill than a public financing bill. Representative Charles Rose (D-NC), Committee on House Administration chairman, called spending limits the "cornerstone" of the bill and emphasized H.R. 3750's matching-fund provision. The latter (like all such provisions) relied on private contributions to determine the amount of funds available to candidates rather than providing an automatic grant. Supporters also argued that the major elements of the bill were already tested. For example, Representative Gerald Kleczka (D-WI) suggested that the bill's "system of spending limits and public financing is not some radical idea the authors of this bill thought up. This is the system which now funds our Presidential elections" (Kleczka 1991, 34680).

H.R. 3750's critics countered that public-benefits portions of the bill were, in fact, akin to direct candidate subsidies because of their effect on the Treasury. Representative Bill Thomas (R-CA.), ranking member of the House Administration Committee, urged his colleagues, as various version of the legislation were being debated, to "make no mistake. There is nothing in this bill, nothing in this bill, that takes away from the taxpayer financing on postal subsidies, on matching funds, and on tax credits, if those are, in fact, the incentives that we are going to have in the bill" (Thomas 1991, 34680). Despite objection from some in the House and Senate, both chambers passed their bills.

In April 1992, a conference committee reported a measure combining the House and Senate bills (U.S. House of Representatives 1992). In terms of public financing provisions, the reported measure largely adopted S. 3's language regarding Senate campaigns and H.R. 3750's language regarding House campaigns. (The bill sent to the president was labeled S. 3.) Both houses of Congress assented to the conference committee's recommendation and sent an act to the president that emphasized direct subsidies only in response to certain opponent spending or independent expenditures (except for matching funds to be made available to House candidates) and provided broadcast vouchers or reduced advertising rates and reduced mailing rates. Spending limits and PAC provisions occupied much of the legislation.

On May 9, 1992, President George H. W. Bush vetoed S. 3. Although Bush called the existing campaign finance structure "seriously flawed," he contended that the measure would not accomplish the goals of increasing competition or balancing resources among candidates. The president also concluded that the measure "would limit political speech protected by the First Amendment and inevitably lead to a raid on the Treasury to pay for the Act's elaborate scheme of public subsidies" (Bush 1993, 736).

Although Congress revisited public financing legislation in the 103rd Congress, legislative momentum on the issue had reached its zenith (at least thus far). In the 103rd Congress, the House and Senate each passed bills (H.R. 3 and S. 3, respectively) that were substantially similar to the legislation vetoed in 1992. Sponsored by Boren, S. 3 proposed reductions in broadcast-advertising and mailing rates. The bill also would have provided direct payments to Senate campaigns, but again only in response to independent expenditures and opposition spending. Sponsored by Gejdenson, H.R. 3 proposed advertising vouchers (based on a matching-provision system). Like the Senate bill, H.R. 3 would have provided direct subsidies in response to independent expenditures or opponent spending. Each chamber passed its bill in 1993. President Bill Clinton's support for public financing seemed particularly promising. Nonetheless, the bills were not reconciled in conference, and the measures died.

As of this writing, Congress has not devoted substantial legislative attention to public financing since. The issue received little attention after Republicans gained control of the House and Senate in 1995 (the 104th Congress). This outcome is not surprising given many Republicans' traditional objections to public financing legislation. In addition, both chambers, and indeed members of both parties, may have simply grown frustrated by several unsuccessful efforts to enact public financing legislation. Finally, although campaign finance issues did receive substantial attention in the late 1990s and early 2000s surrounding BCRA, those debates generally focused on other issues.

Congressional Public Financing in 2008 and Beyond

As the preceding discussion shows, as of this writing, congressional public financing legislation has enjoyed only limited success in Congress. No congressional public financing bill has become law. But supporters have not been deterred. Their opponents have remained equally vigilant.

The 110th Congress (2007–2008) showed renewed interest in public financing. A June 2007 Senate Rules and Administration Committee hearing on S. 1285, introduced by Senator Richard Durbin (D-IL), marked the first congressional hearing on the topic since the 103rd Congress (1993–1994). Two public financing bills (H.R. 1614, sponsored by Representative John Tierney, D-MA; and H.R. 2817, sponsored by Representative David Obey, D-WI), were introduced in the House, but those measures did not receive hearings. In the 111th Congress (2009–2010), the Committee on House Administration held a hearing on H.R. 1826, sponsored by Representative John Larson (D-CT) The committee also considered another Larson bill, H.R. 6116. The Durbin bill also reemerged in the Senate, in the form of S. 752, but the legislation did not receive a hearing.

In some ways, these bills harkened back to those Congress has debated for the past fifty years. In others, they suggested new (or at least renewed) approaches. Like their predecessors, the 110th and 111th Congresses' bills included a combination of matching funds, grants, or advertising vouchers.

Accordingly, it seems that Congress has maintained a consistent vision of how public financing benefits would be structured and delivered since the 1970s. Nonetheless, political context and other factors have shaped the evolution of individual proposals.

At the same time, unlike some of the bills that passed Congress—but did not become law—in the 1970s and 1990s, recent bills' authors appear to be moving toward a more comprehensive approach to public financing. Whereas Congress limited direct subsidies to candidate campaigns and often previously tied public financing provisions to broader reform issues, the more recent bills envision a structure that would cover a substantial portion of (or perhaps all) campaign costs for those who chose to participate. In doing so, although in a very different form than the first congressional public financing bill offered in 1956, the scope of the latest proposals is perhaps not that different from Neuberger's original vision of federally funded campaigns. Recent bills also assume that constitutional challenges could be brought if the legislation became law, and propose expedited review and "severability" mechanisms to prevent other elements from being invalidated if parts a law were held unconstitutional.

Perhaps most notably, H.R. 1826 and H.R. 6116 in the 111th Congress—and S. 752, a Senate counterpart—abandoned spending limits and additional funding in response to opponent fund-raising or independent expenditures. Instead, the bills concentrated on providing public benefits to supplement unlimited fund-raising of contributions of $100 or less. The revamped approach came at least partially in response to increasing concern about the constitutionality of public financing that equalized resources rather than simply providing an alternative funding source compared with traditional private funds.[25] These developments suggest that proponents of public financing may be ready for a renewed debate over extensive public financing legislation, yet mindful that their opponents also are prepared to rebuff those efforts. The history of congressional public financing legislation suggests nothing less.

NOTES

1. The full history of congressional public financing legislation is beyond the scope of this chapter, which presents a discussion of selected bills. Related discussion of the topics addressed in this chapter appears in R. Sam Garrett, "Public Financing of Congressional Campaigns: Background and Analysis," Congressional Research Service report RL33814. Joseph E. Cantor, whose knowledge of campaign finance legislation is unsurpassed, originally served as a coauthor of that report. For additional discussion of related legislative history, see also Mutch 1988, chap. 5).

2. The subheading for the relevant section of Roosevelt's message is "Presidential Campaign Expenses." The accompanying text refers to "Presidential or National campaigns" (Roosevelt 1907, 78).

3. Essentially, "coordinated" spending refers to purchases on which parties and campaigns may communicate and share strategic resources. On coordination, see 2 U.S.C. § 441a(d).

4. Mutch states that "the first bill providing for [public financing of presidential campaigns] was introduced in 1904" (1988, 118). What legislation Mutch is referring to is unclear.

5. Bundlers typically either assemble groups of individuals' campaign contributions ("bundles") or are credited with soliciting certain contributions that go directly to a campaign.

6. FECA is 2 U.S.C. § 431 et seq.

7. BCRA is P.L. 107–155; 116 Stat. 81.

8. Congress enacted major amendments to FECA in 1974, 1976, and 1979.

9. Notably, however, BCRA did not index PAC contributions for inflation. They have remained at $5,000 per calendar year.

10. The "additional" funds are presumably remaining amounts from the previous election cycle.

11. It is beyond the scope of this chapter to address 527s and 501(c)s, but the extent to which their spending is campaign related is a subject of contentious debate.

12. The details of these events are beyond the scope of this chapter.

13. See 80 Stat. 1587 and 81 Stat. 57.

14. On other themes in the FECA debate throughout the 1970s compared with more recent campaign finance measures, see Garrett 2010b.

15. The current presidential public financing system was established in the 1971 Revenue Act. See 85 Stat. 573. FECA amendments later modified elements of the program.

16. As if to underscore the growing concerns about potential corruption surrounding money in politics, the Senate confirmation vote of Gerald Ford's nomination as Richard Nixon's vice president (following the Agnew resignation) interrupted consideration of S.Amdt. 651. The timing was apparently coincidental.

17. For the text of the amendment as introduced, see *Congressional Record* 119, pt. 29, November 27, 1973, p. 38172.

18. Ibid., 38173.

19. On these conditions, see ibid., 38172.

20. Bill referral can vary depending on the issues addressed in individual legislation. In addition to the Committee on Rules and Administration, public financing bills are often referred to the Senate Committee on Finance, which has jurisdiction over tax issues. The Commerce Committee also sometimes receives bills that would affect political advertising or broadcasting issues. In the House, the principal campaign finance committee is the Committee on House Administration. The Ways and Means Committee handles tax issues; the Committee on Energy and Commerce handles telecommunications issues.

21. Today, virtually all public financing proposals include voluntary-participation provisions, due in no small part to the *Buckley v. Valeo* decision.

22. See legislative vote no. 146, *Congressional Record*, April 11, 1974, p. 10952.

23. See 47 U.S.C. § 315(b). See also Williams 1992–1993.

24. The reference to "Mr. President" is to the president of the Senate.

25. The renewed focus on constitutional issues arose after the Supreme Court ruled in *Davis v. FEC* (2008) that the so-called Millionaire's Amendment, a BCRA provision,

unconstitutionally provided additional fund-raising limits for traditionally financed opponents facing wealthy, self-financed opponents. The case did not directly concern public financing but was generally considered to place additional public financing benefits— such as traditional proposals for matching funds provided in response to nonparticipant fund-raising or spending—on questionable constitutional footing.

REFERENCES

Allen, Senator James B. 1973. "Temporary Increase in Public Debt Limit." 93rd Cong. 1st sess., *Congressional Record* 119, pt. 29 (November 27): 38185.

Boren, Senator David. 1991. "Senate Elections Ethics Act of 1991." 102nd Cong. 1st sess., *Congressional Record* 137, pt. 9 (May 23): 12340.

Buckley v. Valeo. 1976. 424 U.S. 1.

Bush, President George H. W. 1993. *Public Papers of the Presidents of the United States: George Bush, 1992–1993.* 2 vols. Washington, DC: Government Printing Office.

Capehart, Senator Homer. 1956. "Federal Campaign Contributions to Relieve Officeholders of Private Obligations." 84th Cong. 2nd sess., *Congressional Record* 102, pt. 2 (February 20): 2854.

Carter, President Jimmy. 1977. "Election Reform." Message to Congress in *Public Papers of the Presidents of the United States: Jimmy Carter, 1977,* 1 vol. Washington, DC: Government Printing Office.

Center for Responsive Politics. "Price of Admission." 2006 financial overview. Available at http://www.opensecrets.org/bigpicture/stats.php?cycle=2006&Display=T&Type=A, accessed July 9, 2008.

Corrado, Anthony. 2005. "Money and Politics: A History of Federal Campaign Finance Law." In *The New Campaign Finance Sourcebook,* ed. Anthony Corrado, Thomas E. Mann, Daniel R. Ortiz, and Trevor Potter. Washington, DC: Brookings Institution Press.

Domenici, Senator Pete. 1974. "Federal Election Campaign Act Amendments of 1974." 93rd Cong. 2nd sess., *Congressional Record* 120, pt. 9 (April 11): 109–151.

"Federal Election Campaign Act Amendments of 1974." 1974. 93rd Cong., 2nd sess., *Congressional Record* 120, pt. 9 (April 11): 10950.

Federal Election Commission. 2007. *Corporate and Labor Organizations.* Campaign guide. January. Available at http://www.fec.gov/pdf/colagui.pdf, accessed July 5, 2008.

———. 2008. "2008 House and Senate Campaign Finance." Available at http://www.fec.gov/DisclosureSearch/mapHSApp.do?election_yr=2008, accessed July 17.

Garrett, R. Sam. 2010a. *Campaign Crises: Detours on the Road to Congress.* Boulder, CO: Lynne Rienner.

———. 2010b. "Campaign Finance Theory and Congressional Practice: Comparing the Legislative Development of 527s and Political Action Committees." Prepared for presentation at the annual meeting of the Southern Political Science Association, Atlanta, January 7–9.

Kennedy, Senator Edward M. 1973. "Temporary Increase in Public Debt Limit." 93rd Cong. 1st sess., *Congressional Record* 119, pt. 29 (November 27): 38177.

Kleczka, Representative Gerald. 1991. "House of Representatives Campaign Spending Limit and Election Reform Act of 1991." 102nd Cong. 1st sess., *Congressional Record* 137, pt. 23 (November 25): 34680.

La Raja. Raymond J. 2008. *Small Change: Money, Political Parties, and Campaign Finance Reform.* Ann Arbor: University of Michigan Press.

Magleby, David B., and Candice J. Nelson. 1990. *The Money Chase: Congressional Campaign Finance Reform*. Washington, DC: Brookings Institution Press.

Matasar, Ann B. 1986. *Corporate PACs and Federal Campaign Finance Laws: Use or Abuse of Power?* New York: Quorum Books.

McConnell, Senator Mitch. 1990. "Senatorial Election Campaign Act." 101st Cong. 2nd sess., *Congressional Record* 136, pt. 14 (July 30): 20303.

McDonald, Michael P., and John Samples, eds. 2006. *The Marketplace of Democracy: Electoral Competition and American Politics*. Washington, DC: Cato Institute and Brookings Institution Press.

Mitchell, Senator George. 1990. "Senatorial Election Campaign Act." 101st Cong. 2nd sess., *Congressional Record* 136, pt. 14 (July 30): 20314.

Mondale, Senator Walter F. 1973. "Temporary Increase in Public Debt Limit." 93rd Cong. 1st sess., *Congressional Record* 119, pt. 29 (November 27): 38183.

Mutch, Robert E. 1988. *Campaigns, Congress, and the Courts: The Making of Federal Campaign Finance Law*. New York: Praeger.

Neuberger, Senator Richard. 1956. "Federal Campaign Contributions to Relieve Officeholders of Private Obligations." 84th Cong. 2nd sess., *Congressional Record* 102, pt. 2 (February 20): 2854.

Roosevelt, President Theodore. 1907. "President's Annual Message." *Congressional Record* 42:67.

Sabato, Larry J. 1984. *PAC Power: Inside the World of Political Action Committees*. New York: W. W. Norton.

Shea, Daniel M., and Michael John Burton. 2001. *Campaign Craft: The Strategies, Tactics, and Art of Political Campaign Management*. Rev. and exp. ed. Westport, CT: Praeger.

Simpson, Senator Alan. 1991. "Senate Elections Ethics Act of 1991." *Congressional Record* 137, pt. 9 (May 23): 12339.

Smith, Bradley A. 2001. *Unfree Speech: The Folly of Campaign Finance Reform*. Princeton, NJ: Princeton University Press.

Stevenson, Senator Adlai, III. 1973. "Temporary Increase in Public Debt Limit." 93rd Cong. 1st sess., *Congressional Record* 119, pt. 29 (November 27): 38225.

Thomas, Representative Bill. 1991. "House of Representatives Campaign Spending Limit and Election Reform Act of 1991." 102nd Cong. 1st sess., *Congressional Record* 137, pt. 23 (November 25): 34680.

U.S. House of Representatives. 1992. "Congressional Campaign Spending Limit and Election Reform Act of 1992." Conference report. 102nd Cong., 2nd sess., rpt. 102-487.

U.S. President's Commission on Campaign Costs. 1962. "Financing Presidential Campaigns." Washington, DC: Government Printing Office.

U.S. Senate Committee on Rules and Administration. 1961. "Proposed Amendments to and Improvements in the Federal Election Laws." Hearings before the Subcommittee on Privileges and Elections, May 11–12. Committee print. Washington, DC: Government Printing Office.

———. 1974. "Federal Election Campaign Act Amendments of 1974." S.Rpt. to accompany S. 3044. No. 93-689, 93rd Cong., 2nd sess., February 21 (legislative day February 19).

Wertheimer, Fred. 1986. "Campaign Finance Reform: The Unfinished Agenda." *Annals of the American Academy of Political and Social Science* 486 (July): 86–102.

Williams, Andrea D. 1992–1993. "The Lowest Unit Charge Provision of the Federal Communications Act of 1934, as Amended, and Its Role in Maintaining a Democratic Electoral Process." *Federal Communications Law Journal* 45 (2): 267–311.

2

❖ ❖ ❖

Small Donors, Large Donors, and the Internet

Rethinking Public Financing
for Presidential Elections after Obama

Michael Malbin

The public funding system for presidential elections collapsed in 2008. The policy question for the future will be whether to revive it at all and, if so, how. It is clear that whatever purposes the system once served, the political context has so changed as to make the system at best insufficient. Some will seek to change the system to serve its original purposes. Others will say that any public financing program, however modified, has become irrelevant or worse. Still others, including this author, argue that the purposes themselves need rethinking. Public policy is, after all, a means to some other end as opposed to an end in itself. I would argue that some of the law's original purposes—most importantly, limiting the amount of spending in politics—cannot be achieved. Others—such as promoting competition, candidate emergence, and public participation—can be helped through some forms of public support, but the system needs a redesign if these are the main goals. The current program has become vestigial. The debate therefore should be over whether the presidential system should be redesigned or repealed. I argue for redesigning in light of both redefined goals and a new context. This chapter concludes with a brief introduction of new legislative paths being pursued in the U.S. Congress that explore some of the trajectories for which this chapter argues.

The presidential public financing system in effect since 1974 is made up of two distinct policy programs. During the nomination contest, participating candidates receive one-for-one federal matching funds for the first $250 the candidate raises from each individual contributor. In return the candidate must abide by a prenomination spending limit that in 2008 came to about $50 million ($42.05 million plus an allowance for legal and accounting costs). In the general election the two major party nominees may receive a flat grant that came to $84.1 million in 2008. In return, a participating candidate must agree to spend only the grant money plus legal and accounting costs. Over the past three decades, either the matching-fund or flat-grant approach has been a model for almost all state and local systems of public financing. Because the same policy and constitutional issues that have bedeviled the presidential system exist elsewhere, the presidential system's collapse and ultimate fate are likely to speak volumes for the future of public financing more broadly.

Any public funding system's success depends on the choices of candidates. In 1976, the U.S. Supreme Court ruled in the landmark case of *Buckley v. Valeo* that the First Amendment prohibits Congress and other legislatures from imposing *mandatory* spending limits on candidates, even if the limits are accompanied by a sweetener like public funds. However, legislatures are free to condition public funds on a candidate's *voluntarily* accepting some limits or obligations in return. As a result, a system will remain useful only if enough candidates decide that the benefits outweigh the costs.

In 2008, almost every one of the two major parties' leading candidates for the nomination refused to accept public matching funds and the attendant spending limits. John McCain accepted public funds for the general election after rejecting them for the primaries, but Barack Obama became the first major party nominee since 1976 to opt out of both phases. In the end, Obama spent nearly four times the $84.1 million public grant during the general-election season.

The system's collapse had been building for some time. George W. Bush in 2000 was the first major party nominee to reject public money for the primaries. Two of the leading candidates in 2004 (Howard Dean and John Kerry) did the same, and Kerry seriously considered opting out for the general election. So 2008 was no surprise, but it was a clear turning point. One factor that made the turning point so obvious was that several candidates said from the start that they would not be participating, without any apparent concern that this might make them look bad to voters. Even typically reform-minded editorial boards did not criticize the decision. Some regretted Congress's failure to amend the law after 2004, but all sympathized with the strategic calculations that led candidates to reject a $50 million spending ceiling as they were running against opponents who said they planned to be spending much more.

The primaries may have left some with the impression that the system's problems could be repaired with a few simple changes—for example, by raising the spending ceiling. But the general election raised deeper questions. These were expressed by many during the election season, but we have taken the liberty of quoting extensively from two articles published during the campaign's closing week. The authors—normally on opposite sides on this issue—were former Federal Election Commission Chairman Bradley Smith and former Senator Bob Kerrey. Smith, who opposes most campaign finance regulation, wrote the following in the *Washington Post*, shortly after Barack Obama's disclosure reports showed him to have raised nearly $640 million in combined primary- and general-election funding as of October 15:

> Obama's epic fundraising should put to rest all the shibboleths about campaign finance reform—that it is needed to prevent corruption, that it equalizes the playing field, or that tax subsidies are needed to prevent corruption. . . .
>
> We should consider it a healthy thing when Americans support their political beliefs with their dollars. What we see in this election is that contributions don't really cause "corruption" and that we don't really want the government deciding who has spoken too much and who has not spoken enough. If Obama's fundraising shows us the emptiness of the arguments for campaign finance "reform," he will have done us a great service, in spite of himself. (Smith 2008)

More surprising than Smith's position, however, was an opinion article in the *New York Post* by former Senator Bob Kerrey, who over the years has been a cochair of Americans for Campaign Reform and a supporter of public campaign financing:

> On the question of public funding of presidential campaigns, we Democrats who strongly support Sen. Barack Obama's candidacy and who previously supported limits on campaign spending and who haven't objected to Obama's opting out of the presidential funding system face an awkward fact: Either we are hypocrites, or we were wrong to support such limitations in the first place.
>
> The next time we speak of the virtue of level playing fields or state our strong belief that democracy can't survive in the modern age unless big money is taken out of campaigns, we'll be counting on our audience's forgetting our silence this year, when the free market was flowing in our direction. . . .

Of course, there's another option: Admit I was wrong on such limitations in the first place. And that's exactly what I'm likely to do.

For the facts in evidence seem to make the case that this presidential campaign is the most exciting, most closely watched and most expensive in my lifetime. That is, there seems to be no correlation between the amount of money spent and disillusionment among the voters. Indeed, the contrary appears to be true. . . .

So maybe I was simply wrong about placing limits on spending and providing public monies in exchange for adhering to these limits. . . . [P]erhaps this will be the moment that causes me to change my views. It certainly feels better than remaining a hypocrite forever. (Kerrey 2008)

These two articles may leave the reader with the impression of an emerging right-to-left consensus on the failures of public financing. To a certain extent, the impression is correct. The 2008 election did create a consensus that old premises need to be rethought. But there is not a similar consensus about what the goals of public policy should be, let alone about what policy mechanisms would best help to further those goals.

To illustrate, let us look again at the quotations from Smith and Kerry. Both seem to argue that the main purpose against which public financing ought to be judged is whether it reduces corruption. Kerrey also spelled out other purposes—such as leveling the playing field and reducing disillusionment—but all, in his understanding, flowed from the spending limit. When higher spending in 2008 seemed to him to be associated with citizen excitement rather than disillusionment, he saw no further reason for public financing and was therefore prepared to consider abandoning it.

Two problems immediately come to mind with this argument. First, public financing for candidates should not ever have been expected to limit private spending on politics, given the First Amendment's protections for independent speech. This has been doubly true since the Supreme Court ruled that political parties have the same right to unlimited independent spending as nonparty groups and individuals.[1] Public financing systems limit the *candidates* who participate in them, but they do not limit the other participants in the system. Presidential candidates who take public funds for the general election have benefited for years from unlimited party spending, first in the form of soft money and then from independent spending. Party spending does not give a candidate the same degree of control as money in the candidate's own account, but it does create real options for getting around the spending cap legally. In contrast, primary candidates do not have such an option. The national party committees do not engage independent spending to support one candidate over another while the primaries are still being contested. Hence the candidates in the primaries face greater pressures than a general-election candidate to opt out if they face an opponent who is doing the same. So if limiting the amount of private money in politics were the only reason for public financing, the system has been undermined for a long time.

This observation leads in two directions. The first harks back to the fact that the system was devised in part as a reaction to President Richard M. Nixon's reliance on major donors in 1972. On that view, the real reason to limit candidate spending was (as Kerrey says) to shift the balance between large donors and small. If so, a more complete version of Kerrey's argument would be that the Obama campaign's use of the Internet showed that public financing is not needed to accomplish such a shift in balance. (We examine later whether the evidence on this issue is settled.) The second path broadens our vision beyond spending.

Goals, Successes, and Failures
of Public Financing, 1976–2004[2]

The goals of the presidential public financing system from the beginning were not confined to fighting corruption or putting limits on spending. After all, the authors of the Federal Election Campaign Act Amendments of 1974 put the same contribution limits on presidential as on congressional candidates, and they mistakenly believed that mandatory spending limits (overturned by the Supreme Court in its 1976 decision in *Buckley v. Valeo*) could be imposed on Congress without public financing. The public financing provisions therefore were not meant as a lever for limits (since they thought they could impose the limits anyway) but to supply alternative funds to help elections serve their purposes without the problematic funds the limits were meant to rule out. That is, *the decision to include public money was not about preventing but enabling.* One of the primary goals was about maintaining competition within a system newly constrained by contribution limits. Before FECA, underdog candidates (such as Eugene McCarthy, the 1968 presidential candidate who was a coplaintiff in *Buckley*) could rely on a few rich patrons to get their campaigns started. Public matching funds were meant to give underdogs an alternative way to remain competitive until they were tested by the voters in early primaries. Second, while the public money was supposed to encourage competition, the spending ceiling was not meant to be so low as to stifle it. Finally, the system was meant to encourage candidates to broaden their fund-raising bases.

Competition

Public matching funds before 2008 worked successfully to provide a meaningful boost to underdog candidates in the primaries—whether Republican or Democrat, conservative, liberal, or moderate. Matching funds typically have been responsible for between one-quarter and one-third of the money raised by participating candidates, with candidates who emphasize small contributions receiving the higher percentages. Examples of the latter have included Democrats Jesse Jackson (1984 and 1988) and Jerry Brown (1992), along with Republicans Pat Robertson (1988), Patrick Buchanan (1992), and Gary Bauer (2000). The high-water mark was established by Ronald Reagan in his 1984 reelection campaign, when he received about 60 percent of his funding from small donors and earned $9.7 million in matching funds, the maximum amount permitted under the limits in effect at the time.

Matching funds have also had a strong impact on competition. A remarkable number of significant candidates, including three future presidents, were underdogs who were just about out of money, running against well-funded opponents, when an infusion of public funds made it possible for them to remain viable. These have included the following:

- Ronald Reagan (1976) had only $43,497 cash on hand at the end of January 1976. President Gerald Ford had fifteen times as much in the bank on that day. If the challenger's campaign had not received $1 million in public money in January, and another $1.2 million in February, his advisers have said they could not have continued. Reagan's strong campaign in 1976 fueled his success in 1980.
- Jimmy Carter (1976) had $42,000 in cash at the end of 1975. The fact that public funds let him continue through the Iowa and New Hampshire primaries propelled the underdog to victory.
- George H. W. Bush (1980) was down to his last $75,000 on December 31, when the now-favored Reagan had seven times that much cash. Public money let Bush earn enough votes to get an offer later to run as vice president.
- Gary Hart (1984) had about $2,200 at the end of December 1983, $2,500 in January 1984, and $3,700 at the end of February. Walter Mondale had $2.1 million in cash on January 31, 1984—more than 800 times as much as his opponent.

- Jesse Jackson (1988) was down to $5,700 at the end of 1987 at a time when the front-runner, Michael Dukakis, had $2.1 million.
- Paul Tsongas (1992) had $80,000 in cash on January 31, compared to Bill Clinton's $1.4 million.
- Pat Buchanan (1992) had $12,000 in cash on January 31 compared to the incumbent President Bush's $8.9 million.
- John McCain (2000) was comparatively the richest of these underdogs, with $350,000 in cash on January 31, 2000. His opponent, George W. Bush, had $20.5 million in cash on the same day, spent down from $31 million the previous month.
- In 2004 John Edwards, Wesley Clark, Richard Gephardt, and Joseph Lieberman would not have been in a position to run competitive races during the early primaries if it had not been for public funds. John Kerry would have been in a similar position against Howard Dean if he had not been rich enough to lend his own money to the campaign.
- John Edwards's (2008) second-place finish in the Iowa caucuses was once again fueled by public matching funds. However, it is likely that if his campaign had remained viable beyond the first races, the spending limit would have prevented him from contesting many primaries effectively in later weeks.

All these candidates garnered significant public support, testing the front-runners, remaining viable until at least some voters could cast real ballots. One key policy question, therefore, is whether the public has been well served by hearing these candidates and others. The list clearly is not a collection of fringe candidates. For three of them (Carter, Reagan, and the elder Bush) matching funds sustained the political careers of future presidents. In every other case, the public learned something about the front-runners because of underdogs' challenges. But by 2008, the public money and spending limit no longer provided enough money to permit most participating candidates to mount full-fledged campaigns. The spread between the financial top tier and the next was simply too great.

Spending Limits, Front-Loading, and Opting Out— A Minihistory

In the hyperspecialized conversations about campaign finance that typically take place in the public arena, we sometimes forget the importance of the fact that 1972 was the first year in which the newly reformed presidential nominating process was to be dominated by primaries. The 1974 campaign finance law's presidential financing provisions were designed to serve a nomination process that had been through only one previous election cycle. The nomination and campaign-finance regimes did fit together for a while. But then the nomination process changed, along with much of the rest of the political environment, although the system for financing presidential elections remained static. Rather than continuing to hold on to an anchor in the midst of a swirling pool, candidates eventually have chosen to let go.

Consider just the impact of the delegate selection calendar. In 1976, Jimmy Carter, a decided underdog, came in first behind "uncommitted" in the Iowa caucuses and then, with more than a month between the two events, won the New Hampshire primary. Using his new visibility to raise funds for the next round of contests, Carter was able to campaign through three and a half more months of relatively evenly spaced primaries until he wrapped up the nomination in June. On the Republican side, the former governor of California, Ronald Reagan, took on a sitting president and came within a hair's breadth of winning. Gerald Ford's victory over Ronald Reagan was in doubt until the GOP convention in August. Small contributions and public matching funds substantially funded both the Carter and Reagan campaigns.

Contrast this leisurely pace with the frenetic nomination process of recent years. In 1976, neither party had selected half of its convention delegates until early May—a full fifteen weeks after the Iowa caucuses and ten after the New Hampshire primary. In 1980, the halfway point was about the same: fourteen weeks after Iowa and nine after New Hampshire, at the end of April. By 1996 the calendar had shifted dramatically. The midpoint in 1996 had moved up to March 12, only four weeks after Iowa and three after New Hampshire (Mayer and Busch 2004). This rapid pace had a dramatic effect on the campaign finance needs of the party out of power.

The eventual GOP nominee in 1996 was Robert Dole. One of his opponents (Steve Forbes) was a self-financed multimillionaire who chose not to be bound by the spending limits. This was the first time a candidate who opted out of the system had put up a serious challenge in the primaries. By March 26, Dole had effectively clinched the nomination, having worked his way through 24 primaries and 13 caucuses that together selected 74 percent of his Republican Party's convention delegates. Like most winners since 1976, Dole had used almost his full spending limit to gain the nomination. But because of the compressed primary season, he now faced a new problem. Past nominees could turn almost seamlessly from the nomination to the convention and then to the publicly funded general election. In contrast,

Dole's victory was coming months before the convention. The nomination contest may have been over practically but not legally. Legally, the candidate is considered to be within the prenomination period, governed by the pre-nomination spending limit, until formally nominated at the party's national convention. Formal nomination was not going to occur for another four months. But Dole at that point was facing an incumbent president who had not been opposed for the nomination. President Clinton could spend mil-lion of dollars in unused primary money to run general election campaign advertisements during what was legally still the prenomination season. Dole, in contrast, had no leeway under the spending ceiling to raise and spend any money in return. By the time Dole received his general-election grant, the contest was all but over.

Three years later, when George W. Bush announced he was going to run for the presidency, the Texas governor faced a strategic situation that looked uncomfortably like Dole's. Bush knew that he too could be running against the self-financed Forbes in the Republican primaries and that whoever won the GOP nomination probably would be up against an incumbent vice presi-dent (Al Gore) in the general election. But in one crucially important respect, Bush's situation was different from Dole's: Bush was able to tap a network of financial supporters from Texas as well as his father's fund-raising base. With confidence in his ability to raise money and a serious concern about being squeezed by the spending limit, Bush decided that the benefits of public money were just not worth the risks. "I'm mindful of what happened in 1996 and I'm not going to let it happen to me," Bush told reporters (Glover 1999).

By avoiding the limit in 2000, Bush was able to spend almost twice as much as a publicly funded candidate. His principal challenger, John Mc-Cain, was an underdog who needed public funds. McCain lost to Bush dur-ing the first week of March ("Super Tuesday") and withdrew from the race. However, had McCain done better with the voters on Super Tuesday, he still would not have been able to continue because he had already spent up to the limit. McCain had made a Faustian bargain: In return for the money that sustained his insurgent campaign in January and February, he had to follow a diet that would starve the campaign by mid-March. The system offered him no escape, even though he was running against a candidate whose spending was not limited.

Of course, the cycle did not stop there. Just as the Dole example weighed on Bush, so did the Bush and McCain examples weigh on the Democrats. In 2003, Howard Dean referred to Bush when he opted out of the public funding system, as Bush had referred to Dole. Then John Kerry in a simi-lar announcement referred to Dean. The situation may have been triggered by front-loading but the issue was more general. Candidates have to weigh the risks and rewards before they decide whether to sign up. Public money is a benefit, especially to a long-shot candidate who cannot raise more money than the spending limit anyway. But for a candidate who can raise more, it would be crazy to abide by a limit that is too low for the political context if the opponent is not doing so too. No public funding system can remain viable if a decision to participate carries with it the risk of political suicide.

If anything, the political context has become tougher in the years since Dole ran. In 2008 more than half the delegates were selected by February 5, a full month earlier than in 1996. This was only three and a half weeks after Iowa and four weeks after New Hampshire. Instead of having the five *weeks* between Iowa and New Hampshire that Jimmy Carter was able to use in 1976, the candidates in 2008 had only five *days*. Then, only one month after New Hampshire, the candidates of 2008 were facing contests in twenty-four different states, including some of the largest, from all parts of the country.

This schedule forces candidates to run a national campaign early, rather than the series of state campaigns envisioned by the Congress that enacted the system in 1974. Knowing there would be almost no time between the first test and the next crucial ones, candidates in the top financial tier felt they had to raise enough money before Iowa to prepare for the massive expenditures to follow. From the beginning, therefore, pundits were predicting (accurately, it turns out) that candidates in the top tier would raise as much as $100 million in calendar year 2007 alone. That means that the top money raisers of 2007 (Hillary Clinton, Barack Obama, and the partially self-financed Mitt Romney) brought in twice as much money before the Iowa caucuses of January 3, 2008, as a publicly funded candidate was allowed under the spending limit for the entire prenomination period through August.

Participation by Small Donors

Front-loading appears to have had a significant effect on not only the amount of money the candidates raise but also how they raise it. One of the stated purposes of the matching fund system was to give candidates an incentive to raise money in small contributions. In 1976, 38 percent of Jimmy Carter's individual contributions and 40 percent of Gerald R. Ford's came in amounts of $200 or less. At the same time, according to the Federal Election Commission, Ford raised only 24 percent of his money, and Carter 18 percent, in contributions of $750 or more.

The leisurely calendar of 1976 helped with this distribution. Because the pace was slow, candidates did not need to raise the bulk of their money until they had a chance to gain public visibility. Small donor fund-raising on a national scale (especially before the Internet) has presupposed name recognition that usually has taken some time and success to develop. As front-loading forced candidates to compress their fund-raising schedules, the mix of contributions began changing. By the late 1980s, when front-loading was becoming noticeable, the leading candidates typically were raising more than half their money from large contributions. The election of 2000 was the last before the contribution limit went up from the $1,000 limit that had been in place since 1974 (with no cost-of-living adjustment). In that election, Al Gore raised 63 percent of his money from $1,000 donors, Bill Bradley raised 66 percent, and George W. Bush raised 72 percent.

The 2004 election saw a significant increase in the importance of small contributions, but not because of matching funds. Because the Bipartisan Campaign Reform Act had doubled the maximum contribution to $2,000 (plus a cost-of-living adjustment), most observers expected to see a greater dependence on large contributions. In fact there was an increase in the percentage of money coming from small contributions, largely because of the Internet and—ironically—because candidates who opted out of public financing were still raising money after they were very well known.

Howard Dean led the way with a strong Internet presence. Dean raised the bulk of his money in the year before the first primary, with about half of his total coming in amounts of $200 or less. But Dean's early performance was an exception. Through the early primaries (January 2007 through February 2008) more than two-thirds of the money raised by all candidates except Dean was coming in amounts of $1,000 or more. George Bush and John Kerry did eventually raise large amounts over the Internet. For both, however, the bulk of the small contributions came after Kerry had sewn up the Democratic nomination and the race had essentially boiled down to a two-person general-election contest. The two candidates were able to keep raising and spending money during the prenomination period because they had rejected public money and were therefore free from the spending limit.

Thus the one-for-one matching fund system over the years stopped being an effective incentive for promoting small contributions. As political imperatives changed, the calendar was helping to push candidates to raise more money early from major donors. The candidates who seemed to be bringing small donors back into the process (Dean, followed by Kerry and Bush) had rejected public funding and then used the Internet's low fund-raising costs to build up their fund-raising networks. The 2008 election would bring this new model of fund-raising to center stage.

The 2008 Election

The 2008 election put many of public financing system's assumptions to a severe test. For example, even if one assumes the system can be changed to lure candidates back into accepting public funds, can one continue to argue after 2008 that some form of public financing is important for promoting competition and participation? Second, when Barack Obama rejected public funds for the general election, his campaign said that his broad fund-raising base was the functional equivalent of public financing? Is this true? And if so, is it reasonable to expect other candidates to be able to replicate his success? We return to these questions after looking at what happened in 2007–2008.

Fund-Raising Juggernauts and Early Money

Presidential candidates raised $1.1 billion in contributions from individuals during the 2008 prenomination season from January 1, 2007, through August 31, 2008. This nearly doubled the $604 million raised in 2004. It was five times as much as the $217 million in private money raised from individuals in 2000 when all the major candidates except Bush opted for public financing. In 2004, President Bush and John Kerry were the first candidates ever to break the $200 million mark. (In 2000, Bush set the previous record of $101 million.) In 2008, Hillary Clinton raised $194 million, and John McCain raised $204 million. Barack Obama raised $409 million before the nomination, which was as much as Clinton's and McCain's receipts combined. (All figures in the remainder of this chapter exclude money raised and set aside for the general election.)

Of course, it took time for the candidates to raise this much money. At the beginning of the campaign, many knowledgeable observers thought presidential races in a front-loaded primary system would quickly narrow into a contest between a front-runner, who could raise a lot of money, and one or perhaps two underdog challengers (Table 2.1). In the year before the first primary, the task for an underdog is to separate oneself from the pack and to remain within striking distance of the front-runner. For the press (and many others) money was seen (often not correctly) as the best early marker for the candidates' relative strength.

Hillary Clinton raised more money than any other candidate during the first quarter, as expected. But second place was a surprise: Barack Obama, a freshman senator, far outdistanced a former candidate for the vice presidency

TABLE 2.1.   EARLY FUND-RAISING, JANUARY–JUNE 2007 (MILLIONS OF DOLLARS)

	January–March	April–June	Total
Democrats			
Obama	24.7	30.9	55.6
Clinton	29.1	21.3	50.3
Edwards	12.6	8.0	20.7
Richardson	6.2	6.9	13.1
Dodd	7.9	2.8	10.7
Biden	3.7	1.8	5.4
Republicans			
Romney	23.3	20.6	44.0
Giuliani	16.9	15.0	31.9
McCain	14.6	10.0	24.7
Brownback	1.9	1.4	3.3
Paul	0.6	2.4	3.0
Tancredo	1.3	1.5	2.8
Huckabee	0.5	0.8	1.3
Hunter	0.5	0.8	1.3

(John Edwards), a governor who had also been a cabinet secretary (Bill Richardson), and two Senate committee chairmen (Christopher Dodd and Joseph Biden). Even more stunning was that Obama had actually raised more than Clinton during the first three months of 2007 if you discounted the $10 million Clinton had transferred from her Senate campaign committee. Then, as if to prove this was no fluke, Obama raised one and a half times as much as Clinton in the second quarter to vault into the financial lead. For the other candidates, the public financing system as currently structured was not going to be able to provide enough money to make up the gap these leaders were opening.

The early picture was more confusing on the Republican side, where there was no clear front-runner. Mitt Romney raised almost as much as Clinton. In fact, by June 2007, Romney, Clinton, and Obama had already raised as much as Howard Dean had in all of 2003, when he was the Democrats' financial front-runner. Rudy Giuliani's numbers were a notch below Romney's. John McCain was third but was nearly out of cash because his spending budget had assumed much higher receipts. By any previous standards these candidates were doing well: Giuliani and McCain raised more in the first six months of 2007 than John Kerry in all twelve months of 2003. Interestingly, Ron Paul and Mike Huckabee at this stage were well down in the financial pack. Future policy makers will have to face the fact that the three GOP candidates whose campaigns lasted the longest in 2008—Huckabee, Paul, and McCain—lost the off-year "financial primary." Without a clear front-runner and break-out-of-the-pack challenger, the three were able to use free media, debates, and the Internet to close the political gap. (The media's saturation coverage of Obama and Clinton made this a less viable path for the remaining Democratic candidates.)

Small and Large Contributions

It has frequently been said that Obama's fund-raising advantage was based on a groundswell of support from an unprecedented number of people who were willing to make small contributions over the Internet. (A small contribution is defined here as one of $200 or less, which is the threshold for disclosure under federal law.) The total amount he received over the primary season in amounts of $200 or less ($205 million) nearly equaled what Clinton or McCain received from all sources combined. Almost three-quarters of the financial advantage Obama ultimately held over Clinton can be explained by his advantage in small contributions. So the basic claim about the importance of small contributions is true. But the full story is more complicated.

Table 2.2 shows receipts by all the leading candidates of 2007–2008 over time. Presidential candidates file reports with the Federal Election Commission quarterly during the off-year and monthly during the election year. To simplify, the table groups the FEC reports in time frames that make sense for the 2008 campaign. Most of the campaigns maintained fairly consistent financial profiles over the first three quarters of 2007. The final quarter of 2007 was the run-up to Iowa and therefore is shown separately. Most of the primaries took place in January and February. Most Republican candidates and all Democratic candidates except Obama and Clinton ended their fund-raising by the end of February. During March through May, the Democratic race was down to two candidates. Clinton did little fund-raising after May and suspended her campaign in June. From June through the end of the prenomination season the field was left to the two presumptive nominees, who were in effect running a general-election campaign against each other.

Table 2.2 makes it clear that all the candidates started off by relying more on large donors than small. Of course, not all candidates followed the same profile. Clinton, Romney, and Giuliani received proportionally the most from $1,000-plus contributors through September 30, but all the candidates emphasized large contributions in the early stage. Obama raised 60 percent of his money during the first nine months of 2007 in amounts $1,000 or more. Even Ron Paul—the libertarian Republican who raised half of his money through the three-quarter mark in small contributions—started during the first quarter with half of his money in amounts of $1,000 or more. For all the candidates with viable campaigns, small contributions increased

TABLE 2.2. LARGE AND SMALL CONTRIBUTIONS OVER THE PRIMARY SEASON: LEADING CANDIDATES' FUND-RAISING, JANUARY 2007–AUGUST 2008

	From All Sources ($ millions)	From Individuals ($ millions)	In Amounts $200 or Less (percent)	In Amounts $1,000 or More (percent)
Democrats				
Obama				
January–September 2007	75.4	74.5	28	60
October–December 2007	22.1	21.6	46	34
January–February 2008	89.3	88.9	53	25
March–May 2008	91.7	91.3	63	18
June–August 2008	134.0	132.8	54	28
Obama subtotals	414.4	409.2	50	31
Clinton				
January–September 2007	73.7	60.7	13	78
October–December 2007	24.0	22.6	17	69
January–February 2008	51.4	45.7	47	43
March–May 2008	59.4	51.1	61	19
Clinton subtotals	208.6	180.1	36	49
Edwards				
January–September 2007	27.1	26.8	32	56
October–December 2007	13.6	4.6	62	18
January–February 2008	7.0	3.9	70	11
Edwards subtotals	47.7	35.2	40	45
Republicans				
McCain				
January–September 2007	29.9	28.0	21	68
October–December 2007	9.5	6.3	38	39
January–February 2008	23.0	21.7	24	60
March–May 2008	54.1	52.8	23	64
June–August 2008	100.2	94.4	38	44
McCain subtotals	216.6	203.2	31	54
Romney				
January–September 2007	62.4	43.7	20	70
October–December 2007	27.1	8.8	18	70
January–February 2008	17.0	7.5	31	49
Romney subtotals	106.5	60.1	21	67
Huckabee				
January–September 2007	2.4	2.3	35	47
October–December 2007	6.7	6.6	39	44
January–February 2008	7.0	6.9	53	30
Huckabee subtotals	16.0	15.8	44	38
Paul				
January–September 2007	8.3	8.2	54	27
October–December 2007	20.0	19.9	66	16
January–February 2008	6.2	6.1	70	9
Paul subtotals	34.5	34.2	64	17
Giuliani				
January–September 2007	42.1	39.2	8	83
October–December 2007	13.8	13.2	7	81
Giuliani subtotals	55.9	52.4	8	82

Note: Table excludes funds raised and sequestered for the general election. Totals include loans, self-financing, public financing, and other items. Percents are of net individual contributions.

over time as the candidates gained name recognition. Obama jumped from receiving 28 percent of his money from contributions of $200 or less over the first three quarters of 2007 (24 percent in the third quarter) to 46 percent in the fourth quarter and then above 50 percent in 2008. Edwards, Huckabee, and Paul also ratcheted up their $200-or-less contributions in the fourth quarter, as did Clinton after the first of the year.

It is worth lingering over these numbers because of their policy implications. The first three quarters were when Obama established himself as one of the two major alternatives to Clinton. Edwards, the other major alternative, was well known to the general public for having been the party's candidate for the vice presidency in 2004. But Obama's visibility was being fueled by the media largely because of his financial success, which rested at the time on contributions of $1,000 or more. This early reliance on large contributions should not be a surprise. As noted earlier, raising large amounts of money through small contributions presupposes visibility. Some have argued that the Internet can do away with this problem. Perhaps, but it has not yet done so. The Internet does open new avenues of communication for gaining visibility. It lets candidates develop networks of volunteers and financial supporters without spending a fortune on postage for direct mail. Peer-to-peer communications, with supporters forwarding fund-raising e-mails to their own friends, lets a candidate piggyback on supporters' networks to reach low-dollar donors. Presumably—since fund-raising, networking, and communications costs are so much lower over the Internet and because it is easier through social networking tools to discover a niche market—an underdog candidate may not have to gain quite as much national recognition as he or she once would have needed for mass fund-raising. But the candidate still has to get the campaign off the ground. Support has to reach some kind of a critical mass. In an underdog campaign for the presidency, the candidate either has to develop a following within a niche (Howard Dean as the antiwar candidate in 2004, Ron Paul as the libertarian Republican), or the candidate needs to become seen as the (or a) credible alternative to the front-runner. And the higher the financial front-runner sets the spending bar, the more money it will take to be perceived as a credible challenger.

All this means that it takes money to raise money. Candidates typically have to start by persuading a few people to give larger amounts before they can branch downward and outward. Might this situation change? After what has been happening to communications in recent years, it would be unwise to dismiss the possibility. But it also would be imprudent to count on it. Unless and until such a change occurs, having the wherewithal to break out of the pack will have to begin either with an established constituency or with those who can give a lot. The alternative is some form of public policy—such as a revised public financing system—to help a potentially strong candidate get started.

Functional Equivalence?

In the end, as already noted, Obama's Internet-based operation raised contributions of $200 or less that nearly equaled what Clinton or McCain raised from all sources combined. But it would be a mistake to see Obama's Internet operation as a one-dimensional fund-raising tool. Many of his donors gave more than once. They also volunteered: The givers were also doers. By the end of the general election campaign the campaign had 13 million addresses on its campaign's e-mail list. The campaign's integrated social networking tools became the engine of its voter mobilization campaign, imitating and improving on the Republican innovations of 2002 and 2004. The Obama staff built a structure *within the campaign* that previously had been handled by ongoing organizations with more permanence than a candidate's campaign committee. Among Republicans this work typically was done by the party; among Democrats it was handled by labor unions and advocacy groups. Because these resources belonged to the candidate, the same tools that helped Obama raise more money than Clinton or McCain also helped him to outorganize them. They were keys to his victory. Obama's nomination rested in large part on his beating Clinton in the caucus states to open a delegate lead she was never able to combat in proportional-representation primaries.

When Obama announced in June 2008 that he was going to reject public financing for the general election, he said that his fund-raising base, with millions of donors giving $200 or less, was the functional equivalent of public financing. He had three million donors by the end of the primary season and four million by the time of the general election. Half his primary money (50 percent) came in contributions of $200 or less. During the general election, 45 percent of Obama's individual contributions were in contributiona of $200 or less. With so many people contributing (and volunteering) there can be no doubt that more people were involved in 2008 than in the past.

But the claim of "functional equivalency" is essentially a claim that Obama's support base was more representative of the general public than that of previous candidates. There is something to the claim, but once again the full picture is complicated. We do not yet have the information needed to draw a full picture of Obama's donors—particularly not of the vast majority of his donors who never gave enough money cumulatively to break the

$201 disclosure threshold. But we are able to make some preliminary and still provisional inferences from the disclosed donor lists.

Table 2.2 presented the percentage of total contributions that candidates received from *contributions* or *transactions* of various size ranges. This is how the press and the Obama campaign staff typically described what they were calling a small-donor revolution. This is also how the Campaign Finance Institute (CFI) and others described candidates' receipts for most of the two-year election cycle. Under this definition, if a donor gives five $100 contributions to a candidate, each one is counted in the $200-or-less category. However, there is another way to look at the numbers, making the *donor* the unit of analysis rather than the single *contribution* or *transaction*. In CFI's various state studies (where disclosure thresholds permit) a donor has been categorized as a "small donor" if he or she gives an aggregate of $100 or less after all of his or her contributions are combined. When CFI reported Obama's donors in this manner, the decision to restrict the use of the term "small donor" to those who gave a total of $200 or less was questioned by some. (For the original release and a follow-up, see CFI 2008 and Malbin 2008.) To clarify the intent, therefore, this chapter refers to "aggregate small donors." In Table 2.3, we separate aggregate donors into three categories for the sake of simplicity. First are those whose contributions aggregated to $200 or less. We use $200 as the cutoff for federal donors, rather than the $100 level we used in state studies, because the federal disclosure threshold makes it impossible to learn about donors whose contributions aggregate to less than $200. Most *donors* for most candidates fall into this category. For the top group we used "$1,000 or more." Most of the *money* typically comes from this group. We picked this number because federal law prohibited contributions above $1,000 before 2004 and we may want eventually (although not in this chapter) to take the time series back to 2000. As a third category, we lumped together all people whose total contributions fell between the other two, aggregated to between $201 and $999. The categories are rough, but they illustrate some important points.

In Table 2.2 we saw that over the full primary season Obama received a substantially higher percentage of his money than other candidates (except Ron Paul) in contributions of $200 or less as well as a substantially lower percentage in amounts of $1,000 or more. Table 2.3 shows that after multiple contributions from the same donors have been aggregated, the differences between Obama and other candidates look more subtle.

Obama received 30 percent of his money for the primary season from donors whose contributions aggregated to $200 or less. This was more than Clinton's 22 percent and McCain's 21 percent in 2008 as well as Bush's 25

TABLE 2.3.   INDIVIDUAL DONORS (AGGREGATED CONTRIBUTIONS) TO LEADING
PRESIDENTIAL CANDIDATES THROUGH AUGUST 31

Candidate	Total Number of Itemized Individual Donors	Total Amount of Itemized Contributions (dollars)	Net Individual Contributions (dollars)	Percent of Individual Contributions from		
				Donors Aggregating to $200 or Less	Donors Aggregating to $201–$999	Donors Aggregating to $1,000 or More
2008						
Democrat						
Obama	404,843	254,282,269	409,153,859	30	28	43
Clinton	170,747	141,384,829	193,997,313	22	23	56
Edwards	33,017	25,038,330	38,582,016	31	22	47
Republican						
McCain	168,194	152,669,105	203,538,725	21	20	60
Romney	44,700	53,796,356	59,783,991	8	13	79
Giuliani	39,250	51,062,011	55.013.148	6	10	83
Paul	32,426	18,348,045	34,336,163	39	28	33
Thompson	17,017	13,648,332	23,202,420	39	18	43
Huckabee	13,744	10,442,938	15,991,901	29	23	48
2004						
Democrat						
Kerry	209,894	164,134,439	215,915,455	20	24	56
Dean	57,448	27,947,961	51,360,995	38	30	28
Edwards	18,589	20,173,933	21,880,659	7	14	78
Republican						
Bush	190,640	183,235,226	256,081,557	25	13	60

Source: Campaign Finance Institute.

percent in 2004, but less than Dean's 38 percent. And while Obama was, in the end, less dependent on aggregate donors of $1,000 or more than Clinton, McCain, Kerry, or Bush, it is nonetheless true that $1,000-or-more donors accounted for a much higher percentage of Obama's money (43 percent) than did his aggregate donors of $200 or less.

While we cannot verify the number of Obama's undisclosed donors, the numbers provided by the campaign staff are consistent with what else we know about this and other campaigns. Based on CFI's analysis of the disclosed records, Obama had about 405,000 different donors during the primary season who gave enough ($201) to trigger disclosure. Subtracting this number from the 3 million donors claimed by the campaign staff for the primary season would mean that more than five out of every six Obama donors, or 87 percent, stopped at $200 or less. These people gave an average total of about $65 per person. Both these figures are comparable to other candidates in past years. In 2000, the typical below-$200 donor averaged about $52. Moreover, the percentage of total donors who stayed in the $200-or-less range was about the same for Obama as for past candidates: In 2004, according to CFI's published estimates, 83 percent of all donors to all candidates gave $200 or less (Graf et al. 2006, 5). In 2000, it was 77 percent, but if you remove Bush it was 84 percent. And then again in 1996, the number for all presidential candidates combined was 84 percent (Campaign Finance Institute, 2003). Obama had an unprecedented *number* of under-$201 donors but the under-$201 group was roughly the same *percentage* of his donor pool as it was for past candidates. He also raised an unprecedented dollar amount from $1,000-and-up donors. His ship was riding higher at all levels, among aggregate small donors and large.

One set of Obama's donors may have been different in kind as well in numbers: The ones CFI had referred to as the repeat donors. Obama received 28 percent of his money from people whose aggregate contributions fell between $201 and $999. This number is slightly higher than John Kerry's (24 percent), higher still than John McCain's (20 percent), and substantially higher than George W. Bush's (13 percent). This middle group explains how Obama's extraordinarily high proportion of under-$201 *contributions* turned into a more ordinary percentage of under-$201 aggregate donors. He had an unusually high proportion of donors who gave under-$201 contributions more than once and whose aggregates ended up between $201 and $999. According to CFI's review of the records, approximately 224,000 of the 405,000 disclosed donors were people who started off by giving at least one contribution of $200 or less and then gave again (usually over the Internet) to cross the $200 mark. Almost all of these (about 206,000 of the 224,000) stayed below $1,000 in the aggregate. In a sense, this was one of Obama's "sweet spots." These repeat donors gave the candidate more than $100 million. We suspect they were also responsible for a fair portion of the campaign's energy and volunteer activism.

But having acknowledged the importance of these repeat donors, it would be premature without survey results to reach any conclusions about how representative they were of nondonating Obama supporters. However, we can note that in our surveys of state donors, the donors who gave $100 or less were in many important ways better representative of the nondonating public than were the donors who gave an aggregate $500 or more. Obama's under-$201 donors (who gave an average of about $65 per person) probably would look in many ways like the under-$101 donors from the states. (Unfortunately, we cannot know for certain because the lack of disclosure precludes sampling them.) It is more problematic just to make assumptions about the repeat donors, who were clearly important. On average, they gave Obama nearly $500 per donor ($490). While this is very close to the $500 that defined an aggregate large donor in CFI's past surveys of state donors, we suspect that the emotions of a presidential campaign will have made these donors different from the $500 donors we have surveyed in the past. But there still may be significant differences between the $500 donors, the $65 donor, and the non-donor. Without a survey, we cannot know.

For the sake of balance, we also need to comment about donors who gave Obama $1,000 or more. A significant portion of this money was raised by so-called bundlers—people who receive recognition for soliciting contributions and directing them to the candidate. According to the Center for Responsive Politics (CRP), 561 "bundlers" had raised a *minimum* of $63 million for Obama by mid-August, and 534 people had raised a minimum of $75 million for McCain. (These figures may include funds given during the primary season that were earmarked for the general election.) The bundlers undoubtedly were responsible for more than these amounts because the campaigns reported the bundlers in ranges and CRP's minimum totals were based conservatively on the low end of each range. A reasonable guess might estimate the real amount at the midpoint for each range. This would yield a total of about $90 million for Obama as of mid-August and more than $100 million for McCain. At the top of the bundlers were 47 of Obama's and 65 of McCain's who were listed by the campaigns in mid-August as being responsible for at least $500,000 each.

In addition to fund-raising directly for their own committees, the candidates were raising money for "joint fund-raising committees." Under current law, a donor in 2008 was able to write a single check to a joint fund-raising committee of up to $67,800 or $70,100, which could then be distributed by the joint committee to candidate and party committees. Because this money may be solicited by the candidate, it is seen by many as having functionally raised the general election contribution limit for presidential candidates. (For a time, Senator McCain even conducted joint fund-raising through his campaign committee's Web site.) With that single check, a donor in 2008 could give up to $2,300 for a candidates' primary campaign, another $2,300 for the candidate's general election campaign *if* the candidate has opted out of public financing, $28,500 for a national party committee, and up to $10,000 for any of a number of state party committees, up to the annual maximum contribution of $65,500 for all party committees combined. The advocacy organization Public Citizen listed 2,205 people as having contributed at least $25,000 to joint fund-raising committees supporting Obama and 1,846 people as having made similar contributions to joint fund-raising committees supporting McCain (http://whitehouseforsale.org).

According to records filed with the Federal Election Commission, Democratic joint fund-raising committees supporting Obama had raised $228 million, of which $87 million went to the candidate and $104 million to the national party. Republican committees supporting McCain raised $221 million, of which $22 million went to the candidate before the general election, $120 million went to the national party, and $24 million to state parties. How the parties would spend the money was strongly influenced by whether the candidates accepted public financing. Because John McCain had accepted public financing, political party independent spending was more important for him than for Obama. As of election day, the Republican National Committee had reported $53 million in independent spending to support McCain, compared to less than $500,000 spent independently by the Democratic National Committee to support Obama. The committees also spent money for coordinated advertising, voter mobilization, and other activities. This was in addition to the $84.1 million in public money that went to McCain as well as the $337 million Obama raised for the general election in private contributions.

Whither Public Financing and Why

The presidential public financing system collapsed in 2008 because the system no longer served most candidates' needs. Since any system with spending limits must be voluntary under the Constitution, no system can accomplish much unless candidates see benefits for themselves outweighing costs. But a system that *only* gives benefits to candidates would not justify spending public money unless it also served the public's interest. So the key questions for a policy maker considering a revised public financing program must be, What are the public interests to be served and how might a system be designed to serve them?

Some have argued that spending limits remain important, but they have to be increased to become more realistic. The problem is in knowing at what level a limit is "realistic" for a specific election context. Without specifying dollar amounts, we can imagine limits in three kinds of ranges. In one, a limit is so low as to prevent serious candidates from running a competitive race. The public financing system in Wisconsin reached this level some years ago, and the presidential system has now reached it. Alternatively, a spending limit might be set so high as to constrain no one and therefore serve no useful purpose. Somewhere in a middle ground, a spending limit will modify behavior. Candidates will weigh the cost of public funding against the constraints and calculate the constraint to be worth the benefit. But whether the constraint is accepted will vary markedly with the context. For example, state legislative candidates in Minnesota typically accept public financing with low spending limits. Their decisions seem collectively to relate to the manner in which legislative candidates in that state typically campaign, expectations of the public, and other factors not easily translated. But Minnesota also has calibrated its spending limits upward periodically by statute in a context where legislators of both parties seem willing to look for limits that most of the legislators consider reasonable. The legislators thus have been adjusting to a changing context in a background of unusual bipartisan cooperation. By contrast, the presidential system was never adjusted, even as the primary calendar and the media and constitutional contexts changed. As contexts changed, so did the candidates' assessments of costs and benefits. And once some candidates opted out, the cost of staying in went up markedly.

Some state laws try to respond to the situation in which a participating candidate runs against one who opts out by providing extra money to the participating candidate—sometimes two or three times as much as the state's standard level of public funding. Recently, constitutional concerns have been raised about such an approach.[3] But even if constitutional, this approach puts off the question without answering it. Whether or not two or three times the statutory limit will be "enough" will depend on context—including the spending potential of one's opponent. If the limit is higher than a candidate would spend anyway, then the limit serves no purpose. If it does constrain seriously, candidates at some point will either opt out or help their political parties raise money to be spent in unlimited independent expenditures. We do not and probably cannot ever know enough to calibrate firm limits well in a manner that will endure. The inherent problem is that the limits are fixed or pegged to a nonpolitical cost index, while the context is changing. Having said this, there are alternative ways to address the problem. We return to these shortly, because the problem is worth addressing only if the program brings about other public benefits deemed worth the effort.

I would argue that public funding could continue to serve the positive goals we have discussed, provided the system is structured properly to do so. I am not arguing that public financing is the only useful means to serve these ends but that it is one useful and often effective means. For example, the public funding system once strengthened competition for the presidency. It helped future presidents of both parties sustain underdog campaigns against front-runners until the public was ready to vote. The system could serve competition in this way again, but only if it provides enough money for the underdogs to run viable campaigns. The system could also be redesigned to foster participation by small donors and reduce candidates' dependence on large donors. Some will argue that this is superfluous in the age of the Internet. It is true that President Obama had many small donors without public funding, but (a) small contributions did not kick in even for him in a major way until the fourth quarter of 2007; (b) even for Obama, the financial contributions made by those who gave an aggregate of $200 or less were much less than those who aggregated to $1,000 or more; and (c) there is no reason to believe that even Obama's significant level of success will transfer to other candidates—particularly those running for less visible offices.

Before candidates began opting out of presidential public financing because of the spending limit, we saw that the system's one-for-one matching fund had stopped giving them enough of an incentive to orient their fundraising toward small contributors. But the presidential primary matching fund is not the only matching fund model to consider. For example, New York City's public financing system offers a six-to-one match for the first $175 a donor gives to a participating candidate. Under this formula, a $175 contribution is worth $1,225 to the candidate. With this kind of a match, the incentives change radically. Suddenly, it would "pay" even more for the candidate to look for the small donor than a $1,000 one. In addition, if the public matching funds were made available early enough, it would be possible for candidates to build up their initial visibility without relying so heavily on major donors and bundlers.

Eventually, any policy designer (and candidate) will have to face up to the spending limit. Even a six-for-one match would not be enough of an incentive for a serious candidate if it meant accepting an impossible limit. Again there are alternatives. One, favored by the American Civil Liberties Union, is to see public financing as a floor with no ceiling. Another, proposed in 2003 by the previously cited Campaign Finance Institute Task Force on Financing Presidential Elections, would have used multiple matching funds (like New York's), set a higher spending limit, and allowed candidates to raise and spend as much money as an opponent if the opponent opts out. Finally, Fred Wertheimer, president of Democracy 21, floated an intriguing set of ideas in an opinion article published shortly after the 2008 election. His proposal contained the following elements: (1) a four-for-one match for $200; (2) a "spending ceiling" of $250 million for the primaries and another $250 million for the general election; (3) a requirement that public money cease after candidates have reached the $250 million mark; but (4) after this point permitting candidates to raise and spend an unlimited amount of money as long as it is contributed by donors who give no more than $200 in the aggre-gate (Wertheimer 2008). A proposal based on these ideas was expected to be introduced by Senators Russell Feingold (D-WI) and Susan Collins (R-ME). While the details may change before introduction, the general structure is designed thoughtfully to get around the problems that have sunk the current system while at the same time supporting competition and promoting small donor participation.

A congressional public financing bill introduced by in 2009 by Sena-tors Richard Durbin (D-IL) and Arlen Specter (R-PA) similarly sought to enhance competition and the role of small donors by (1) providing a basic flat grant for candidates who wish to participate and who pass a qualify-ing threshold; (2) reducing the maximum permissible contribution from pri-vate sources to $100 for participating candidates; (3) providing four-to-one matching funds above the flat grant for small contributions, up to a maxi-mum amount of public funds per candidate; and (4) permitting candidates to spend unlimited amounts as long as the funds continue to come from donors who give no more than $100 each.

By putting these ideas forward at the end of this chapter, I am not endorsing them as the best of all possible solutions. Rather, they are put for-ward to show that the collapse of the current public financing system does not signal a fatal flaw with public financing per se. There are many ways to design a system that can further important goals while respecting the consti-tutional limits. To do so, however, it is important to recognize that the goals themselves have to be part of the conversation. Hard and fixed spending lim-its may be popular, but they do not accomplish the goals that their support-ers once claimed for them. But other goals that are at least as important can be furthered though proper design. While public financing may be a tough sell, that is a political more than a design flaw.

NOTES

1. *Colorado Republican Federal Campaign Committee v. Federal Election Commis-sion*, 518 US 604 (1996); *Federal Election Commission v. Colorado Republican Federal Cam-paign Committee* 533 US 431 (2001); *McConnell v. Federal Election Commission*, 540 US 93 (2003).

2. This section of the chapter is adapted from material in two reports published by the Campaign Finance Institute's Task Force on Financing Presidential Nominations (Cam-paign Finance Institute 2003, 2005). The present author was also the principal author of both task force reports.

3. The Supreme Court in *Davis v. Federal Election Commission* (2008) overturned the so-called Millionaire's Amendment provision in the Bipartisan Campaign Reform Act,

which had increased the contribution limit for money given to candidates who are running against a self-financed opponent.

REFERENCES

Campaign Finance Institute. 2003. Task Force on Financing Presidential Nominations. *Participation, Competition, Engagement: How to Revive and Improve Public Funding for Presidential Nomination Politics.* Washington, DC: Campaign Finance Institute.

———. 2005. Task Force on Financing Presidential Nominations. *So the Voters May Choose: Reviving the Presidential Matching Fund System.* Washington DC: Campaign Finance Institute.

———. 2008. "CFI Analysis of Presidential Candidates' Donor Reports—REALITY CHECK: Obama Received about the Same Percentage from Small Donors in 2008 as Bush in 2004." November 24. Available at http://www.cfinst.org/pr/prRelease.aspx?ReleaseID=216.

Glover, Mike. 1999. "Bush Says He'll Forgo Matching Funds." *Associated Press State and Local Wire,* July 15.

Graf, Joseph, Grant Reeher, Michael J. Malbin, and Costas Panagopoulas. 2006. *Small Donors, Online Donors and First-Timers in the Presidential Election of 2004.* A Project of the George Washington University's Institute for Politics, Democracy and the Internet in Collaboration with the Campaign Finance Institute. Available at http://ipdi.org/UploadedFiles/Small%20Donors%20Report.pdf. Also available at http://www.cfinst.org/president/#reports.

Kerrey, Bob. 2008. "Dems' Campaign-Finance Hypocrisy." *New York Post,* October 28. Available at http://www.nypost.com/seven/10282008/postopinion/opedcolumnists/dems_campaign_finance_hypocrisy_135631.htm. Accessed March 24, 2009.

Malbin, Michael J. 2008. "Remarks Prepared for Making Elections Work: The Law and the Process after November. A Conference Co-sponsored by the AEI-Brookings Election Reform Project, Election Law Journal and the University of California Washington Center." December 4. Available at http://www.cfinst.org/president/SmallDonors_Remarks120408.aspx.

Mayer, William and Andrew Busch. 2004. *The Front-Loading Problem in Presidential Nominations.* Washington, DC: Brookings Institution Press.

Smith, Bradley A. 2008. "Obama's Huge Haul Should End This Fight." *Washington Post,* October 26, Outlook Section, p. B01.

Wertheimer, Fred. 2008. "The $200 Campaign Finance Fix." *Washington Post,* November 13, p. A23.

3

◇ ◇ ◇

Public Financing in the States and Municipalities

ROBERT M. STERN

hen it comes to public financing of campaigns, the states and local governmental agencies are clearly the laboratories of reform. Public financing of elections exists in one form or another in twenty-four states and sixteen local jurisdictions. The Center for Governmental Studies has compiled these laws in a comprehensive but easy-to-use chart format that summarizes pertinent information on state and local public financing programs.

The first states to adopt public financing of campaigns (in 1974) were Minnesota and New Jersey, whose laws are still alive and relatively well today. North Carolina is the most recent state to adopt a law (although California voters considered a public financing measure put on the ballot by the California legislature in June 2010).

In terms of localities, Tucson, Arizona, adopted its public financing law in 1985, while Chapel Hill, North Carolina, is the latest to adopt a law in 2008. Six of the sixteen local jurisdictions with public financing laws are located in California.

Public financing laws vary tremendously. Some merely give tax credits to their citizens for making campaign contributions. Others provide direct subsidies to candidates who agree only to take the public funds. The discussion in this chapter centers on programs that give direct subsidies to candidates.

Partial versus Full Public Financing

Jurisdictions take two different approaches to financing candidate elections with public subsidies. The traditional approach gives matching or partial public financing to candidates who qualify for the program. Private contributions are permitted to be raised, and these are matched with public dollars, such as $1 for every $1 in private contributions received by the candidate up to a certain threshold.

A number of jurisdictions at the state level (Arizona, Connecticut, Maine, New Mexico, North Carolina and Vermont) and the local level (Albuquerque, New Mexico; Chapel Hill, North Carolina; Miami-Dade County, Florida; and Portland, Oregon) have enacted legislation known as "clean money" or full public financing. These programs require candidates to raise a large number of very small contributions ($5 to $10 is typical) and then forgo raising any further private funds (or in the case of Connecticut limiting such contributions to no more than $100).

Maine was the first state to adopt full public financing of elections in 1996. Its law was challenged in court because the opponents felt that the amount of public financing awarded each candidate was so large that it practically forced candidates to accept the program. The United States Court of Appeal rejected the claims and found the measure valid.[1] Arizona's full public financing law has been under attack since it first was implemented in 2000. So far the courts have upheld its provisions except for a successful challenge that voided the use of lobbyist fees to fund the program.[2]

Full public financing in Massachusetts encountered rather unique political and legal problems—all unrelated to any questions about the constitutional validity of the public financing program. Instead, implementation of full public financing in Massachusetts was thwarted by a reluctant legislature. The initiative process in Massachusetts, like that of only a few other states, does not permit initiative legislation to establish a budget or allocate funds. Although voters ratified the initiative by a two-to-one margin, the legislature refused to pay for it. While the Massachusetts Constitution does not permit the allocation of budgets through initiative legislation, Article 48 of the Constitution seemed to require the legislature either to repeal the law or fund it.[3]

Based on such a reading of the Massachusetts Constitution, full public financing proponents asked the Supreme Judicial Court to order the state to fund the law. Several of the justices seemed perplexed by the lawsuit. One justice noted that the voter-approved law is "flagrantly being ignored."

But another justice questioned, "What do we do if we order the Legislature to fund this and they refuse to do so? Do we put the Legislature in jail?" (Klein 2001).

In the end, the court threw down the gauntlet on January 25, 2002, and ruled that the legislature must either fund the program or repeal it within two weeks. The legislature refused to fund the program but eventually put a measure on the ballot to repeal the law. The voters approved amendments to the law in 2002 that applied the law to only statewide officials, not legislative races.

The courts have accepted the constitutionality of voluntary partial public financing of candidate campaigns since the 1976 *Buckley v. Valeo* decision.[4] The courts have rather consistently extended the tenets of *Buckley* to apply to full public financing programs as well.

Eligible Offices and Applicable Elections

State public financing programs vary in terms of which elective offices are included in the programs and whether the program applies to primary or general elections or both. The most ambitious programs apply to all state elective offices and all elections. Yet most public financing states have opted to include only some offices and elections.

In some jurisdictions, such as Minnesota, public financing applies to all state offices but only in the general election. Minnesota has a strong tradition of partisan politics, and the two major parties view the general election as a more critical stage to balance financial resources between candidates than the primary election (Meyer 2008). (It is worth noting, however, that this rationale badly backfired for the two major parties in the 1998 gubernatorial election, when public subsidies enabled a third-party candidate—Jesse Ventura—to capture the gubernatorial mansion.)

In one jurisdiction, New Jersey, only candidates for the office of governor are eligible to receive public funds (although New Jersey has experimented with legislative campaign financing in two elections) (Levinson 2008a). Other jurisdictions limit public funding to only statewide candidates. The rationale behind limiting the offices eligible for public financing usually is based on targeting offices that are uniquely important in the policy arena or particularly susceptible to the problems associated with private financing of campaigns. An additional rationale often is to reduce the costs of public financing programs.

As shown in Table 3.1, sixteen states provide some form of public financing in candidate campaigns. Seven of these states include all state offices in

TABLE 3.1.   PUBLIC FINANCING OF STATE ELECTIONS

All state offices	Arizona
	Connecticut
	Hawaii
	Maine
	Minnesota
	Nebraska
	Wisconsin
Statewide offices	Florida
	Massachusetts
	New Mexico (only Public Regulation Commission but not governor)
	North Carolina (certain offices but not governor)*
	Rhode Island
Governorship	Maryland (and lieutanant governor)
	Michigan (and lieutenant governor)
	New Jersey
	Vermont (and lieutenant governor)
State appellate courts	New Mexico
	North Carolina
	Wisconsin

*North Carolina provides public funding to candidates for auditor, superintendent of public instruction, and commissioner of insurance, but not governor.

the public financing program, five states include statewide elective offices, and four states include only gubernatorial elections. Another eight states provide public subsidies to party committees. Three states—New Mexico, North Carolina (Horwitz 2008) and Wisconsin—currently provide some public funds to state appellate court candidates.

Sources of Public Funds

States have several options in finding sources of funds for a public financing program. These sources include, but are not limited to, allocations from the state general fund, tax checkoffs, tax add-ons, tax rebates, election-related fines, funds from abandoned property, and an Arizona innovation, surcharges on civil and criminal fines and forfeitures. To fund candidates for the Public Regulation Commission, New Mexico imposes fees on utility inspections, carriers, and insurance premiums. Most states provide some combination of these funding sources.

The most reliable source of public funds (except in Massachusetts when the program applied to legislative candidates), and the most equitably distributed across taxpayers, is a direct allocation in the state budget from the general fund. All taxpayers share the burden of paying, and the state general fund contains a sufficient pool of funds to finance the program. However, this source of public funds can fall prey to the politically sensitive charge of "raising taxes." In fact, opponents of public financing programs often describe these programs as "taxpayer-funded campaigns," while proponents prefer such terminology as "public financing" or "clean elections."

In an effort to evade the "taxpayer" controversy, many states have pursued alternative sources of funds to pay for public financing programs. One of the most popular is the voluntary tax checkoff. With a tax checkoff, taxpayers may choose to earmark a dollar or two that they have already paid to the general fund to the public financing program. At one time, the tax checkoff provided an important source of funds for the federal public financing program and many of the states, including Wisconsin.

Over the years, however, the number of taxpayers willing to earmark their tax dollars to public financing programs has waned. In the presidential public financing program, the tax checkoff participation rate fell from 27.5 percent of taxpayers earmarking funds for the program in 1976 to 8 percent in 2006. This dropoff in participation rates in states with a tax checkoff system has been equally dramatic. In Minnesota, for example, 27.2 percent of taxpayers earmarked dollars for the state public financing program in 1976; but participation fell to 8.2 percent in 1999, the year after Jesse Ventura was elected governor. It has dropped even further since. In Wisconsin, the participation rate has fallen from 18.4 percent to 6 percent in 2006. The declining interest in utilizing tax checkoffs is found among all states employing this source of public funds. It now provides only a limited source of revenue for the states.

Tax add-ons have a far worse record. With a tax add-on, taxpayers may choose to pay an additional dollar or two in taxes to support the public financing program. Tax add-ons have never been a serious source of funding for public financing programs in any state and have averaged less than 1 percent in participation rates.

Other minor sources of revenue for some state public financing programs include candidate filing fees, surplus funds left over after a campaign ends and voluntary contributions to the program. Separately, these minor sources of revenue cannot support a public financing program. But when tax checkoffs, tax add-ons, and other types of financing are combined, they can provide significant assistance in offsetting the costs of public financing. Nevertheless, a steady and larger source of revenue is needed to pay for an effective public financing program.

Arizona has found one such source of revenues: a 10 percent surcharge on all civil and criminal fines and forfeitures.[5] Borrowing a method used in many states to finance state court systems, Arizona added an additional 10 percent surcharge, on top of an already existing court surcharge on a wide array of fines and forfeitures, ranging from petty traffic violations to white-collar crime to other felony offenses. The surcharge pays for nearly 70 percent of Arizona's public financing program.

Qualification of Candidates for Public Financing

In all but one existing public financing systems, candidates must agree to expenditure limitations (Richmond, California is the exception) and demonstrate some level of viability as a serious candidate to qualify for public funds. Many states also require candidates to limit the use of their own personal funds and to have an opponent in order to be eligible for public financing. The greatest differences between states in qualification procedures are the means of demonstrating viability as a serious candidate.

All public financing states establish a fundraising qualification threshold for candidates to demonstrate viability. But these thresholds vary widely between full public financing and partial public financing systems, from state to state, and by level of office.

Since partial public financing systems consist of matching private contributions with public subsidies, the qualification threshold for eligibility to receive public funds usually involves reaching two fundraising thresholds: (1) raising a substantial sum of private dollars, and (2) raising that qualifying sum in small contributions from others.

Nebraska is unique among partial public financing systems in its qualification process as well as how it functions.[6] As long as all candidates agree to the spending ceilings, no candidate receives public subsidies. But if a participating candidate is opposed by a candidate who has rejected the spending ceilings, then the participating candidate qualifies for public financing.

Qualification thresholds for full public financing systems are very different from partial programs because of their objective of removing all, or nearly all, private money from campaigns. In several states, participating candidates must (1) agree to the voluntary spending ceilings, (2) accept no private contributions in excess of $100 to be used exclusively as seed money to set up a qualification organization, (3) raise a specified number of $5 qualifying contributions, and (4) agree not to accept any more private contributions upon qualification for public financing.

As shown in State Chart 2 (see the State and Local Charts at the end of the chapter), it is often the number, not the amount, of qualifying contributions that are important in these full public financing systems. The emphasis is on demonstrating that a significant number of citizens support the candidacy, even if these citizens may not have the financial resources to be major contributors. A $5 qualifying contribution is thought to demonstrate that support rather than a simple signature because it shows at least a minimal commitment. Studies of the ballot initiative process have documented that citizens will sign a petition on almost any subject, as long as signing requires no sacrifice, simply to get the petition circulator out of the way (Center for Governmental Studies 2008). Requiring $5 rather than just a signature is designed to reinstill integrity into this form of the petition process. The candidate then turns over the qualification contributions to the state.

The numbers of qualifying contributions required in each full public financing program usually range depending on the office. Ideally, the appropriate number of required qualifying contributions should meet two mutual objectives. The number should not be so high as to be onerous and disable all but the well-connected candidates from being able to qualify. At the same time, the number should not be so low that frivolous candidates can qualify and flood the public financing system.

Qualification for Vermont's public financing system depends on an equation based on amounts raised—but small amounts, nonetheless. Candidates for governor must raise $35,000 from at least 1,500 qualified individuals in qualifying contributions of $50 or less in order to be eligible for public subsidies. Candidates for lieutenant governor must raise $17,500 from at least 750 qualified individuals in qualifying contributions for eligibility.

Allocation of Public Funds

Jurisdictions offer two basic forms of allocating public subsidies in public financing programs: matching funds and bloc grants. Each of these forms of allocating funds must also address the additional issues of amount of disbursement, timing of disbursement, and a maximum cap on disbursements.

Matching Funds

Most, but not all, partial public financing systems operate on a matching fund allocation basis.[7] Once a candidate qualifies for public subsidies, the candidate may then submit records of private contributions that the state matches with public funds according to a specified formula. Frequently, a partial public financing program may match a small private contribution on a one-to-one basis or higher. For example, Rhode Island matches each private contribution of $500 or less with twice that amount in public subsidies for participating candidates.

Most matching fund programs strive not only to minimize the influence of private contributions on candidates but also to maximize the power and importance of small contributors by multiplying the value of their contributions. The matching fund program in New York City is a classic example of attempting to maximize the value of small contributions. At one point, the city's public financing program had a one-to-one match of all private contributions of $1,000 or less. The city revised its law to provide a matching ratio of $6 in public funding for every $1 in private contributions up to the first $175 given by any city resident. The revised formula encourages candidates to seek smaller contributions from a greater number of contributors without increasing the costs of the program.

In addition to maximizing the value of small contributions, matching fund programs have several additional advantages over other forms of allocation formulas. Unlike bloc grant programs, candidates receive public subsidies in a matching fund program only when they raise money, limiting the possibility that a frivolous candidate could receive substantial public funds. Further, candidates who lose popularity over the course of the election, as demonstrated by decreasing fundraising ability, will receive proportionately less in public subsidies.

Bloc Grants

Full public financing programs deliver their public subsidies to candidates in the form of bloc grants. Under a bloc grant formula, once candidates qualify for public financing, they receive the public subsidies in one lump sum or in large chunks according to a set timetable. Full public financing systems could not operate in any other manner, since there are no private contributions to match.

The bloc grant formula in full public financing systems enjoys several strategic advantages over a matching fund formula.[8] First, participating candidates are given equivalent and complete campaign budgets up front in the beginning of the campaign period. Several states, including Arizona, Connecticut, Maine, New Mexico and North Carolina, deliver their full allocation of public subsidies to eligible candidates at the beginning of each election. This approach has the dramatic impact of placing all participating candidates on an equal footing. One key objection to a matching fund formula is that challengers and lesser-known but viable candidates are likely to fall behind incumbents and well-established candidates at the starting line because they face greater difficulty in soliciting private contributions to be matched. A slow start can compound itself in partial public financing systems by making it seem that the candidate is not viable. This is not the case in a full public financing bloc grant formula, where participating challengers and incumbents begin the campaign season with identical campaign coffers.

Second, the full public financing bloc grants virtually eliminate private money from campaigns and, presumably, any special influence that such private contributions may buy. A partial financing matching fund formula, on the contrary, preserves an important though reduced role of private contributions in campaigns.

Finally, the bloc grant formulas of full public financing systems free candidates from all fundraising burdens and allow the candidates to focus on communicating with voters. Candidates in nonpublic financing systems are estimated to spend up to half of their time on fundraising rather than campaigning. This share is proportionately reduced when a larger share of public funds is provided, and nearly vanishes in a full public financing system.

Voluntary Spending Ceilings

As shown in State Chart 2, spending ceilings vary considerably from state to state. Differences in demographics, media expenses, and other election-related factors make a single spending ceiling formula possible. Some states fix their spending ceilings at an absolute dollar amount, adjusted for inflation. Other states set their ceilings according to an amount per resident expenditure, such as Maryland's 37.2 cents per resident. Other states set different spending ceilings for primary and general elections for the same office. Only one jurisdiction, Richmond, California, does not impose spending limits on candidates who accept public funding.

Usually the spending ceiling in the primary election will be lower than that of the general election, but not always. The full public financing system in Arizona provides candidates with some discretion in spending more or less in the primary or general election, depending on which election is the most competitive. A candidate may opt to reallocate up to 50 percent of the spending ceilings from the general to the primary elections if the district is classified as primarily a one-party district.

One of the more interesting nuances in spending ceilings is employed in Minnesota—that is, incumbents have a slightly lower spending ceiling than challengers. First-time challengers may spend roughly 10 percent more than incumbents in Minnesota's public financing program, and if there was a competitive primary, candidates can spend 20 percent more than the ceiling. Vermont is another state that gives challengers an advantage over incumbents: 15 percent.

Excessive Spending by Opponents

An appropriate spending ceiling will also provide a mechanism for lifting the ceilings on participating candidates upon certain conditions. It is difficult to justify hamstringing a participating candidate who is facing excessive spending by opponents with an absolute spending limit. This excessive spending can come from a wealthy non-participating opponent or from outside groups waging their own independent expenditure campaigns. Arizona, Connecticut, Florida, Maine, Michigan,[9] Minnesota, New Mexico, North Carolina, Rhode Island and Wisconsin all lift the voluntary spending ceilings on specific races when spending grows excessive in those races. Most of these states raise the spending limits only when nonparticipating opponents exceed the recommended ceilings. Arizona, Connecticut, Maine, New Mexico, North Carolina, Rhode Island and Vermont also lift the ceilings when independent expenditures skew campaign activity disproportionately for or against a candidate.

In most public financing states, "lifting" of the spending limits is capped at two or three times the original ceiling. The rationale of placing a secondary cap on lifting the spending ceilings is twofold. First, it is assumed that the benefits of campaign spending follows a bell curve—that is, campaign spending becomes redundant and produces declining electoral benefits beyond a certain point. Second, many of these programs, especially the full public financing systems, provide additional public funds to participating candidates.[10]

Independent Expenditures

Arizona, Connecticut, Florida, Maine, New Mexico and North Carolina provide a complicated formula for calculating when independent expenditures "trigger" the lifting of spending ceilings. These states not only lift the spending ceilings for participating candidates who are opposed by independent expenditures but also provide additional public funds to participating candidates to match the excessive independent spending. In a clause of the

Arizona law, entitled "Equal funding for candidates," independent expenditures for or against participating candidates are treated as expenditures against or for each opposing candidate, and participating candidates have their public fund allocations adjusted appropriately to provide equal financing among participating candidates. Independent expenditures for or against multiple participating candidates require that the elections agency allocate the expenditures for and against participating candidates "based on the relative size or length and relative prominence of the reference to candidates for different offices."[11] Implementing this provision has caused some consternation among elections administrators, but rules and regulations have been developed.

Contribution Limits

Though not an inherent component of public financing, all public financing systems (except Nebraska) include a set of contribution limits that apply across the board to participating as well as nonparticipating candidates. Only full public financing programs require participating candidates to eschew private contributions altogether (except for small qualifying contributions and seed money). Contribution limits are usually part of any system of campaign finance reform, and are equally as important in a comprehensive public financing program. The attractiveness of participating in a public financing system would suffer considerably if candidates who opted out of the system could raise private campaign contributions in unlimited amounts.

Contribution limits in public financing systems range from a low of $100 from any individual per election cycle for candidates in Connecticut to a high of $10,000 per election to gubernatorial candidates in Wisconsin. Most states have contribution limits from individuals to candidates between $250 and $1,000 per election. Wisconsin's unusually high contribution limit could be another factor discouraging candidates from participating in the public financing program.

Conclusion

No one campaign financing system is the panacea to solve the problems of improper influence on governmental officials, too much money being spent, too few candidates running for office, too many independent expenditures being made, and too little information getting to the voters.

Most states have adopted some type of reform law, such as contribution limitations on candidates, that goes beyond disclosure, while all states require disclosure of contributions and expenditures (with the exception of North Dakota, which does not require disclosure of expenditures). Many states and local communities are experimenting with public financing systems. While several states now provide clean money, or full public financing to candidates, other jurisdictions believe that partial matching fund programs are better. Many have enhanced their programs, and some are wrestling with legislation to modify the law.

Public financing laws, whether partial or full, will always prove controversial. Most incumbents do not want competition and recognize that public financing provides needed funds to their underfunded opponents. Some taxpayers believe that no tax money should be used to subsidize any politician or campaign. Some reformers believe in an all-or-nothing approach; if there is not total public financing of campaigns, it is not worth enacting partial public financing. Others believe that any reform is better than no reform. In any event, the states and localities that have adopted these laws are proving to be the laboratories of reform that are necessary to prove whether these programs are worth the taxpayer money being spent on them.

NOTES

1. Daggett v. Comm. on Governmental Ethics and Elections Practices, 205 F.3rd 445 (2001).

2. Lavis v. Bayless, CV 2001-006078 (Maricopa County, December 19, 2001).

3. Art. 48, § 2 of the Massachusetts Constitution reads, in part: "Excluded Matters.—No measure that relates to religion, religious practices or religious institutions; or to the appointment, qualification, tenure, removal, recall or compensation of judges; or to the reversal of a judicial decision; or to the powers, creation or abolition of courts; or the operation of which is restricted to a particular town, city or other political division or to particular districts or localities of the commonwealth; or that makes a specific appropriation of money from the treasury of the commonwealth, shall be proposed by an initiative petition; but if a law approved by the people is not repealed, the general court shall raise by taxation or otherwise and shall appropriate such money as may be necessary to carry such law into effect."

4. Buckley v. Valeo, 424 U.S. 1 (1976).

5. Arizona's 10 percent surcharge on civil and criminal fines and forfeitures to pay for its public financing program sparked the popular, but misleading, campaign theme: "Let criminals pay for politicians."

6. Nebraska Revised Statutes § 32-1603(1) et seq.

7. A few states with partial public financing systems, such as Michigan, Minnesota, Vermont and Wisconsin, provide candidates with bloc grants rather than matching funds.

8. Although no existing partial public financing system provides bloc grants to eligible candidates at the beginning of the election, it is certainly possible to develop a disbursal formula for a partial public financing system in which a substantial bloc of funds is given to qualified candidates very early in the election.

9. Spending limits are lifted for publicly financed candidates in Michigan only when a nonparticipating candidate spends more than $340,000.

10. Minnesota had a similar trigger mechanism, in which participating candidates faced with excessive spending received additional public funds to coincide with the lifting of spending ceilings. A federal appeals court, however, invalidated the provision that granted additional public funds to offset excessive spending. In Day v. Halohan, 34 F.3rd 1356, cert. denied (1994), the U.S. Court of Appeals of the 8th Circuit ruled that because Minnesota's public financing program already enjoys near universal candidate participation in the public financing system, the provision allowing public funds to match half of excessive independent expenditures serves no compelling state interest. The same court cast its own decision in Day into doubt when, two years later, it upheld a lifting of the spending ceiling when a nonparticipating opponent exceeds the limits. Rosenstiel v. Rodriguez, 101 F.3rd 1544 (1996). Similar trigger matching fund formulas for independent expenditures have been upheld for other states in subsequent court rulings. See, for example, Daggett v. Commission on Governmental Ethics and Election Practices, 205 F.3rd 445 (2000).

11. Arizona Revised Statutes, Title 16, Chap. 6, Art. 2, § 16-952.

REFERENCES

Center for Governmental Studies. 2008. *Democracy by Initiative: Shaping California's Fourth Branch of Government.* 2nd ed. Los Angeles: Center for Governmental Studies.

Horwitz, Sasha. 2008. "Public Campaign Financing: North Carolina Judiciary, Balancing the Scales." Los Angeles: Center for Governmental Studies.

Klein, Rick. 2001. "Justices Hit Lawmakers on Clean Elections." *Boston Globe*, December 4, p. B1.

Levinson, Jessica A. 2008a. "Public Campaign Financing: New Jersey Governor, Weeding Out Big Money in the Garden State." Los Angeles: Center for Governmental Studies.

———. 2008b. "Public Financing: New Jersey Legislature, A Pilot Project Takes Flight." Los Angeles: Center for Governmental Studies.

Meyer, Anna N. 2008. "Public Campaign Financing: Minnesota, Damming Big Money in the Land of 10,000 Lakes." Los Angeles: Center for Governmental Studies.

STATE AND LOCAL CHARTS

The charts on the following pages summarize the laws of twenty-four states and sixteen local jurisdictions that have public financing programs.

The local charts contain information for only jurisdictions with public financing laws on the books. Public financing programs in six local jurisdictions—Cincinnati, Ohio; King County, Washington; Petaluma, California; Sacramento County, California; Seattle, Washington; and Cary, North Carolina—have been terminated or suspended, three by statewide ballot measure, one by local ballot measure, one by city council repeal, and one by suspension under legal settlement.

STATE CHART 1. POPULATION, DATE ENACTED, TAX PROVISIONS, DISTRIBUTION OF FUNDS

State	Population[1]	Enacted	Tax Provisions				Funding Mechanism	Public Funds Allocation
			Credit	Deduction	Checkoff	Surcharge		
Arizona	6,338,755	1998	$5 reduction in tax for $5 clean elections checkoff; voluntary donation to fund, a tax credit not to exceed 20% of the tax amount on the return of $500 per taxpayer, whichever is higher[2]	$100 individual, $200 joint Money designated as surcharge is deductible	$5 for clean elections fund[2]	$2, $5, $10, additional amounts may be donated[3]	Checkoff; voluntary donations; surcharge on civil and criminal penalties	Clean elections fund grants to qualifying candidates for statewide and legislative office. Funding is available for primary and general elections.[4]
Arkansas	2,834,797	1996	$50 individual, $100 joint for contributions to candidates, small donor PACS, approved PACS, and organized political parties[5]	—	—	—	—	—
Connecticut	3,405,565	2005	—	—	—	—	Appropriation from the general fund, revenue from abandoned property, and voluntary contributions[6]	Lump-sum grants to candidate committee for state candidates for senator or representative.[7] In 2010 and thereafter to qualifying candidates for senator, representative, governor, lieutenant governor, attorney general, state comptroller, secretary of state, and state treasurer.[7] Funding is available for primary and general elections.[8]

(continued on next page)

STATE CHART 1. *Continued*

State	Population[1]	Enacted	Tax Provisions				Funding Mechanism	Public Funds Allocation
			Credit	Deduction	Checkoff	Surcharge		
Florida	18,251,243	1986[9]	—	—	—	—[10]	Direct appropriations from the general fund if necessary; proceeds from filing fees; proceeds from assessments[11]	Matching funds to qualifying candidates for governor, lieutenant governor, attorney general, chief financial officer, and corporations commissioner. Individual contributions are matched on a 2-to-1 basis for qualifying contributions and on a 1-to-1 basis for subsequent contributions of $250 or less. Funding is available for primary and general elections.[12]
Hawaii	1,283,388	1979	—	$250 for contributions to central or county party committees, or $1,000 for aggregate contributions to candidates who abide by limits, up to $250 per candidate[13]	$2 individual, $4 joint[14]	—	Checkoff, appropriated funds; other moneys[15]	To qualifying candidates for governor, lieutenant governor, and mayor in an amount equaling 10% of the spending limit. To qualifying candidates for senator, representative, and county council member, in an amount equaling 15% of the spending limit. To qualifying candidates for the office of Hawaiian affairs in an amount of no more than $1,500. To qualifying candidates for the board of education and all other offices in an amount of no more than $100. Funding is available for primary and general elections.[17,18]

State	Population[1]	Enacted	Tax Provisions				Funding Mechanism[16]	Public Funds Allocation
			Credit	Deduction	Checkoff	Surcharge		
Idaho	1,499,402	1975	—	—	$1 individual[16]	—	Checkoff[16]	Each political party, through its central committee, shall be eligible for payments from the fund in the following manner: (1) Each party shall receive the amount of the fund which has been designated by the contributing individuals and credited to the separate account in the fund maintained for the party. (2) 90% of the fund which has not been designated, but is credited to the general election campaign fund, shall be distributed to the central committees in proportion to the share of the votes cast for the candidate of the party for the office of governor in the last election for governor, provided that no party shall receive more than 50% of the fund so distributed. Funding is available only for general elections.[17]

STATE CHART 1. *Continued*

State	Population[1]	Enacted	Tax Provisions				Funding Mechanism[18]	Public Funds Allocation
			Credit	Deduction	Checkoff	Surcharge		
Iowa	2,988,046	1987	—	—	$1.50 individual, $3 joint[18]	—	Checkoff[18]	All contributions directed to the Iowa election campaign fund by taxpayers who do not designate any one political party to receive their contributions shall be divided by the director of revenue equally among each account currently maintained in the fund. With certain conditions any candidate for a partisan public office may receive campaign funds from the Iowa election campaign fund through the state central committee of the candidate's political party. However, the state central committee of each political party shall have discretion to choose which of the party's candidates for public office shall be allocated campaign funds out of money received by that party from the Iowa election campaign fund.[19] Funding is to be used only in general elections.[20]
Maine	1,317,207	1996	—	—	$3 individual, $6 joint[21]	Any amount designated by taxpayer[22]	Checkoff; general fund; surplus candidate seed money; unspent candidate funds; voluntary donations; fines[23]	Lump-sum grants for governor, senator, and representative in primary and general elections.[24] Surcharge: to a political party designated by the taxpayer

| | | | Tax Provisions | | | | Funding | |
State	Population[1]	Enacted	Credit	Deduction	Checkoff	Surcharge	Mechanism	Public Funds Allocation
Maryland	5,618,344	1974	—	—	—	Add-on not to exceed $500 per tax filer[25]	Direct appropriations; fines; tax add-ons	Matching funds on a 1-to-1 basis are distributed to candidates for governor and lieutenant governor in the primary and general elections if they are opposed. If unopposed, matching funds are given on a 1-to-3 basis.[26]
Massachusetts	6,449,755	2003	$1 credit for $1 contribution checkoff to the State Election Campaign Fund[27]	—	$1 individual, $2 joint[27]	—	Direct appropriations; checkoff; monies from former public campaign finance fund	Matching funds to qualifying candidates for certain offices (governor, lieutenant governor, attorney general, auditor, secretary, treasurer, and receiver general) disbursed on a 1-to-1 basis for all qualifying contributions up to office-based limits.[28] Funding is available for primary and general elections.[29]
Michigan	10,071,822	1976	—	—	$3 individual, $6 joing[30]	—	Checkoff[30]	Matching funds to qualifying candidates for governor in the primary election and to candidates for governor and lieutenant governor in general election.[31] Distributed on a pro rata basis if sufficient funding is not available.[30] Candidates receive a 2-to-1 match for small contributions (under $100) in the primary up to $990,000 and a flat grant of $1.125 million for the general election.[32]

(continued on next page)

STATE CHART 1. *Continued*

State	Population[1]	Enacted	Tax Provisions				Funding Mechanism	Public Funds Allocation
			Credit	Deduction	Checkoff	Surcharge		
Minnesota	5,197,621	1974	Refund up to $50 for contributions to political parties and qualified candidates, $100 joint[33]	—	$5 individual, $10 joint, into either party or general accounts as designated by taxpayer[34]	—	Direct appropriations; checkoff; anonymous contributions to candidates and committees[35]	Lump-sum grant to qualifying candidates for governor, lieutenant governor, attorney general, other statewide offices, and senator and representative; to the state committee of a political party for multicandidate expenditures; and to state general fund for administrative purposes, after the primary elections (funding is available in the general election only). If 98% of tax returns have not been filed one week after the primary election, the remaining funds are to be distributed by December 15.[36] Candidates may receive public funding equal to 50% of the spending limit, and may raise private funds equal to 50% of the spending limit.[36]

| | | | | Tax Provisions | | | Funding | |
State	Population[1]	Enacted	Credit	Deduction	Checkoff	Surcharge	Mechanism	Public Funds Allocation
Nebraska	1,774,571	1992	—	—	—	Any amount $1 or greater not exceeding amount of income tax refund[37]	Direct appropriations; taxpayer contribution of income tax refund; amounts repaid to campaign finance limitation cash fund by candidates[38]	Lump-sum grant to qualified candidates for governor, secretary of state, attorney general, auditor of public accounts, state legislature, Public Service Commission, board of regents of the University of Nebraska, and state board of education who agree to abide by the statutory spending limitation.[39] If a nonabiding opponent spends more than 40% of the spending limit, the publicly funded candidate will receive the money the opponent spends minus the expenditures limit. Funding is available in the general election.[40]
New Jersey	8,685,920	1974	—	—	$1 individual, $2 joint	—	Direct appropriations and checkoff	Matching funds to qualified candidates for governor on a 2-to-1 basis for both the primary and the general elections, up to $2.7 million in the primary and $6.4 million in the general election.[41]

(continued on next page)

State	Population[1]	Enacted	Tax Provisions				Funding Mechanism	Public Funds Allocation
			Credit	Deduction	Checkoff	Surcharge		
New Mexico	1,969,915	2003	—	—	$2 individual, $4 joint	—	Qualifying contributions; unspent monies; direct appropriations; utility inspection and supervision fees; carrier inspection fees; insurance premium tax[42]	Clean money grant to qualified candidates for the Public Regulation Commission, justice of the Supreme Court, and justice of the Court of Appeals.[43] Contested primary elections: Public Regulation Commission: $0.25 for each voter of the candidate's party in the district of the office for which s/he is running ($25,552–$36,730 Democrat; $16,807–$21,245 Republican); judicial offices: $0.15 for each voter of the candidate's party in the state ($79,727 Democrat; $76,272 Republican). Uncontested primary elections: certified candidates are eligible to receive 50% of the amount specified above.[44] Contested general elections: Public Regulation Commission: $0.25 for each voter in the district of the office for which the candidate is running ($57,486–$64,778); judicial offices: $0.15 for each voter in the state. ($161,185). Uncontested general elections: certified candidates will receive 50% of the amount specified above.[45]

State	Population[1]	Enacted	Tax Provisions				Funding Mechanism	Public Funds Allocation
			Credit	Deduction	Checkoff	Surcharge		
North Carolina (judicial election program)	9,061,032	2002	—	$25 for political contributions	$3 individual, $6 joint[46]	Up to amount of income tax refund due	Money from the North Carolina Candidates Financing Fund— taxpayer designations, unspent Public Campaign Financing Fund Revenues, returned monies, voluntary donations, money from surcharge on attorney membership fees.[47]	Clean money grant to participating candidates. Court of Appeals candidates may receive 125 times the candidate's filing fee ($160,000) in public funding, and participating Supreme Court candidates may receive approximately 175 times the candidate's filing fee ($240,100).[48] The money is distributed in a lump-sum grant.[49] Funding is available only for the general election.[50]
North Carolina (statewide candidate program)	9,061,032	2007	—				Money from the North Carolina Voter Owned Elections Fund— voluntary donations, appropriations from the general fund, $1,000,000 for the 2007–08 fiscal year and $3,580,000 for the 2008–09 fiscal year appropriated by the legislature, unspent public funds given to certified candidates, funds ordered to be returned to the fund as a result of a violation[51]	Clean money grant to qualified candidates for auditor, superintendent of public instruction, and commissioner of insurance.[52] Candidates in contested general elections are given funds equal to the average amount of campaign expenditures by candidates who won the preceding three general elections for that office, but no less than $300,000. One-third of the funds are distributed within five business days after the candidate is certified to appear on the ballot, the rest on August 1, before the general election. Funding is available only for the general election.[50]

(continued on next page)

STATE CHART 1. *Continued*

State	Population[1]	Enacted	Tax Provisions				Funding Mechanism	Public Funds Allocation
			Credit	Deduction	Checkoff	Surcharge		
Ohio	11,466,917	1987	$50 individual, $100 joint, for contributions to statewide and legislative candidates	—	$1 individual, $2 joint[53]	—	Checkoff	Lump-sum grant divided equally among major political parties each calendar quarter. Party allocation divided: 50% to state executive committees of party and 50% to county executive committees of party according to proportion of income from tax return checkoffs in each county.[54] The grants may not be used to support a particular nominee in the primary period, but may be used for operating and administrative costs.[55]
Oklahoma	3,617,316	1995	—	$100[56]	—	—	—	—
Oregon	3,747,455	1995	Lesser of (1) total contributions with a maximum of $50 individual, $100 joint, or (2) the taxpayer's liability for contribution to a major or minor party, a candidate for any office, or registered political committee.[57]	—	—	—	—	—

		Tax Provisions				
State	Population[1]	Enacted	Credit	Deduction	Checkoff	Surcharge	Funding Mechanism	Public Funds Allocation

State	Population[1]	Enacted	Credit	Deduction	Checkoff	Surcharge	Funding Mechanism	Public Funds Allocation
Rhode Island	1,057,832	1988	—	—	$5 individual, $10 joint[58]	—	Checkoff	First $2 ($4 for a joint return) of checkoff allocated to major political parties. Distributed to eligible political party designated by taxpayer. If a party is not designated, 5% of the amount is allocated to each party for each state officer elected, and the remainder to each party in proportion to the votes its candidate for governor received in previous election. Maximum of $200,000 allocated to all political parties.[58] Remainder to qualifying candidates in general election for governor, lieutenant governor, secretary of state, attorney general, and general treasurer as state matching funds.[59] Qualified statewide candidates are eligible for 2-to-1 public matching grants for contributions of $500 or less and a 1-to-1 match for contributions in excess of $500.[60] Funding is available only for the general election.[61]

(continued on next page)

STATE CHART 1. *Continued*

State	Population[1]	Enacted	Credit	Deduction	Checkoff	Surcharge	Funding Mechanism	Public Funds Allocation
				Tax Provisions				
Utah	2,645,330	1998	—	—	$2[62]	—	Checkoff to political party designated by taxpayer[62]	To designated political party, without restrictions on use.[63] The funds are distributed annually, on or before August 15.[64]
Vermont[65]	621,254	1997	—	—	—	Up to amount of income tax refund or over-payment[66]	Surcharge; public funding penalties; unexpended campaign finance grants; portion of corporation annual reporting fees; gifts; and state appropriations[67]	Lump-sum grant to contested, qualifying candidates for governor and lieutenant governor. Governor candidates: nonincumbent—$75,000 minus qualifying contribution for primary; $225,000 for general election. Lieutenant governor candidates: nonincumbent—$25,000 minus qualifying contributions for primary; $75,000 for general election. Incumbents receive grants of 85% of those listed above. If funds are insufficient, they are to be distributed proportionally to all qualified candidates.[68]

| | | | Tax Provisions | | | | Funding | |
State	Population[1]	Enacted	Credit	Deduction	Checkoff	Surcharge	Mechanism	Public Funds Allocation
Virginia	7,712,091	1999	$25 individual, $50 joint, for contributions to candidates	—	—	$25 individual, $50 joint, of income tax refund[69]	Surcharge	To designated political party, without restrictions on use.
Wisconsin	5,601,640	1977	—	—	$1 individual, $2 joint	—	Checkoff[70]	Lump-sum grant to qualifying candidates for state executive office, state legislative office and state supreme court candidates in a general election. Money from the Wisconsin election campaign fund is distributed to candidates in varying percentage amounts depending on the office.[71]

(continued on next page)

Source: Center for Governmental Studies, Los Angeles, California.
[1] Based on estimated 2007 census figures from the U.S. Census Bureau, which can be found at the American Factfinder website: http://factfinder.census.gov.
[2] Arizona Revised Statutes § 16-954.
[3] Arizona Revised Statutes § 43-612.
[4] Arizona Revised Statutes § 16-951.
[5] Arkansas Code Annotated § 7-6-222.
[6] Connecticut General Statutes Chapter 157 § 9-701.
[7] Connecticut General Statutes Chapter 157 § 9-702.
[8] Connecticut General Statutes Chapter 157 § 9-705.
[9] The Election Campaign Financing Trust Fund expired effective November 4, 1996, by operation of s. 19(f), Article III of the State Constitution. The courts determined that Florida's public campaign finance laws remained in force despite the elimination of the trust fund, funded through the general fund instead of the trust fund. Secretary of State v. Milligan, 704 So.2d 152 (Fla.App. 1 Dist. 1997).
[10] Florida Statutes § 199.052(13) "'The annual intangible tax return shall include language permitting a voluntary contribution of $5 per taxpayer, which contribution shall be transferred into the Election Campaign Financing Trust Fund. A statement providing an explanation of the purpose of the trust fund shall also be included" was deleted as of 2003. Florida's intangible personal property tax is an annual tax based on the current market value, as of January 1, of intangible personal property owned, managed, or controlled by Florida residents or persons doing business in Florida. http://www.myflorida.com/dor/taxes/ippt.html.
[11] Florida Statutes Annotated § 106.32.
[12] Florida Statutes Annotated § 106.35.

STATE CHART 1. *Continued*

[13] Hawaii Revised Statues § 235-7(g).

[14] Hawaii Revised Statutes § 235-102.5(a) ("the check-off does not constitute an additional tax liability.").

[15] Hawaii Revised Statutes § 11-217.

[16] Idaho Code § 63-3088.

[17] Idaho Code § 34-2503.

[18] Iowa Code § 68A.601.

[19] Iowa Code § 68A.602.

[20] Iowa Code § 68A.605.

[21] 36 Me. Rev. Stat. Ann § 5286.

[22] 36 Me. Rev. Stat. Ann § 5283.

[23] 21-A Me. Rev. Stat. Ann § 1124.

[24] 21-A Me. Rev. Stat. Ann § 1125.

[25] Maryland Code, Election Law, § 15-103.

[26] Maryland Code, Election Law, § 15-104.

[27] Massachusetts General Laws 62 § 6C.

[28] Massachusetts General Laws 55C § 5.

[29] Massachusetts General Laws 55C § 2.

[30] Mich. Comp. Laws § 169.261.

[31] Mich. Comp. Laws § 169.203.

[32] Mich. Comp. Laws § 169.264 and Mich. Comp. Laws § 169.265.

[33] Minnesota Statutes § 290.06.

[34] Minnesota Statutes § 10A.31. According to Minnesota's Campaign Finance and Public Disclosure Board, 8.4 percent of taxpayers participated in the checkoff. Record available at http://www.cfboard.state.mn.us/forms/incometax01.pdf

[35] Minnesota Statutes § 10A.15: "A political committee, political fund, principal campaign committee, or party unit may not retain an anonymous contribution in excess of $20, but must forward it to the board for deposit in the general account of the state elections campaign fund."

[36] Minnesota Statutes § 10A.31.

[37] Nebraska Revised Statutes § 77-27,119.04.

[38] Nebraska Revised Statutes § 32-1610.

[39] Nebraska Revised Statutes § 32-1611: A certified candidate's opponent must go over 40 percent of the spending limit in order to receive public funds. Funds are first distributed to candidates for legislative races and then to statewide candidates if funds are left over.

[40] Nebraska Revised Statutes § 32-1611.

[41] New Jersey Statutes 19:44A-33.

[42] New Mexico Statutes § 1-19A-10.

[43] New Mexico Statutes § 1-19A-14.

[44] 2008 fund distribution derived from secretary of state records, available at http://www.sos.state.nm.us/pdf/FUNDDISTRIBUTIONGEN.pdf.

[45] Ibid.. http://www.sos.state.nm.us/pdf/FUNDDISTRIBUTIONPRI.pdf.

[46] North Carolina General Statutes § 105-159.2.

47 North Carolina General Statutes § 163-278.63.

48 Calculations based on 2008 North Carolina candidate filing fees, derived from the State Board of Elections, available at http://www.sboe.state.nc.us/content.aspx?id=64

49 North Carolina General Statutes § 163-278.65.

50 North Carolina General Statutes § 163-278.99.

51 North Carolina General Statutes § 163-278.98-§ 163-278.99E.

52 North Carolina General Statutes § 163-278.95.

53 Ohio Revised Code § 5747.081.

54 Ohio Revised Code § 3517.17.

55 Ohio Revised Code § 3517.18.

56 Oklahoma Statutes § 2358.3.

57 Oregon Revised Statutes § 316.102.

58 General Laws of Rhode Island 1956, § 44-30-2.

59 Actual distributions are far below these maximums.

60 General Laws of Rhode Island 1956, § 17-25-19.

61 General Laws of Rhode Island 1956, § 17-25-22.

62 Utah Code 1953 § 59-10-1311.

63 Utah Code 1953 § 59-10-1312.

64 The funds must be distributed "on or before four months after the due date for filing a return" (Utah Code 1953 § 59-10-1312). The deadline for returns is April 15; thus the funds must be distributed by August of the same date.

65 In 2007, the governor eliminated the funding for the program.

66 32 Vermont Statutes § 5862c.

67 17 Vermont Statutes Annotated § 2856.

68 17 Vermont Statutes Annotated § 2855.

69 Virginia Code § 58.1-344.3.

70 In 2006, 6 percent of taxpayers in Wisconsin participated in the checkoff program.

71 Wisconsin Statutes 11.50.

STATE CHART 2. QUALIFYING THRESHOLD, RESIDENCY RESTRICTIONS, SPENDING LIMITS

State	Qualifying Threshold	Residency Restrictions on Matchable Contributions	Spending Limits
Arizona	*Qualifying contributions:* To become eligible for public financing, candidates must raise the following amounts in $5 contributions: *Governor:* $22,050. *Secretary of state and attorney general:* $13,775. *Treasurer and superintendent of public instruction:* $8,250. *Mine inspector:* $2,750. *Legislature:* $1,100. *Corporation commissioner:* $8,250[1] *Seed money:* Contribution limits of $100 in the following amounts: *Governor:* $40,000. *Other candidates:* 10% of the sum of the primary election spending limit and the original general election spending limit.[2]	Yes, for qualifying contributions	A clean election candidate may spend only clean elections funds. *Governor:* $490,940 (primary). *Secretary of state:* $103,361 (primary). *Attorney general:* $103,361 (primary). *Treasurer, superintendent of public instruction:* $51,675 (primary). *Mine inspector:* $23,890 (primary). *Member of legislature:* $12,921 (primary). *Corporation commissioner:* $82,680 (primary).[3] General election amounts are 50% greater.
Arkansas	N/A	N/A	N/A
Connecticut	*House:* $5,000 in contributions of $5 to $100. *Senate:* $15,000 in contributions of $5 to $100. *Governor:* $250,000 in contributions of $100 or less. *Lieutenant governor, attorney general, state comptroller, state treasurer, secretary of state:* $75,000 in contributions of $100 or less.[4]	Yes, for qualifying contributions. For candidates for the House, at least 150 contributions must come from individual state residents. For candidates for the Senate, at least 300 contributions must come from individual state residents. For candidates for governor, at least $225,000 in contributions must come from individual state residents. For candidates for lieutenant governor, attorney general, state comptroller, state treasurer, and secretary of state, $67,500 or more must come from individual state residents.[4]	During the qualifying period, the expenditures are limited to the required amount of qualifying contributions, plus allowable personal funds the candidate provides to the candidate committee. During the primary-election period, expenditures are limited to the amount of the primary grant and any unspent qualifying contributions or personal funds provided by the candidate. During the general-election period, expenditures are limited to the amount of the general-election grant and any unspent qualifying contributions or personal funds provided by the candidate.[5] *For major party candidates:* *House:* In the qualifying period, $6,000; in the primary, $10,000 plus unspent funds from the qualifying period; in the general election, $25,000 plus unspent funds from the primary period. *Senate:* In the qualifying period, $17,000: in the primary, $35,000 plus unspent funds from the qualifying period; in the general election, $85,000 plus unspent funds from the primary period. *Governor:* In the qualifying period, $270,000; in the primary, $1,250,000 plus unspent funds from the qualifying period; in the general election, $3,000,000 plus unspent funds from the primary period. *Lieutenant governor, attorney general, state comptroller, state treasurer, secretary of state:* In the qualifying period, $85,000; in the primary, $375,000 plus unspent funds from the qualifying period; in the general election, $750,000 plus unspent funds from the primary period.[6]

State	Qualifying Threshold	Residency Restrictions on Matchable Contributions	Spending Limits
Florida	*Governor:* $150,000 of contributions of not more than $500. *Cabinet office:* $100,000 of contributions of not more than $500[7]	Yes, for qualifying and matchable contributions	*Governor and lieutenant governor (on the same ticket, considered a single candidate for purposes of public financing):* $2.00 per registered voter (approximately $20 million). *Cabinet officer:* $1.00 per registered voter (approximately $10 million).[8] These numbers apply to the primary and general elections.
Hawaii	*Governor:* $100,000 in amounts of $100 or less. *Lieutenant governor:* $50,000 in amounts of $100 or less. *Senator:* $2,500 in amounts of $100 or less. *Representative:* $1,500 in amounts of $100 or less. *Mayor:* $5,000 to $50,000 in amounts of $100 or less (depending on the number of voters in the city). *Prosecuting attorney:* $5,000 to $30,000 in amounts of $100 or less (depending on the number of voters in the district). *County council:* $1,500 to $5,000 in amounts of $100 or less (depending on the number of voters in the district). *Board of education:* $500 in amounts of $100 or less. *Office of Hawaiian Affairs:* $500 in amounts of $100 or less.[9]	No	Estimates provided apply to 2008 primary and general elections: *Governor:* $2.50 per registered voter ($1,461,725 per election). *Lieutenant governor:* $1.40 per registered voter per election ($818,566). *Senator:* $1.40 per ($23,814–$48,159). *Representative:* $1.40 per ($11,456–$20,874). *Mayor:* $2.00 per ($68,798–$794,780). *Prosecuting attorneys:* $1.40 per. *County council:* $1.40 per ($11,623–$98,385). *Board of education:* $0.20 per.[10] ($37,360–79,478). *Office of Hawaiian Affairs:* $0.20 per ($116,938).[11]
Idaho	N/A	N/A	N/A
Iowa	N/A	N/A	N/A
Maine	*Representative:* At least 50 registered voters from the candidate's electoral division must provide a qualifying contribution. Total contributions are not to exceed $500. *Senate:* At least 150 registered voters from the candidate's electoral division must provide a qualifying contribution. Total contributions are not to exceed $1,500. *Governor:* At least 3,250 registered voters from the state must provide a qualifying contribution. Total contributions are not to exceed $50,000.[12] Individuals may not make donations exceeding $500 to gubernatorial candidates and $250 to a candidate for any other office.[13]	Yes, for matching contributions	Clean elections candidates may spend only clean election funds once they qualify for the program:[14] *Governor:* $200,000 (primary); $400,000 (general).[12] *State senator:* $7,746 (primary); $20,082 (general). *State house representative:* $1,504 (primary); $4,362 (general). (Fluctuates based on average spent in races in previous two years, in addition to other limiting factors.)

(continued on next page)

STATE CHART 2. *Continued*

State	Qualifying Threshold	Residency Restrictions on Matchable Contributions	Spending Limits
Maryland	*Governor and lieutenant governor:* To be eligible, candidates must raise contributions of up to $250 from individuals only, equal to 10% of the spending limit, which in 2006 was $2,086,871.[15]	No	*Governor and lieutenant governor:* $2,086,871 for 2006, which is 0.372[16] times the population of Maryland, as determined by annually by the state board.[17] These limits apply to both the primary and general elections.
Massachusetts[18]	*Governor:* $75,000 (primary): $125,000 (general) in contributions of $250 or less. *Attorney general:* $37,500 (primary): $62,500 (general) in contributions of $250 or less. *Lieutenant governor, state secretary, treasurer, receiver general, and auditor:* $15,000 (primary); $25,000 (general) in contributions of $250 or less.[19]	No	*Governor:* $1,500,000. *Attorney general:* $625,000. *State secretary, treasurer, receiver general, and auditor:* $375,000.[20] These limits apply to both the primary and general elections.
Michigan	*Governor and lieutenant governor (running together):* $75,000 in qualifying contributions of $100 or less.[21]	Yes, for qualifying and matchable contributions	*Governor and lieutenant governor (running together):* $2,000,000.[22] The primary and general elections each have separate expenditure limits of $2,000,000.
Minnesota	*Governor and lieutenant governor (running together):* $35,000 in contributions of $50 or less. *Attorney general:* $15,000 in contributions of $50 or less. *Secretary of state, state auditor:* $6,000 in contributions of $50 or less. *Senate:* $3,000 in contributions of $50 or less. *Representative:* $1,500 in contributions of $50 or less.[23]	Yes, for qualifying contributions	*Governor and lieutenant governor (running together):* $2,393,800. *Attorney general:* $399,000. *Secretary of state and state auditor:* $199,500. *State senator:* $59,900. *State representative:* $30,100.[24] Minnesota provides public funding only for general elections. The expenditure limits apply to only general elections.
Nebraska	Candidates must raise 25% of the spending limit for the office in question from state residents (includes businesses), at least 65% coming from individuals.[25] The contribution limit is 50% of the expenditure limit.	Yes	*Governor:* $2,297,000. *State treasurer, secretary of state, attorney general, and auditor of public accounts:* $209,000. *Member of legislature:* $89,000. *Public Service Commission and state board of education:* $100,000. *Board of Regents of University of Nebraska:* $70,000.
New Jersey	*Governor:* $300,000 in contributions of $3,000 or less, the first $96,000 of which is not matched.[26] These amounts are adjusted for inflation.	No	*Governor:* $4,400,000 (primary); $9,600,000 (general).[26] These amounts are adjusted for inflation.

State	Qualifying Threshold	Residency Restrictions on Matchable Contributions	Spending Limits
New Mexico	*Public Regulation Commission:* $1,150–$1,300 in $5 contributions.[27] *Judicial offices:* $5, 375 in $5 contributions.[27]	Yes, for qualifying contributions[28]	*Public Regulation Commission:* Clean money candidates are limited to public funding, and up to 10% additional funds from political party contributions. The public funds distributed are based on number of registered voters. *Contested primary elections: Public Regulation Commission:* $25,552–$36,730 Democrat; $16,807–$21,245 Republican. *Judicial offices:* 79,727 Democrat; $76,272 Republican. *Uncontested primary elections:* certified candidates are eligible to receive 50% of the amount specified above.[29] *Contested general elections: Public Regulation Commission:* $57,486–$64,778. *Judicial offices:* $161,185 *Uncontested general elections:* certified candidates will receive 50% of the amount specified above.[29]
North Carolina (judicial)	At least 350 contributions of $10 to $500 from registered voters, that total at least 30 times the filing fee for the office, or approximately $38,000 for Court of Appeals candidates and $40,000 for Supreme Court candidates[30]	Yes, for qualifying contributions[30]	*Court of Appeals:* 125 times the filing fee for that office or $160,000 plus seed money and rescue funds. *Supreme Court:* 175 times the filing fee, or $233,625 plus seed money and rescue funds.[31] Public funds are distributed during the general election only, and the expenditure limit applies to that period.
North Carolina (statewide)	Contributions of $10 to $200 from at least 750 voters statewide before the primary election. The total amount of contributions must be equal to or exceed 25 times the amount of the filing fee for the specified office (filing fee in the last election for these positions was $1,045).[32]	Yes, for qualifying contributions[33]	*Auditor, superintendent of public instruction, and commissioner of insurance:* September 1 through primary election date, the maximum expenditure limit is $239,800. From the primary election date through the general election date, candidates can spend only the public funds grant, which is approximately $300,000.[34]
Ohio	N/A	N/A	N/A
Oklahoma	N/A	N/A	N/A
Oregon	N/A	N/A	N/A
Rhode Island	At least 250 contributions of at least $25 (and not more than $1,000), as follows: *Governor:* totaling at least $300,000. *Lieutenant governor, secretary of state, attorney general, and general treasurer:* totaling at least $65,000.[35]	No, for qualifying and matchable contributions	*Governor:* $1,500,000. *Lieutenant governor, secretary of state, attorney general, and general treasurer:* $375,000.[36] These limits apply in the general election.

(continued on next page)

STATE CHART 2. *Continued*

State	Qualifying Threshold	Residency Restrictions on Matchable Contributions	Spending Limits
Utah	N/A	N/A	N/A
Vermont	*Governor:* $35,000 collected from no fewer than 1,500 qualified individual contributors making a contribution of no more than $50 each. *Lieutenant governor:* $17,500 collected from no fewer than 750 qualified individual contributors making a contribution of no more than $50 each.[37]	Yes, contributors must be registered to vote in Vermont, and no more than 25% of the total number of qualified individual contributors may be residents of the same county.[38]	*Governor:* A candidate for governor shall limit campaign expenditures to no more than $300,000 in any two-year general election cycle. *Lieutenant governor:* A candidate for lieutenant governor shall limit campaign expenditures to no more than $100,000 in any two-year general election cycle.[39]
Virginia	N/A	N/A	N/A
Wisconsin	A candidate must receive 6% of total primary votes cast, be opposed for the general election, and receive a percentage of the spending limit in contributions of $100 or less: *Governor:* $53,910. *Lieutenant governor:* $16,174. *Attorney general:* $26,950. *State treasurer, secretary of state, superintendent of public instruction. Supreme Court:* $10,781. *State senator:* $3,450. *State representative:* $1,725.[40]	Nonresidents who contribute more than $25 must designate a resident agent within the state.[41]	*Governor:* $1,078,200. *Lieutenant governor:* $539,000. *Secretary of state, state treasurer, state superintendent, or Supreme Court justice:* $215,625. *State senator:* $34,500. *State representative:* $17,250.[42] These limits apply to expenditures made during both the primary and general elections.

Source: Center for Governmental Studies, Los Angeles, California.

[1] For 2008, according to Citizens Clean Elections Acts and Rules updated January 2008, at http://www.ccec.state.az.us/ccecweb/ccecays/ccecPDF.asp?docPath=docs/2008Act.pdf page 15.
[2] Arizona Statutes § 16-945
[3] For 2008, according to Citizens Clean Elections Acts and Rules updated January 2008, at http://www.ccec.state.az.us/ccecweb/ccecays/ccecPDF.asp?docPath=docs/2008Act.pdf page 27.
[4] Connecticut General Statutes Chapter 157 § 9-704 (3 and 4).
[5] Connecticut General Statutes Chapter 157 § 9-702 (c).
[6] Connecticut General Statutes Chapter 157 § 9-705 and Connecticut General Statutes Chapter 157 § 9-710. Grant amounts, and therefore spending limits, differ for major party, minor party, petitioning candidates, and by percent of vote in previous elections.
[7] Florida Statutes § 106.33.
[8] For a candidate facing no general election opposition, but opposition in the primary, the limit will be 60 percent of the primary. Florida Statutes § 106.34.
[9] Hawaii Revised Statutes § 11-219.
[10] Hawaii Revised Statutes § 11-209.
[11] 2008 spending limits derived from Hawaii's Campaign Spending Commission records, available at http://hawaii.gov/campaign/2008explimits.htm.
[12] 21 Me. Rev. Stat. Ann § 1125.

13 21 Me. Rev. Stat. Ann § 1015.

14 The legislative clean elections distribution for a given year is the average amount of campaign expenditures made by each similarly situated candidate during the previous two elections. For 2006, the clean elections distributions were as follows. *Primary election*: contested candidates for state representative, $1,504; uncontested candidates for state representative, $512; contested candidates for state senator, $7,746; uncontested candidates for state senator, $20,082; uncontested candidates for state senator, $8,033. *General election*: contested candidates for state representative, $4,362; uncontested candidates for state representative, $1,745; contested candidates for state senator, $1,927.

15 According to Summary of Campaign Financing Laws, Maryland State Board of Elections at http://www.elections.state.md.us/campaign_finance/public_funding.html.

16 The expenditure limit is 0.30 (adjusted annually with the CPI) times the population of Maryland; 0.30 adjusted for 2006 was equal to 0.372.

17 The Maryland State Board of Elections relies on data from the Division of Health Statistics of the Maryland Department of Health and Mental Hygiene, published in *Maryland Vital Statistics*, which is published annually. The most recent report (2005) estimated the Maryland population at 5,600,388.

18 Massachusetts Clean Elections Law, repealed as of July 1, 2003 (M.G.L.A. 55A, MA ST 55A), has been replaced by Massachusetts Limited Public Financing of Campaigns for Statewide Elective Office (M.G.L.A. 55C, MA ST 55C).

19 Massachusetts General Laws 55C §§ 4, 6.

20 Amounts given are applied separately to the general election and the primary, so the combined limit is double the amounts given. (M.G.L.A. 55C § 1A, MA ST 55C § 1A).

21 M.C.L.A. §§ 169.212, 265.

22 M.C.L.A. §§ 169.203, 267. "For purposes of sections 61 to 71, 'candidate' only means, in a primary election, a candidate for the office of Governor and, in a general election, a candidate for the office of Governor or Lieutenant Governor. However, the candidates for the office of Governor and Lieutenant Governor of the same political party in a general election shall be considered as 1 candidate."

23 Minnesota Statutes § 10A.323.

24 Minnesota Statutes § 10A.25.

25 Nebraska Revised Statutes § 32-1604.

26 The New Jersey Election Law Enforcement Commission adjusts these amounts based on a price index, the given amounts are for 2005 (NJ ST 19:44A-7.1, NJ ST 19:44A-7.1). http://www.elec.state.nj.us/pdffiles/publicfinancedocs/CostIndex_2005.pdf.

27 1-19A N.M.S.A. §§ 2, 4.

28 Contributions are limited to registered voters who are eligible to vote for the office the candidate is seeking. 1-19A N.M.S.A. § 2.

29 2008 fund distribution derived from Secretary of State records, available at http://www.sos.state.nm.us/pdf/FUNDDISTRIBUTIONPRI.pdf.

30 North Carolina General Statutes § 163-278.64(b).

31 No funds distributed in uncontested primaries or general elections and only in specified circumstances during contested primaries. N.C.G.S. § 163-278.65.

32 North Carolina General Statutes § 163-278.98.

33 North Carolina General Statutes § 163-278.96.

34 North Carolina General Statutes § 163-278.98e3.

35 General Laws of Rhode Island § 17-25-20.

36 General Laws of Rhode Island § 17-25-19.

37 17 Vermont Statutes Annotated § 2854(a).

38 17 Vermont Statutes Annotated § 2854(b).

39 17 Vermont Statutes Annotated § 2805a.

40 The candidates for the following offices must raise 5 percent of the spending limit for that office: governor, lieutenant governor, secretary of state, state treasurer, attorney general, state superintendent of public instruction, and Supreme Court justice. All others: 10 percent. The amounts are as follows: governor, $53,910; lieutenant governor, $16,174; secretary of state, $10,781; state treasurer, $10,781; attorney general, $26,950; state superintendent of public instruction, $10,781; Supreme Court justice, $10,781; state senator, $3,450; and state representative, $1,725. Wisconsin Statutes Annotated §§ 11.26, 11.31, 11.50.

41 Wisconsin Statutes Annotated § 11.07.

42 Wisconsin Statutes Annotated § 11.31.

STATE CHART 3. CONTRIBUTION LIMITS, CANDIDATE PERSONAL CONTRIBUTIONS, MAXIMUM PUBLIC FUNDS AVAILABLE

State	Contribution Limits	Candidate Personal Contributions	Maximum Public Funds Available
Arizona	*Nonstatewide offices: Legislative:* $488 from an individual or political committee. *Other nonstatewide offices:* $390 from an individual or political committee. *Statewide offices:* $1,010 from an individual or political committee.[1]	$1,230 statewide or $610 legislative for clean elections candidates, otherwise unlimited[2]	*Governor:* $638,222 in primary; $957,333 in general election. *Secretary of state:* $165,378 in primary; $248,067 in general election. *Attorney general:* $165,378 in primary; $248,067 in general election. *Treasurer:* $82,680 in primary; $124,020 in general election. *Superintendent of public instruction:* $82,680 in primary; $124,020 in general election. *Corporation commissioner:* $82,680 in primary; $124,020 in general election. *Mine inspector:* $41,349 in primary; $62,024 in general election. *Legislature:* $12,921 in primary; $19,382 in general election.[2] For a qualifying, third-party candidate, 70% of the sum of the primary election spending limit and the general election spending limit for his or her respective office. For an unopposed, participating candidate in the primary, five dollars times the number of qualifying contributions for that candidate. In the general election, an amount equal to five dollars times the number of qualifying contributions for that candidate.[3]
Arkansas	*All candidates:* $2,000 per election[4]	Unlimited	N/A
Connecticut	*House:* $250. *Senate:* $1,000. *Governor:* $3,500. *Lieutenant governor, attorney general, state comptroller, state treasurer, secretary of state:* $2,000.[5]	*House:* $1,000. *Senate:* $2,000. *Governor:* $20,000. *Lieutenant governor, attorney general, state comptroller, state treasurer, secretary of state:* $10,000.[6]	*House:* $10,000 in the primary ($25,000 if the district is dominated by the opposing party); $25,000 in the general election (30% of that amount if the candidate runs unopposed and 60% of that amount if the candidate runs against a minor party candidate). *Senate:* $35,000 in the primary ($75,000 if the district is dominated by the other party); $85,000 in the general election (30% of that amount if the candidate runs unopposed and 60% of that amount if the candidate runs against a minor party candidate). *Governor:* $1,250,000 in the primary, and $3,000,000 in the general election (30% of that amount if unopposed and 60% if running against a minor party candidate). *Lieutenant governor, attorney general, state comptroller, state treasurer, secretary of state:* $375,000 in the primary, and $750,000 in the general election (30% of that amount if unopposed and 60% if running against a minor party candidate).[7]
Florida	*Candidates and committees:* $500 per election (individuals)[8]	$425,000 limit to qualify for public financing, otherwise unlimited	Matching funds eligibility is not expressly capped by statute, but is finite because of spending limits.[9] In 2006, total amounts distributed in the primary and general elections were as follows: *Governor:* $7,415,325. *Chief financial officer:* $1,943,964. *Attorney general:* $1,381,011. *Commissioner of agriculture:* $393,459.[10]

State	Contribution Limits	Candidate Personal Contributions	Maximum Public Funds Available
Hawaii	*Four-year statewide office:* $6,000 per election. *Four-year nonstatewide office:* $4,000 per election. *Two-year office:* $2,000 per election. *Noncandidate committees:* $1,000 per election.[11]	Contributions from a candidate's immediate family limited to $50,000, including loans[12]	Based on expenditure limit: *Governor:* $154,248 in each the primary and general. *Lieutenant governor:* $86,379 for each election. *Mayor:* $7,317–$83,219 for each election (depending on the population of the city). *Senator:* $3,666–$7,683 for each election. *Representative:* $1,705–$3,223 for each election. *County council member:* $1,844–15,517 for each election. *Hawaiian affairs:* $1,500 for each election. *Board of education:* $50 for each election.[13]
Idaho	Unlimited	Unlimited	N/A
Iowa	Unlimited	Unlimited	N/A
Maine	*Governor and lieutenant governor (running together):* $500 per election. *Senator and representative:* $250 per election. Aggregate limit of $25,000 per calendar year.[14]	None allowed for certified clean election candidates, otherwise unlimited	*Governor:* $200,000 (primary); $400,000 (general). Legislative candidates receive the average expenditures made by legislative candidates in contested races in the previous two elections.[15] *Representative:* $1,504 contested (primary); $512 uncontested (primary). *Senator:* $7,746 contested (primary); $1,927 uncontested (primary). *Representative:* $4,144 contested (general); $1,658 uncontested (general). *Senator:* $19,078 contested (general); $7,631 uncontested (general).
Maryland	*Candidates and committees:* $4,000 per election cycle. Aggregate limit of $10,000 per election cycle.[16]	Unlimited	In a primary election, opposed candidates (governor and lieutenant governor) receive $1.00 for every $1.00 in eligible private contributions; unopposed candidates (governor and lieutenant governor) receive $1.00 for every $3.00 in eligible private contributions. In a general election, opposed candidates receive equal portions of the remaining fund; if unopposed, candidates receive no funding.[17]
Massachusetts	*Candidates:* $500 per calendar year. *Party committees:* $5,000 per calendar year. Aggregate limit of $12,500 per calendar year.[18]	Unlimited	The following amounts are available in the primary and general election periods, separately: *Governor and lieutenant governor:* $750,000. *Attorney general:* $312,500. *State secretary, treasurer, receiver general, and auditor:* $187,500.[19]
Michigan	*Statewide office:* $3,400. *Senator:* $1,000. *Representative:* $500.[21] *Judicial candidates:* $100 for lawyers.	$50,000 per gubernatorial campaign from the candidate and the candidate's family, regardless of public funding[21]	*Governor and lieutenant governor:* $990,000 in the primary election;[22] $1,125,000 in the general election.[23]

(continued on next page)

State	Contribution Limits	Candidate Personal Contributions	Maximum Public Funds Available
Minnesota	*Governor and lieutenant governor (running together):* $2,000 in election year, otherwise $500.[24] *Attorney general:* $1,000 in election year, otherwise $200.[25] *Secretary of state, state auditor, state senator, and state representative:* $500 in election year, otherwise $100.[26]	*Governor and lieutenant governor (running together):* $20,000.[24] *Attorney general:* $10,000.[25] *Secretary of state, state auditor, state senator, and state representative:* $5,000[26]	Calculated for each general election according to the following statutory formula: *Governor and lieutenant governor together:* 21% of available funds. *Attorney general:* 4.2% of available funds. *State auditor:* 2.4% of available funds. *Secretary of state:* 2.4% of available funds. *State senator:* 23.33% when state senators serve four-year terms and 35% for two-year terms. *State representative:* 46.66% when state representatives serve four-year terms and 35% for two-year terms.[27] In 2006, the distributed amounts totaled $4,796,523.17.[28]
Nebraska	No more than 50% of the spending limit[29]	Unlimited	Maximum funds determined by opponent spending.[30] Specifically in the last election, candidates could receive up to three times the spending limits: *Governor:* $6,891,000. *State treasurer, secretary of state, attorney general, and auditor of public accounts:* $627,000. *State legislators:* $267,000. *Public Service Commission and state board of education:* $300,000. *Board of Regents of University of Nebraska:* $210,000.[31]
New Jersey	*Governor:* $3,400 per election. *All other offices:* $3,000 per election.[32]	$25,000 if the candidate accepts public financing, otherwise unlimited[33]	To qualified candidates for governor on a 2-to-1 basis for both the primary and general elections, up to $2.7 million in the primary and $6.4 million in the general election.[35]
New Mexico	Unlimited for nonparticipating candidates. Clean money candidates are limited to $100 seed money contributions, subject to a total limit of $5,000.[35]	Clean money candidates may make personal contributions as long as such contributions do not exceed the total seed money limit of $5,000; otherwise unlimited	*Contested primary elections: Public regulation commissioner:* $0.25 for each voter in the district of the candidate's party in the district of the office for which s/he is running ($25,552–$36,730 for Democrats and $16,807–$21,245 for Republicans).[36] *Justice of the Supreme Court and justice of the Court of Appeals:* $0.15 for each voter of the candidate's party in the state ($79,727 for Democrats and $76,272 for Republicans). *Uncontested primary elections:* certified candidates receive funds equal to 50% of the amount specified above.[37] *Contested general elections: Public regulation commissioner:* $0.25 for each voter in the district of the office for which the candidate is running ($57,486–$64,778). *Justice of the Supreme Court and justice of the Court of Appeals:* $0.15 for each voter in the state ($161,185). *Uncontested general elections:* certified candidates receive funds equal to 50% of the amount specified above.[38]

State	Contribution Limits	Candidate Personal Contributions	Maximum Public Funds Available
North Carolina (judicial)	*Court of Appeals or Supreme Court:* $1,000 per election (from individuals); $2,000 per election (from candidate's parent, child, brother, or sister).[39]	Participating candidates, candidates' spouses, parents, children, and siblings can contribute $1,000 to the campaign. This money is to be contributed during the qualifying period, as only fund money can be spent after a candidate qualifies.[40]	*Court of Appeals:* 125 times the candidate's filing fee (varies by district) and up to twice this amount in the general election, or up to $76,000 in the primary. *Supreme Court:* 175 times the candidate's filing fee (varies by district) and up to twice this amount in the general election, or up to $80,000 in the primary[41]
North Carolina (statewide)	*Auditor, superintendent of public instruction, and commissioner of insurance:* $200 for qualifying contributions and $4,000 thereafter up to a total of $20,000[42]	Participating candidates, candidates' spouses, parents, children, and siblings can contribute $1,000 to the campaign during the qualifying period. This money is to be contributed during the qualifying period, as only fund money can be spent after a candidate qualifies.[40]	*Auditor, superintendent of public instruction, and commissioner of insurance:* The amount of funds the candidate can receive is based on the average amount of campaign-related expenditures made by all candidates who won the immediately preceding three general elections for the specific office, with a minimum amount of $300,000.
Ohio	*Statewide office and General Assembly:* $10,670 per election. *County political party:* $10,670 per election. *State political party:* $32,010 per calendar year. *Political action committee:* $10,670 per calendar year[43]	Unlimited[44]	N/A
Oklahoma	For all state candidates, a "family" (an individual, his/her spouse, and any children under the age of 18) may give a maximum of $5,000[45]	Unlimited	N/A
Oregon	Unlimited	Unlimited	N/A

(continued on next page)

State	Contribution Limits	Candidate Personal Contributions	Maximum Public Funds Available
Rhode Island	*Individual contribution:* $1,000 per calendar year. Aggregate limit of $10,000 total per calendar year.[46]	No more than 5% of the expenditure limit if a candidate accepts public financing; otherwise unlimited[47]	The following amounts are available for the general election only: *Governor:* $750,000. *Lieutenant governor, secretary of state, attorney general, and general treasurer:* $187,500.[48]
Utah	Unlimited	Unlimited	Unlimited
Vermont	*Governor, lieutenant governor, secretary of state, state treasurer, auditor of accounts, and attorney general:* $400 per two-year election cycle. *State senator and county office:* $300. *State representative and local office:* $200. *Noncandidate political committee or political party:* $2,000.[49]	Unlimited	*Governor:* $75,000 (primary); $225,000 (general). *Lieutenant governor:* $75,000 (primary); $75,000 (general).[55]
Virginia	Unlimited	Unlimited	N/A
Wisconsin	*Governor:* $10,000. *Lieutenant governor:* $10,000. *Attorney general:* $10,000. *Secretary of state, state treasurer, Supreme Court justice, state superintendent of public instruction:* $10,000. *State senator:* $1,000. *State representative:* $500.[51]	Twice the individual contribution limit if a candidate accepts public financing; otherwise unlimited[52]	45% of disbursement level specified for the office.[53] Specifically the grant may not exceed the following: *Governor:* $485,190. *Lieutenant governor:* $145,563. *Attorney general:* $242,550. *Secretary of state, state treasurer, Supreme Court justice, and state superintendent of public instruction:* $97,031. *State senator:* $15,525. *State representative:* $7,763.54. These amounts are available in the general election only.

Source: Center for Governmental Studies, Los Angeles, California.

[1] Adjusted biennially per Arizona Revised Statutes § 16-905. These amounts reflect contribution limits on individuals; additional contribution limits can be found under the same citation, available at http://www.azleg.state.az.us/FormatDocument.asp?inDoc=/ars/16/00905.htm&Title=16&DocType=ARS.

[2] Adjusted pursuant to Arizona Revised Statutes § 16-959(a). Numbers listed accurate as of September 2007, available at http://www.azsos.gov/election/2008/Info/CCEC_Biennial_Adjustment_Charts.htm.

[3] Arizona Revised Statutes §16-951.

[4] Arkansas Code § 7-6-203.

[5] Contribution limits for nonparticipating candidates derived from Secretary of State records, available at http://www.ct.gov/seec/lib/seec/contribution_limits_2007.pdf.

[6] Connecticut General Statutes Chapter 157 § 9-710 (c).

[7] Connecticut General Statutes Chapter 157 § 9-705.

[8] For these purposes, same-ticket candidates for governor and lieutenant governor are considered a single candidate. Florida Statutes § 106.08.

[9] The Florida Supreme Court responded to a legal challenge with "The Republican Party argues that the failure to identify a specific dollar amount to be transferred renders the funding provision null. We do not agree. Section 106.34 sets limits on the amounts candidates can spend. Section 106.35 establishes formulas and thus controls the distribution of funds to qualified candidates. These sections adequately specify, control, and limit the funds transferred." *Republican Party of Florida v. Smith*, 638 So.2d 26 (Fla. 1994).

[10] Florida Division of Elections, Public Campaign Finance reports. The most recently reported statistics are for 2006. Available at, http://election.dos.state.fl.us/campaign-finance/matching-funds2006.shtml.

[11] Hawaii Revised Statutes § 11-204(a).

[12] Hawaii Revised Statutes § 11-204(c).

[13] Hawaii Revised Statutes § 11-218.

[14] Aggregate limit does not apply to candidates or candidates' domestic partners when supporting the candidates' own campaign. Maine Revised Statutes § 1015.

[15] Maine Revised Statutes § 1125.8. Please note that the amounts distributed to legislative candidates reflect a 5 percent reduction in initial distribution amounts for the 2008 November election. This change is part of the budget recently enacted by the legislature and signed by the governor. The payment amounts for the primary election have not been changed. Information about the initial distribution of funds is available at http://www.state.me.us/ethics/mcea/initialdist.htm.

[16] Maryland Code, Election Law, § 13-266(b).

[17] Maryland Code, Election Law, § 15-106.

[18] Annual Campaign Contribution Limits, Office of Campaign and Political Finance for the Commonwealth of Massachusetts, available at http://www.mass.gov/ocpf/guides/fs_contrib_limits.pdf.

[19] Amounts given are applied separately to the general election and the primary, so the combined limit is double the amounts given. (M.G.L.A. 55C §§ 1A, 5).

[20] Campaign Finance, Election Cycle Contribution Limits for State Elective Offices, Michigan Department of State, available at http://www.michigan.gov/documents/limits_charts_-_state_elective_65033_7.pdf.

[21] MI ST § 169.269 (6). "As used in this subsection, 'immediate family' means a spouse, parent, brother, sister, son, or daughter. A candidate and members of that candidate's immediate family may not contribute in total to that person's candidate committee an amount that is more than $50,000.00 in value for an election cycle."

[22] MI ST § 169.264.

[23] MI ST § 169.265.

[24] Handbook for Governor and Lt. Governor Candidates, Minnesota Campaign Finance and Public Disclosure Board, February 2008, available at http://www.cfboard.state.mn.us/handbook/hb_cand_governor_lt_governor.pdf.

[25] Handbook for Attorney General Candidates, Minnesota Campaign Finance and Public Disclosure Board, February 2008, available at http://www.cfboard.state.mn.us/handbook/hb_cand_attorney_general.pdf.

[26] Candidate Handbooks, Minnesota Campaign Finance and Public Disclosure Board; available at http://www.cfboard.state.mn.us/CandRefGuide.html.

[27] Minnesota Statutes § 10A.31.

[28] Minnesota Campaign Finance and Public Disclosure Board; available at http://www.cfboard.state.mn.us/publicsubsidy/2006_Final_Pubsub_Pymt.pdf.

[29] Nebraska Revised Statutes § 32-1608.

[30] Nebraska Revised Statutes § 32-1606.

[31] Calculated from Nebraska Revised Statutes § 32-1604.

[32] The New Jersey Election Law Enforcement Commission adjusts these amounts based on a price index, the given amounts are for 2009 (NJ ST 19:44A-7.1, NJ ST 19:44A-7.1). http://www.elec.state.nj.us/pdffiles/publicfinancedocs/CostIndex_2009.pdf.

[33] N.J. Senate, No. 1176—L.1980, c. 74.

[34] New Jersey Statutes 19:44A-33.

[35] 1-19A N.M.S.A. § 5.

(continued on next page)

101

STATE CHART 3. *Continued*

[36] Amounts vary depending on the candidate's district.

[37] Numbers derived from the New Mexico Secretary of State, available at http://www.sos.state.nm.us/pdf/FUNDDiSTRIBUTIONPRI.pdf.

[38] Numbers derived from the New Mexico Secretary of State, available at http://www.sos.state.nm.us/pdf/FUNDDISTRIBUTIONGEN.pdf.

[39] 2008–2009 Campaign Finance Manual, North Carolina State Board of Elections, available at http://www.sboe.state.nc.us/content.aspx?id=7.

[40] North Carolina General Statues § 163-278.98 (e)(4a).

[41] North Carolina General Statues § 163-278.65.

[42] North Carolina General Statues § 163-278.96.

[43] Contribution Limit Chart, Ohio Secretary of State, February 2007, available at http://www.sos.state.oh.us/SOS/Campaign%20Finance/CFGuide/Resources/limchart.aspx.

[44] Candidates for statewide or general assembly office who receive or expend personal funds of more than $100,000 in a primary or $150,000 in general election for statewide office, or more than $25,000 per election for general assembly must file a personal funds notice.

[45] 2008–2009 Constitutional Ethics Rules: Instruction Manual on Campaign Reporting, State of Oklahoma, available at http://www.ok.gov/oec/documents/MAN08-09.cfd.pdf, page 6.

[46] Rhode Island Statutes § 17-25-10.1.

[47] Rhode Island Statutes § 17-25-20.10.

[48] Rhode Island Statutes § 17-25-19(b).

[49] Vermont Statutes § 2805.

[50] The grant for a primary election period is reduced by an amount equal to the candidate's qualifying contributions. Incumbents are entitled to only 85 percent of the total funds they would otherwise receive. Candidates in uncontested elections and candidates who lose in the primary are not eligible for public funds. Vermont Statutes § 2855.

[51] Contribution Limits for State Offices, Elections Division, Wisconsin Government Accountability Board, available at http://elections.state.wi.us/docview.asp?docid=1818&locid=47.

[52] Wisconsin Statutes Annotated § 11.26.10.

[53] Wisconsin Statutes Annotated § 11.50.9.

[54] Figures based on amounts delineated in Wisconsin Statutes Annotated § 11.31.

State	High-Spending Opponent Trigger Provision	Independent Expenditure (IE) Trigger Provision	Debate Requirement
Arizona	If a nonparticipating candidate exceeds the expenditure limit, equivalent funds (minus 6% for a nonparticipating candidate's estimated fund-raising costs) are distributed to a participating candidate up to a maximum of three times the expenditure limit.[1]	Independent expenditures made against a participating candidate entitle that candidate to matching funds, and independent expenditures in favor of a candidate entitle all other participating candidates to matching funds, with the same restrictions as apply in the case of a high-spending opponent.[2]	Participating candidates must participate in debates prior to the primary and general elections.[3]
Arkansas	N/A	N/A	N/A
Connecticut	If a nonparticipating opponent spends in excess of 100% of the grant amount, the participating candidate gets an additional 25% of the applicable grant amount. If the opponent spends in excess of 125% of the applicable grant amount, the participating opponent gets an additional 25% of the applicable grant amount (meaning 50% of the original grant amount). This formula continues until the nonparticipating candidates spends 175% more than the applicable grant amount, at which point no more supplemental funds are available.[4]	A participating candidate can receive additional public funds based on independent expenditures if the candidate's non-participating opponent's expenditures exceeds the amount of the independent expenditures are more than the applicable grant amount. A participating candidate can receive additional funds matching the amount of the independent expenditure, up to the applicable primary or general election grant amount.[5]	No
Florida	If a nonparticipating candidate exceeds the expenditure limit, equivalent funds are distributed to participating candidate up to a maximum of twice the expenditure limit.[6]	No	No
Hawaii	No	No	No
Idaho	N/A	N/A	N/A
Iowa	N/A	N/A	N/A
Maine	If any candidate exceeds the clean money distribution, the excess is matched, up to a limit of two times the original distribution.[7]	A participating candidate can receive additional public funds based on independent expenditures if an opponent's contributions or expenditures plus the independent expenditures made on the opponent's behalf are greater than funds received by a participating candidate plus the independent expenditures made on behalf of that candidate.	No
Maryland	No	No	No

(continued on next page)

State	High-Spending Opponent Trigger Provision	Independent Expenditure (IE) Trigger Provision	Debate Requirement
Massachusetts[8]	No	No	No
Michigan	No	No	No
Minnesota	Expenditure limits are eliminated.[9]	No	No
Nebraska	If any candidate exceeds the expenditure limit, equivalent funds are distributed to the qualified candidates up to three times the expenditure limit.[10]	No	No
New Jersey	No	No	Yes[11]
New Mexico	If a nonparticipating candidate exceeds the public funds distribution, additional funds are distributed to match the excess, up to twice the original public funds distribution.[12]	Independent expenditures are treated like expenditures made directly by a nonparticipating candidate in order to determine whether participating candidates are entitled to additional matching funds.[12]	No
North Carolina (judicial)	If a nonparticipating candidate opposing a certified candidate spends campaign money in excess of the expenditure limit, then the certified opponent receives matching funds in amounts equal to the excess spending, up to twice the spending limit.[13]	Independent expenditures made in opposition to a participating candidate or in support of an opponent to that candidate entitle that candidate to matching funds up to twice the original public funds distribution.[14]	No
North Carolina (statewide)	If a nonparticipating candidate opposing a certified candidate spends campaign money in excess of the expenditure limit, then the certified candidate will be entitled to receive a matching amount of public funds to remain competitive, which is limited to two times the original grant in general elections, and to an amount equal to the qualifying contributions in a primary.[15]	If independent committee expenditures are made in opposition to a participating candidate or in support or a noncertified candidate, then the certified candidate will be entitled to receive a matching amount of public funds to remain competitive, which is limited to two times the original grant in general elections, and to an amount equal to the qualifying contributions in a primary.[16]	No
Ohio	N/A	N/A	N/A
Oklahoma	N/A	N/A	N/A
Oregon	N/A	N/A	N/A

State	High-Spending Opponent Trigger Provision	Independent Expenditure (IE) Trigger Provision	Debate Requirement
Rhode Island	If a nonparticipating candidate exceeds the expenditure limit, the limit is lifted to the extent the nonparticipating candidate exceeds it.[17]	Independent expenditures are counted against the expenditure limit of the candidate.[18]	No
Utah	N/A	N/A	N/A
Vermont	No	Independent expenditures are counted against the expenditure limit of the candidate on whose behalf the expenditure was made.[19]	No
Virginia	N/A	N/A	N/A
Wisconsin	If an opponent is eligible for public financing but does not accept it, qualified candidates for the same office who accept public financing are no longer subject to expenditure limits.[20]	No	No

Source: Center for Governmental Studies, Los Angeles, California.

[1] Arizona Revised Statutes § 16-952.

[2] Arizona Revised Statutes § 16-952(C).

[3] Arizona Revised Statutes § 16-956.

[4] Connecticut General Statutes Chapter 157 § 9-713.

[5] Connecticut General Statutes Chapter 157 § 9-714 (2).

[6] Florida Statutes § 106.355.

[7] Maine Revised Statutes 21-A, § 1125.

[8] Massachusetts Clean Elections Law, repealed as of July 1, 2003 (M.G.L.A. 55A, MA ST 55A), has been replaced by Massachusetts Limited Public Financing of Campaigns for Statewide Elective Office (M.G.L.A. 55C, MA ST 55C).

[9] Minnesota Statutes § 10A.25.10.

[10] Nebraska Statutes § 32-1606.

[11] A participating candidate must forfeit and repay all public funds if he or she does not participate in the debate unless the Election Law Enforcement Commission determines that the candidate's failure to participate occurred under reasonable or justifiable circumstances. (N.J.S.A. 199:44A-47 NJ ST 19:44A)

[12] New Mexico Statutes § 1-19A-14.

[13] North Carolina General Statutes § 163-278.67(b).

[14] North Carolina General Statutes § 163.278.67(a).

[15] North Carolina General Statutes § 163-278.99B.

[16] North Carolina General Statutes § 163-278.99B (2).

[17] General Laws of Rhode Island § 17-25-24.

[18] General Laws of Rhode Island § 17-25-23.

[19] 17 Vermont Statutes Annotated § 2801. While Vermont's mandatory expenditure limits for nonparticipating candidates were ruled unconstitutional, Vermont's expenditure limits for participating candidates remain in effect.

[20] Wisconsin Statutes Annotated § 11.50.2(i).

LOCAL CHART 1. POPULATION, DATE ENACTED, PUBLIC FUNDS ALLOCATION, MAXIMUM AMOUNT

Jurisdiction	Population[1]	Enacted	Public Funds Allocation[2]	Maximum Public Funds Available
Albuquerque, NM	504,949	2005	*City council:* $1 per registered district voter per participating candidate. *Mayor:* $1 per registered city voter per participating candidate.[3]	*City council and mayor:* $450,000 per candidate (overall amount in program equals 1% of the city's general fund).[4]
Austin, TX	709,893	1992	*City council and mayor:* Equal distribution of available funds among qualifying candidates in a runoff election. The public funds are distributed as a lump-sum grant. If no eligible candidate is in a runoff election, the funds are reserved for future elections.[5]	No maximum is established by law.
Boulder, CO	94,673	2000	*City council:* $1 in public funds for every $1 in contributions.[6]	*City council:* A candidate may receive no more than 50% of the (CPI-adjusted) spending limit in public funds.[6]
Chapel Hill, NC	48,715	2008	*Mayor:* A qualified candidate receives a lump-sum grant of $9,000.[7] *Town council:* A qualified candidate receives a lump-sum grant of $3,000.	*Mayor:* $9,000 lump-sum grant. *Town council:* $3,000 lump-sum grant.[7]
Long Beach, CA	472,494	1994	*City council, mayor, citywide offices:* $1 in public funds for every $2 in contributions (primary); $1 in public funds for every $1 in contributions (runoff).[8]	A candidate may receive no more than 33% of the primary spending limit and 50% of the runoff-election spending limit in public funds, which equals the following: *City council:* $17,207 (primary); $13,036 (runoff). *Mayor:* $86,037 (primary); $65,180 (runoff). *Other citywide office:* $65,180 (primary); $32,590 (runoff).[9]
Los Angeles, CA	3,849,378	1990	*City council:* $1 in public funds for every $1 in contributions from individuals, up to $250 (primary); lump-sum grant of one-fifth of the maximum matching funds available, plus a $1-to-$1 match for individual contributions, up to $250 (general). *Mayor and citywide offices:* $1 in public funds for every $1 in contributions from individuals, up to $500 per contributor (primary); lump-sum grant of one-fifth of the maximum matching funds available, plus a $1-to-$1 match for individual contributions, up to $500 (general).[10]	*City council:* $100,000 (primary); $125,000 (general); up to $25,000 more to match noncandidate and nonparticipating candidate expenditures in the general election. *Mayor:* $667,000 (primary); $800,000 (general); up to $200,000 more to match noncandidate and nonparticipating candidate expenditures in the general election. *Controller:* $267,000 (primary); $300,000 (general); up to $60,000 more to match noncandidate and nonparticipating candidate expenditures in the general election. *City attorney:* $300,000 (primary); $350,000 (general); up to $70,000 more to match noncandidate and nonparticipating candidate expenditures in the general election.[11]

Jurisdiction	Population[1]	Enacted	Public Funds Allocation[2]	Maximum Public Funds Available
Miami-Dade County, FL	2,402,408	2001	*County commission:* A qualified candidate receives a lump-sum grant of either $50,000 or $75,000 for the general election, depending on which qualification threshold is met. A qualified candidate receives an additional $50,000 if a runoff election is held. *Mayor:* A qualified candidate receives a lump-sum grant of $300,000 for the general election, and an additional $200,000 if a runoff election is held.[12]	*County commission:* $75,000 (general); $50,000 (runoff). *Mayor:* $300,000 (general); $200,000 (runoff)[12]
New Haven, CT	124,001	2006	*Mayor:* A qualified candidate receives matching funds as follows: For contributions over $25: $50 (until the candidate reaches the expenditure ceiling). For contributions under $25: 2-to-1 match.[13]	*Mayor:* $125,000 in matching funds (primary); $125,000 (general); $15,000 lump-sum grant (one for primary and one for general)[13]

New York, NY	8,214,426	1988	*City council, mayor, and citywide offices:* $6 in public funds for every $1 in contributions from "a natural person resident in the city of New York," up to $1,050 in public funds per contributor ($522 per contributor in the case of a special election).[14]	Under normal circumstances, a candidate may not receive public funds that exceed 55% of spending limit,[14] which in 2009 equals the following:
				
				   City council: $88,550 per election. *Borough president:* $762,300 per election. *Mayor:* $3,386,900 per election. *Public advocate and comptroller:* $2,117,500 per election.
				
				   However, if a high-spending opponent spends 50% over the spending limit ("Tier One"), the participating candidate is eligible to receive matching funds in a 5:1 ratio in the following maximum amounts (2009):
				
				   City council: $107,333 per election. *Borough president:* $924,000 per election. *Mayor:* $4,105,333 per election. *Public advocate and comptroller:* $2,566,667 per election.
				
				   Additionally, if a high-spending opponent spends 300% over the spending limit ("Tier Two"), the participating candidate is eligible to receive matching funds in a 6:1 ratio in the following maximum amounts (2009):
				
				   City council: $201,250. *Borough president:* $1,732,500. *Mayor:* $7,697,500. *Public advocate and comptroller:* $4,812,500.

(continued on next page)

LOCAL CHART 1. *Continued*

Jurisdiction	Population[1]	Enacted	Public Funds Allocation[2]	Maximum Public Funds Available
Oakland, CA[15]	397,067	1999	*City council:* $1 in public funds for every $1 in contributions, up to $100 in public funds per contributor[16]	Candidates may not receive public funds exceeding 30% of the applicable spending limit,[16] which equaled the following as of 2007: *City council:* $30,300–$35,100 per election (depending on the population of the district). *School board:* $20,100–$23,400 per election (depending on the population of the district).
Portland, OR[17]	537,081	2005	*Commissioner, mayor, auditor:* Candidates receive the maximum amount of funds for contested primary and general elections, minus the total amount of qualifying contributions[18] and seed money[19] received by the candidate in a predetermined schedule before each election.[20]	Contested primary (and special nominating) elections: *Mayor:* $200,000. *Commissioner:* $150,000. *Auditor:* $150,000. General elections: *Mayor:* $250,000. *Commissioner:* $200,000. *Auditor:* $200,000.[21]
Richmond, CA	96,648	2003	*City council and mayor:* When $15,000 total in matchable contributions are received, $5,000 is disbursed. When $20,000 in total matchable contributions are received, $5,000 is disbursed. When $25,000 in total matchable contributions are received, $5,000 is disbursed. When $30,000 in total matchable contributions are received, $5,000 is disbursed. When $35,000 in total matchable contributions are received, $5,000 is disbursed.	*City council and mayor:* $25,000 in matching funds per election.
Sacramento, CA	453,781	2003	*City council and mayor:* $1 in public funds for every $1 in contributions received within 88 days of the election, up to $250 in public funds per contributor.[22]	*City council:* $32,800 per election. *Mayor:* $109,6000 per election.[22]
San Francisco, CA	744,041	2000	*Board of Supervisors:* A Board of Supervisors candidate receives $50,000 on certification of eligibility, then $4 in public funds for each of the first $5,000 raised in individual contributions, then $1 in public funds for each $1 in individual contributions raised, up to a maximum of $43,750. *Mayor:* A mayoral candidate receives $50,000 on certification of eligibility, then $4 in public funds for each $1 of the first $100,000 raised in individual contributions, then $1 in public funds for every $1 in individual contributions raised up to $400,000 or a maximum of $850,000 in total public funds.[23]	*Board of Supervisors:* $43,750. *Mayor:* $850,000.

Jurisdiction	Population[1]	Enacted	Public Funds Allocation[2]	Maximum Public Funds Available
Suffolk County, NY[24]	1,469,715	1998	Upon reaching the threshold for eligibility, a candidate receives the following amount of public funds per election, in a lump-sum grant: *County legislature:* $10,000. *Executive:* $200,000. *Comptroller, treasurer, district attorney:* $70,000.[25]	*County legislature:* $10,000. *Executive:* $200,000. *Comptroller, treasurer, district attorney:* $70,000.[25]
Tucson, AZ	518,956	1985	*City council and mayor:* $1 in public funds for every $1 in contributions.[26]	There is no maximum amount established explicitly by law, but under the matching-funds formula, it would be impossible for a candidate to receive more than 50% of the spending limit in public funds. Consequently, the maximum public funds available to a candidate would be as follows: *City council* (for 2007 elections): $45,091 per election cycle. *Mayor* (for 2007 elections): $90,194 per election cycle.[26]

Source: Center for Governmental Studies, Los Angeles, California.

[1] Based on estimated 2006 census figures from the U.S. Census Bureau, which can be found at the American Factfinder Web site: http://factfinder.census.gov, unless otherwise indicated.

[2] In jurisdictions that use a matching funds system, as opposed to a lump-sum grant system, the amount of public funding a candidate may receive per contributor is typically limited by the size of the jurisdiction's contribution limit. For example, in Boulder, a candidate may receive $1 in public funds for every $1 in private contributions up to the jurisdiction's $100 contribution limit. Therefore, a candidate in Boulder could not receive more than $100 in public funds per contributor. In an effort to encourage candidates to solicit smaller contributions from a larger number of donors, some jurisdictions place a limit on the size of a contribution that will be matched which is lower than the general contribution limit (e.g., Los Angeles and New York City). For the purposes of interpreting this column, assume that contributions up to the contribution limit are matchable unless otherwise noted.

[3] Albuquerque, N.M., City Charter Article XVI, § 12 (2007).

[4] *Id.* at § 10.

[5] Austin, TX, City Code § 2-2-34(A).

[6] Boulder, CO, Revised Code § 13-2-20(a).

[7] Chapel Hill Town Ordinance § 2-94.

[8] Long Beach, CA, Municipal Code § 2.01.410(D).

[9] *Id.* at §§ 2.01.410(A) (3), (B) (2) and (C) (2).

[10] Los Angeles, CAa, Municipal Code §§ 49.7.20 and 49.7.19(B).

[11] *Id.* at 49.7.22.

[12] Miami-Dade County Candidate's Handbook on Public Financing, April 2007, available at http://www.miamidade.gov/elections/Library/publicfinancing.pdf.

[13] New Haven, CT, Code of General Ordinances, Title II, Article XVII, § 2-253.

[14] New York City, NY, Administrative Code § 3-705(2).

[15] In October 2008, the Oakland city council approved a resolution allowing a one-time transfer of $226,000 for the public campaign finance program to the general fund. In July 2003, the city council temporarily suspended the program for the 2004 elections because of a budget crisis.

[16] Oakland, CA, Municipal Code § 3.13.110.

(continued on next page)

LOCAL CHART 1. *Continued*

[17] In May 2005, Portland, Oregon, became the first U.S. city to enact a full public financing program for local candidates. After raising a certain number of qualifying contributions of $5, candidates become eligible to receive all the money necessary to run a campaign, up to a predetermined spending limit.

[18] A "qualifying contribution" is defined as a contribution of no more than $5 in cash, or in the form of a check or money order made payable by any resident to the candidate or principal campaign committee of the candidate. See Portland, OR, City Code § 2.10.010(Y).

[19] A "seed money contribution" is defined as a contribution of no more than $100 made by a person to a political committee or candidate. *Id.* at § 2.10.010(AB).

[20] *Id.* at § 2.10.100.

[21] *Id.* at § 2.10.110.

[22] Sacramento, CA, City Code § 2.14.140.

[23] San Francisco, CA, Campaign and Governmental Conduct Code § 1.144.5 (2007).

[24] Although the law is still officially on the books, the Suffolk County public financing program has been consistently underfunded and virtually inoperable since its inception. For a more in-depth analysis of the problems with the Suffolk County program, see Center for Governmental Studies, *Dead on Arrival? Breathing Life into Suffolk County's New Campaign Finance Reforms* (2002).

[25] Suffolk County, NY, Charter § C41-4(C) (2007).

[26] Tucson, AZ, Charter, Chapter 16, Subchapter B, § 5(a) (2005).

LOCAL CHART 2.   QUALIFYING THRESHOLD, RESIDENCY RESTRICTIONS, SPENDING LIMITS

Jurisdiction	Qualifying Fund-Raising Threshold[1]	Residency Restriction on Matchable Contributions	Funding Mechanism	Spending Limits[2]
Albuquerque, NM	To become eligible for public financing, candidates must raise $5 qualifying contributions from city residents as follows: *City council:* 1% of registered city voters in district. *Mayor:* 1% of registered city voters.	Yes, for qualifying contributions	Qualifying contributions; unspent moneys; seed money; appropriations equal to one tenth of 1% of the approved general fund; voluntary contributions from members of the public	*City council:* $1.00 per registered voter in the district (approximately $55,000). *Mayor:* $1.00 per registered city voter (approximately $495,000).
Austin, TX	None[3] (public financing program candidates receive funds if in a runoff).	N/A	Lobbyist registration fees; donations from individuals and business entities; liquidated damages and criminal fines for campaign violations; voluntary $1 checkoff on utility bills; candidate filing fees[4]	*City council:* $75,000 (general), an additional $50,000 for a runoff. *Mayor:* $120,000 (general), an additional $80,000 for a runoff.[5]
Boulder, CO	10% of spending limit in contributions of $25 or less.[6]	No	City council allocation[7]	$0.15 per registered voter when legislation was passed, adjusted based on the CPI[7]
Chapel Hill, NC	*Mayor:* At least 150 qualifying contributions (contributions of $5 to $20 made by a Chapel Hill resident) that add up to at least $1,500. *Town council:* At least 75 qualifying contributions (contributions of $5 to $20 made by a Chapel Hill resident) that add up to at least $750.[8]	Yes, for qualifying contributions[9]	Town council allocation[10]	*Mayor:* Seed money (maximum $1,500), qualifying contributions (maximum $4,500), public funds grant ($9,000), and any rescue funds. *Town council:* Seed money (maximum $750), qualifying contributions (maximum $2,250), public funds grant ($3,000), and any rescue funds[11]
Long Beach, CA	*Council:* $5,000 in contributions of $100 or less. *Mayor:* $20,000 in contributions of $200 or less. *Other citywide office(s):* $10,000 in contributions of $150 or less.[12]	No	City council allocations "from time to time"[13]	*City council:* $56,000 (primary); $26,072 (runoff). *Mayor:* $260,720 (primary); $130,360 (runoff). *Other citywide office(s):* $130,360 (primary); $65,180 (runoff).[14]

(continued on next page)

111

LOCAL CHART 2. *Continued*

Jurisdiction	Qualifying Fund-Raising Threshold[1]	Residency Restriction on Matchable Contributions	Funding Mechanism	Spending Limits[2]
Los Angeles, CA	*City council:* $25,000 in contributions of $250 or less. *Mayor:* $150,000 in contributions of $500 or less. *City attorney and controller:* $75,000 in contributions of $500 or less.[15]	No	The city charter mandates $2 million in annual appropriations to fund the public financing program. The annual appropriations are held in a trust fund, the balance of which may never exceed $8 million. Both the annual appropriation and the total balance amounts are adjusted for changes in the cost of living.[16]	*City council:* $330,000 (primary); $275,000 (general). *Mayor:* $2,251,000 (primary); $1,800,000 (general). *Controller:* $900,000 (primary); $676,000 (general). *City attorney:* $1,013,000 (primary); $788,000 (general).[17]
Miami-Dade County, FL	*County commission:* 300 contributions between $100 and $500 from 200 registered voter residents of Miami-Dade County for a total of at least $300,000, in order to receive $50,000 in public funds for the general election. If total qualifying contributions reach $50,000, the candidate is eligible for $75,000 in public funds for the general election. *Mayor:* 1,500 contributions between $100 and $500 from 1,500 registered voter residents of Miami-Dade County. *Runoff:* A candidate who was not a participant in the election may receive public funds in a runoff without meeting the threshold requirement, provided that the candidate did not exceed the spending limit in the primary and agrees to abide by the runoff spending and personal contribution limits.[18]	Miami-Dade County uses a lump-sum grant program, rather than a matching funds program. However, the contributions that a candidate must receive in order to qualify for a public funding grant must be made by registered voter residents of the county.[18]	Appropriations from general revenues "in an amount sufficient to fund qualifying candidates."[19]	*Commissioner:* $200,000 (general); $150,000 (runoff). *Mayor:* $650,000 (general); $450,000 (runoff).[18]
New Haven, CT	*Mayor:* 200 contributions from separate individuals who are electors of no less than $25 and no more than $300.[20]	Yes, for qualifying contributions and matching funds[21]	Annual budget appropriation[22]	*Mayor:* $300,000 (primary); $300,000.[22]

Jurisdiction	Qualifying Fund-Raising Threshold[1]	Residency Restriction on Matchable Contributions	Funding Mechanism	Spending Limits[2]
New York, NY	In order to reach the following threshold requirements, the contributions must be between $10 and $175 and made by natural persons who are residents of New York City. *City council:* at least 75 contributions from council residents totaling $5,000. *Borough president:* at least 100 contributions totaling an amount equal to $0.02 multiplied by the resident population of the borough (for 2009, $10,000–49,307).[23] *Mayor:* at least 1,000 contributions totaling $250,000. *Public advocate and comptroller:* at least 500 contributions totaling $125,000.[24]	Yes, for qualifying contributions[25]	Annual budget appropriation[26]	Limits apply to only participating candidates. The following apply to 2009 primary and general elections: *Mayor:* $6,158,000 per election. *Public advocate and comptroller:* $3,850,000 per election. *Borough president:* $1,386,000 per election. *Council:* $161,000 per election.[27] Additional spending limits apply to the two years preceding the election year.
Oakland, CA	Contributions of $100 or less totaling at least 5% of the applicable spending limit.[28]	Yes (principal residence or primary place of business must be within the city of Oakland)[29]	City council appropriation "sufficient to fund all candidates for the city office eligible to receive limited matching funds"[30]	2007 election year limits: *District city council member:* $101,000 to $117,000 (depending on the population of the district). *School board director:* $67,000 to $78,000 (depending on the population of the district).[31]
Portland, OR	To become eligible for public financing, candidates must raise $5 qualifying contributions from city residents as follows: *Mayor:* 1,500 residents. *Commissioner:* 1,000 residents. *Auditor:* 1,000 residents.[32]	Yes, for qualifying contributions[33]	City council appropriation; civil penalty fund revenues; voluntary private contributions[34]	*Commissioner:* $150,000 (primary); $200,000 (general). *Mayor:* $200,000 (primary); $250,000 (general). *Auditor:* $150,000 (primary); $200,000 (general).[35]
Richmond, CA	*Mayor and city council:* When $15,000 total in matchable contributions are received, $5,000 is disbursed. When $20,000 in total matchable contributions are received, $5,000 is disbursed. When $25,000 in total matchable contributions are received, $5,000 is disbursed. When $30,000 in total matchable contributions are received, $5,000 is disbursed. When $35,000 in total matchable contributions are received, $5,000 is disbursed.	No	Annual budget appropriation	None

(continued on next page)

LOCAL CHART 2. Continued

Jurisdiction	Qualifying Fund-Raising Threshold[1]	Residency Restriction on Matchable Contributions	Funding Mechanism	Spending Limits[2]
Sacramento, CA	*City council:* Candidates must raise at least $7,500 in contributions of $250 or less. *Mayor:* Candidates must raise at least $10,000 in contributions of $250 or less.[36]	No	City council appropriation[37]	*City council:* $82,000. *Mayor:* $548,000.[38]
San Francisco, CA	*Board of supervisors:* Candidate must raise $5,000 in contributions between $10 and $100 from at least 75 residents of the city, and be opposed by another eligible candidate who has either established eligibility or has raised or spent an amount subject to certain amount, $5,000 or more for board of supervisors candidates.[39] *Mayor:* Candidates must raise at least $25,000 in qualifying contributions from at least 250 contributors, and be opposed by another candidate who has either established eligibility or has received contributions or made expenditures that in the aggregate equal or exceed $50,000.[40]	Yes, for qualifying contributions[41]	Election campaign fund established by ordinance. Ordinance directs the mayor and board of supervisors to appropriate an amount sufficient to provide funding to all eligible candidates[42]	*Board of supervisors:* $86,000.[43] *Mayor:* $1,375,000.
Suffolk County, NY[48]	The following thresholds must be met by contributions from natural-person residents of the county of between $10 and $500: *County legislature:* 50 contributions totaling at least $5,000. *Executive:* 500 contributions totaling at least $75,000. *Comptroller, treasurer, district attorney:* 300 contributions totaling at least $30,000.[45]	Yes, for qualifying contributions[46]	Voluntary taxpayer donations to the campaign finance fund[47]	*County legislator:* $17,000 (primary); $34,000 (general).[52] *Executive:* $338,000 (primary); $563,000 (general). *Other countywide offices:* $113,000 (primary); $225,000 (general). Additional spending limits apply to the year preceding the election year.[49]
Tucson, AZ	The following thresholds must be met with contributions from city residents: *City council:* 200 contributions of $10 or more. *Mayor:* 300 contributions of $10 or more.[50]	Contributions received toward meeting the matching funds qualification threshold must be from Tucson residents. Once a candidate exceeds the qualification threshold, nonresident contributions are matchable.[51]	Mayor/council annual budget appropriations[52]	*City council:* $0.20 (may be adjusted using the CPI annually) per registered voter in the city per election cycle: $90,181 (2007). *Mayor:* $0.40 (may be adjusted using the CPI annually) per registered voter in the city per election cycle: $180,388 (2007). No candidate may spend more than 75% of these limits prior to the primary election.[53]

Source: Center for Governmental Studies, Los Angeles, California.

[1] In order to be eligible to receive public financing, candidates must first demonstrate a modicum of public support. Various qualification thresholds are used to ensure that public funds are not allocated to candidates with no support base. Most jurisdictions require candidates to raise a minimum amount of campaign funds in small contributions. Some jurisdictions (e.g., Austin) require that candidates receive enough votes in a general election to proceed into a runoff election before becoming eligible to receive public funds.

[2] The spending limits in these jurisdictions are binding on only candidates who voluntarily agree to abide by such limits in exchange for public financing. The U.S. Supreme Court has interpreted the First Amendment of the federal Constitution to prohibit mandatory spending limits. See *Buckley v. Valeo,* 424 U.S. 1, 49 (1976). The *Buckley* Court did rule, however, that Congress may "condition acceptance of public funds on an agreement by the candidate to abide by specified expenditure limitations." *Id.* at 57 n. 65. The local governments included in this chart have relied on this rationale to implement voluntary public financing programs with spending limits. The following jurisdictions apply a cost of living adjustment ("COLA") to the spending limits: *Boulder, see* Boulder, CO, Revised Code § 13-2-21(b)(1) (2007); *Long Beach,* see Long Beach, CA, Municipal Code § 2.01.1210 (2007); *Miami-Dade County,* see Miami-Dade, FL, County Code § 12-22(e)(3) (2007); *New York City, see* New York City, NY, Administrative Code § 3-706(1)(e) (2007); *Oakland, see* Oakland, CA, Municipal Code § 3.12.200 (2007); *San Francisco,* see San Francisco, CA, Campaign and Governmental Conduct Code § 1.130(f) (2007); *Suffolk County,* see Suffolk County, NY, Charter § C41-5(A)(4) (2007); and *Tucson,* see City of Tucson, AZ, Charter, Chapter 16, Subchapter B, § 3(c) (2007). The spending limits listed in this chart are the most current adjusted limits. The original limits can be found in the cited ordinances and charters.

[3] Austin, TX, Code § 2-2-34.

[4] Austin, TX, Code § 2-2-32.

[5] Austin, TX, Code § 2-2-7.

[6] Boulder, CO, Revised Code § 13-2-21(a) (2007).

[7] *Id.* at 13-2-20(a).

[8] Chapel Hill Town Ordinance § 2-91.

[9] Chapel Hill Town Ordinance § 2-86.

[10] Chapel Hill Town Ordinance § 2-87.

[11] Chapel Hill Town Ordinance § 2-96 (b)-(c).

[12] Long Beach, CA, Municipal Code § 2.01.410.

[13] *Id.* at § 2.01.910.

[14] These limits are current as of January 2006, except for the city council primary elections figure, which was recalculated in 2008. Long Beach, CA, Municipal Code § 2.02.410 (2007).

[15] Los Angeles, CA, Municipal Code § 49.7.19.

[16] Los Angeles, CA, City Charter, Art. IV §§ 471(c) (1) and (2) (2007).

[17] Los Angeles, CA, Municipal Code § 49.7.13.

[18] Miami-Dade County Candidate's Handbook on Public Financing, April 2007, available at http://www.miamidade.gov/elections/Library/publicfinancing.pdf.

[19] Code of Miami-Dade County, FL § 12-22(b).

[20] New Haven, CT, Title II, Article XVIII, § 2-253.

[21] *Id.* at § 2-245.

[22] *Id.* at § 2-249.

[23] Contribution Limits, Spending Limits, and Public Funds Requirements, 2009 Citywide Elections, NYC Campaign Finance Board, available at http://www.nyccfb.info/candidates/candidates/limits/2009.htm.

[24] New York City, NY, Administrative Code § 3-703(2) (a).

[25] *Id.* at § 3-702(3).

[26] *Id.* at § 3-709.

[27] The spending limits given here are the limits that apply to the 2003 city council elections and the 2005 citywide office elections. *Id.* at § 3-706(1) (a).

(continued on next page)

LOCAL CHART 2. *Continued*

[28] Oakland, CA, Municipal Code §§ 3.13.080(C), 3.13.110.

[29] *Id.* 3.13.110(a).

[30] *Id.* at § 3.13.060.

[31] *Id.* at § 3.12.200. The statute specifies the spending limit amount per resident, adjusted for changes in the cost of living. The city's limits are based on the city clerk's resident population count of 399,484.

[32] Portland, OR, City Code § 2.10.070.

[33] *Id.* § 2.10.010(G).

[34] *Id.* at § 2.10.040.

[35] *Id.* at § 2.10.110.

[36] Sacramento, CA, Sacramento City Code § 2.14.130 (2007).

[37] *Id.* at § 2.14.215.

[38] *Id.* at § 2.14.050.

[39] San Francisco, CA, Campaign and Governmental Conduct Code § 1.140 (2007).

[40] *Id.* at § 1.140.5.

[41] *Id.* at § 1.104(k).

[42] *Id.* at § 1.138.

[43] Because San Francisco implemented ranked choice voting (also known as instant runoff voting) in the 2004 elections, there was no runoff election. Therefore, the public financing provisions relating to runoff elections were not applicable. San Francisco also offers voluntary spending limits to candidates for the offices of board of education and other citywide offices, but does not offer public financing to candidates for these offices. See id. at § 1.130.

[44] Although the law is still officially on the books, the Suffolk County public financing program has been consistently underfunded and virtually inoperable since its inception.

[45] Suffolk County, NY, Charter §§ C41-1 (definition of "threshold contribution") and C41-2(A) (8) (a) (2007).

[46] *Id.* at § C41-1 (definition of "matchable contribution").

[47] *Id.* at § C41-8(J).

[48] *Id.* at §§ C41-5(A) and (B) (2007).

[49] Figures updated quadrennially.

[50] City of Tucson, AZ, Charter, Chapter 16, Subchapter B, § 4(a) (2007).

[51] *Id.* at §§ 4(b) and 5(a).

[52] *Id.* at § 6.

[53] *Id.* at § 3.

LOCAL CHART 3.   SPENDING LIMITS PER RESIDENT, CONTRIBUTION LIMITS, CANDIDATE PERSONAL CONTRIBUTIONS

Jurisdiction	Spending Limits per Resident[1]	Contribution Limits[2]	Candidate Personal Contributions[3]
Albuquerque, NM	*City council:* $1.00 per registered voter in the district (approximately $55,000). *Mayor:* $1.00 per registered city voter (approximately $495,000).	No candidate shall allow total contributions from any one person with the exception of the contributions from the candidate himself or herself of more than 5% of the total annual salary for such office.[4]	$500 in seed money allowed.
Austin, TX	*City council:* $0.63 (general), an additional $0.14 for a runoff.[5] *Mayor:* $0.28 (general), an additional $0.17 for a runoff.	*Contributions from person to Council candidates:* $50 per election. *Mayor candidates:* $1,000 per election.[6]	May not exceed 5% of spending limit.[7]
Boulder, CO	$0.15 per registered voter when legislation was passed, adjusted based on the CPI.[8]	$100 per candidate in a given election[9]	May not exceed 20% of spending limit.[10]
Chapel Hill, NC	None	$20 per resident, per candidate, per election	Statute is silent.[11]
Long Beach, CA	*City council:* $0.99–$1.50 (primary); $.14 (runoff).[12] *Mayor:* $0.55 (primary); $0.28 (runoff). *Other citywide office:* $0.28 (primary); $0.13 (runoff).[13]	*Contributions from persons to Council candidates:* $350 per election. *Mayor candidates:* $650 per election. *Other citywide office candidates:* $450.[14]	Limited by only the total spending limit.
Los Angeles, CA	*City council:* $1.29 (primary); $1.07 (general).[15] *Mayor:* $0.85 (primary); $0.47 (general). *Controller:* $0.23 (primary); $0.18 (general). *City attorney:* $0.26 (primary); $0.20 (general).[16]	Contributions from persons to: *City council candidates:* $500 per election. *Mayor, city attorney, controller candidates:* $1,000 per election. *PACs that support or oppose any candidate (includes PACs that make IEs):* $500 per calendar year. Total contributions made "in connection with all candidates" in any single election: the greater of $1,000 or ($500 multiplied by the number of city council offices on the ballot + $1,000 multiplied by the number of citywide offices on the ballot). A candidate may not accept contributions from PACs which combined exceed: *City council:* $150,000. *City attorney or controller:* $400,000. *Mayor:* $900,000.[17]	*Council:* $25,000. *Citywide office:* $100,000.[18]
Miami-Dade County, FL	*Commissioner:* $1.08 (general); $0.81 (runoff). *Mayor:* $0.27 (general); $0.19 (runoff).[19]	$500 per election[20]	May not exceed $25,000.[20]

(continued on next page)

LOCAL CHART 3. *Continued*

Jurisdiction	Spending Limits per Resident[1]	Contribution Limits[2]	Candidate Personal Contributions[3]
New Haven, CT	*Mayor:* $2.42 (primary); $2.42 (general).	*Mayor:* $300 per election.[21]	$15,000 per primary or general election[22]
New York, NY	Election year limits through 2009: *Mayor:* $0.70 per election. *Public advocate and comptroller:* $0.44 per election. *Borough president:* $0.78 per election.[23] *Council:* $0.93 per election.[24] Additional spending limits apply to the two years preceding the election year.	*Citywide office:* $4,950 per election cycle. *Borough president:* $3,850 per election year. *Council:* $2,750 per election cycle.[25] Participating candidates may not accept contributions from PACs unless the PAC voluntarily registers with the Campaign Finance Board and the contribution does not exceed the contribution limit applicable to the office.[26]	May not exceed three times the applicable contribution limit.[27]
Oakland, CA	2007 election year limits: *District city council member:* $1.27 to $1.47 (depending on the population of the district). *School board director:* $0.17 to $0.19 (depending on the population of the district).[28]	Contributions from persons to (annually adjusted using 1999 index-year figures below): *Nonparticipating candidates and PACs that make IEs:* $100 per election. *Participating candidates:* $500 per election.[29] Contributions from "broad-based political committees"[30] to: *Nonparticipating candidates:* $250 per election. *Participating candidates:* $1,000 per election.[31]	May not exceed 5% of the spending limit.[32]
Portland, OR	*Commissioner:* $1.12 (primary); $1.49 (general). *Mayor:* $0.37 (primary); $0.46 (general). *Auditor:* $0.27 (primary); $0.37 (general).	Participating candidates may not accept campaign contributions, except for qualifying contributions and seed money. Nonparticipating candidates are bound by state law, which does not impose any contribution limits on local candidates.[34]	Limited by only the total spending limit; can contribute only $100 in seed money.[34]
Richmond, CA	None	Individuals to candidates or committees that make independent expenditures: $2,500 per election cycle.	Unlimited
Sacramento, CA	*City council:* $1.45.[35] *Mayor:* $1.21.	*Individuals to mayoral candidates:* $1,150. *Individuals to city council candidates:* $900. *PAC to mayoral candidates:* $5,850. *PAC to city council candidates:* $3,500.[36]	*Mayor:* $30,000. *City council:* $7,500.[37]
San Francisco, CA	*Supervisor:* $1.27.[38] *Mayor:* $1.21.	*General election:* $500: contributions from corporations prohibited. *Aggregate limit for general election:* $500 multiplied by the total number of offices being elected, per contributor. *Contributions to PACs (includes PACs that make IEs):* $500 per year per committee and $3,000 total to all committees per year.[39]	Limited by only the total spending limit (note, however, that there is a preliminary injunction granted regarding the enforcement of these limitations).

Jurisdiction	Spending Limits per Resident[1]	Contribution Limits[2]	Candidate Personal Contributions[3]
Suffolk County, NY	*Executive:* $0.23 (primary), $0.38 (general). *Other county-wide offices:* $0.08 (primary), $0.15 (general). *County legislator:* $0.20 (primary), $0.42 (general).[40] Additional spending limits apply to the year preceding the election year.[41]	The following contribution limits apply to only public financing program candidates: *County legislator:* $1,100 per election. *Executive:* $2,750 per election. *Comptroller, treasurer, district attorney:* 1,650 per election.[42] Participating candidates are prohibited from accepting contributions from PACs, lobbyists, or firms doing business or proposing to do business with the county.[43]	May not exceed the contribution limit applicable to the office.[44]
Tucson, AZ	*Mayor:* $0.40 (may be adjusted using the CPI annually) per registered voter in the city per election cycle: $180,388 (2007). *Council:* $0.20 (may be adjusted using the CPI annually) per registered voter in the city per election cycle: $90,181 (2007). No candidate may spend more than 75% of these limits prior to the primary election.[45]	*From individuals:* $390 per election. *From PACs:* $390 per election. *From small donor PACs:*[46] $2,000 per election. *Total from political party committees:* $10,020 per election. *Total contributions from non-party PACs:* $10,020 per election. *Total contributions to candidates or PACs who contribute to other candidates:* $3,740.[47]	May not exceed 3% of the applicable spending limit in any election cycle.[48]

(continued on next page)

Source: Center for Governmental Studies, Los Angeles, California.

[1] Most jurisdictions have enacted spending limits in the form of total dollar amounts, but a few have enacted spending limits on the basis of the number of voters or residents in the jurisdiction. This column was included to provide a standard unit for comparison between the programs of different jurisdictions. The figures given are based on estimated 2006 census figures from the U.S. Census Bureau, which can be found at the American Factfinder Web site: http://factfinder.census.gov.

[2] The limits listed in this column are limits on contributions from persons to candidates, unless otherwise noted. The term "person" is defined broadly in most jurisdictions to included humans, corporations, partnerships, political committees and other organizations. The term "PAC" is used as an abbreviated reference to a political committee. The following jurisdictions apply a COLA to the contribution limits: *Cincinnati,* see Cincinnati, OH, City Charter, Art. XIII § 4(f)(2) (adopted by voters November 2001); *Long Beach,* see Long Beach, CA, Municipal Code § 2.01.1210 (2007); *New York City,* see New York City Administrative Code § 703(7) (2007); *Oakland,* see Oakland, CA, Municipal Code §§ 3.12.050(G) and 3.12.060(G) (2007); *Suffolk County,* see Suffolk County, NY, Charter § C41-2(F) (2007); and *Tucson,* see Arizona Revised Statutes § 16-905(I) (2007). The contribution limits listed in this chart are the most current adjusted limits. The original limits can be found in the cited ordinances and charters.

[3] Applies to only candidates voluntarily participating in the public financing program.

[4] Albuquerque, NM, Code of Ordinances, Article XIII, § 4(e) (2007).

[5] Based on total population, divided by six city council districts.

[6] Austin, TX, Code § 2-2-8(A).

[7] Austin, TX, Code § 2-2-7(C).

[8] Boulder, CO, Rev. Code §13-2-21(a).

[9] *Id.* at § 13-2-17.

[10] *Id.* at § 13-2-21(b) (2).

[11] *Id.*

[12] City of Long Beach, CA. Adjusted Expenditure Ceilings Pursuant to Proposition M. Updated June 6, 2006.

[13] Long Beach, CA, Municipal Code § 2.02.410 (2007).

[14] The contribution limits listed here are the COLA-adjusted limits that took effect on January 2, 2006. Long Beach, CA, Municipal Code § 2.01.310 (2005).

LOCAL CHART 3. *Continued*

[15] Based on total population, divided by 15 city council districts.

[16] Los Angeles, CA. Municipal Code § 49.7.13 (2007).

[17] Los Angeles, CA. City Charter, Art. IV §470(c) (2007).

[18] Los Angeles, CA. Municipal Code § 49.7.19(A)(3).

[19] Based on total population, divided by 18 county legislator districts.

[20] Miami-Dade County Candidate's Handbook on Public Financing, April 2007, available at http://www.miamidade.gov/elections/Library/publicfinancing.pdf.

[21] New Haven, CT. Title II. Article 18. § 2-249.

[22] *Id.* 2-251.

[23] Based on total population, divided by five borough districts.

[24] Based on total population, divided by 51 council districts.

[25] The contribution limits given here are the limits that apply to the 2007 city council elections and the 2009 citywide office elections. New York City, NY. Administrative Code § 3-703(1) (f).

[26] *Id.* at §§ 3-703(1) (k) and 3-707.

[27] *Id.* at § 3-703(1) (h).

[28] *Id.* Oakland, CA. Municipal Code § 3.12.200. The statute specifies the spending limit amount per resident, adjusted for changes in the cost of living. The city's limits are based on the city clerk's resident population count of 399,484.

[29] *Id.* at § 3.12.050 (A) and (B).

[30] A "broad-based political committee" is a committee of persons that has been in existence for more than six months, receives contributions from 100 or more persons, and acting in concert makes contributions to five or more candidates. *Id.* at §3.12.040. See also *id.* at § 3.12.060(C).

[31] *Id.* at §§ 3.12.060 (A) and (B).

[32] *Id.* at § 3.13.090.

[33] Based on total population, divided by four commissioners.

[34] Portland, OR. City Code § 2.10.050(A).

[35] Based on total population, divided by eight council members.

[36] *Id.* at § 2.13.050.

[37] *Id.* at § 2.14.165.

[38] San Francisco, CA. Campaign and Governmental Conduct Code 1.114 (2005). Based on total population, divided by eleven supervisorial districts.

[39] *Id.* at § 1.114.

[40] Based on total population, divided by 11 supervisorial districts.

[41] Figures updated quadrennially.

[42] Suffolk County, NY. Charter § C41-2(A) (6) (2005).

[43] *Id.* at § C41-2(G).

[44] *Id.* at § C41-2(A) (8).

[45] *Id.* at § 3.

[46] A "small donor PAC" is a committee that receives contributions of $10 or more from at least 500 individuals. Arizona Revised Statutes § 16-905(I) (2005).

[47] *Id.* at §§ 16-905(A)-(E).

[48] Tucson, AZ. City Charter, Chapter 16, Subchapter B, § 2 (2005).

LOCAL CHART 4.   HIGH-SPENDING OPPONENTS, INDEPENDENT EXPENDITURES, DEBATE REQUIREMENTS

State	High-Spending Opponent Trigger Provision	Independent Expenditure (IE) Trigger Provision	Debate Requirement[1]
Albuquerque, NM	When a participating candidate's opposing funds[2] in aggregate are greater than the funds distributed plus seed money, the participating candidate is entitled to receive matching funds in the amount that the opposing funds exceed the funds distributed plus seed money.	When a participating candidate's opposing funds in aggregate are greater than the funds distributed plus seed money, the participating candidate is entitled to receive matching funds in the amount that the opposing funds exceed the funds distributed plus seed money.	No
Austin, TX	Opponent expenditures or receipt of contributions in excess of the voluntary contribution and expenditure limits excuses participating candidates from further compliance with applicable limits.[3]	If a person spends more than $10,000 in one race, the spending limits are no longer binding on any candidates in the race.[4]	Yes[5]
Boulder, CO	None	None	No
Chapel Hill, NC	When privately financed candidates raise or spend 140% of the spending limit for a certified candidate, a certified candidate for mayor gets an additional $4,000 and a certified candidate for town council gets an additional $2,000.[6]	When independent expenditure committees raise or spend 140% of the spending limit for a certified candidate, a certified candidate for mayor gets an additional $4,000 and a certified candidate for town council gets an additional $2,000.[7]	No
Long Beach, CA	None	None	No
Los Angeles, CA	Opponent expenditures or receipt of contributions in excess of the applicable spending limit eliminates the spending limit for all other candidates in the race, and makes participating candidates eligible to receive matching funds at a rate of 3-to-1 up to the maximum if the opponent exceeds the spending limit by 50%.[8]	If an IE committee spends more than $50,000 in a city council race, $100,000 in a city attorney or controller race, or $200,000 in a mayoral race, the spending limits are no longer binding on any candidate running for the office, and for the general election, participating candidates become eligible to receive matching funds at a rate of 3-to-1 up to the maximum.[8]	Yes[9]
Miami-Dade County, FL	None	None	No
New Haven, CT	If opponent expenditures exceed the applicable spending limit, the participating candidate may apply for, receive, and expend an additional $25,000 bonus grant from the fund or have the expenditure ceiling lifted. (A candidate who has already spent $300,000 is not eligible for the bonus grant.)[10]	None	No

(continued on next page)

LOCAL CHART 4. *Continued*

State	High-Spending Opponent Trigger Provision	Independent Expenditure (IE) Trigger Provision	Debate Requirement[1]
New York, NY	Opponent expenditures or receipt of contributions in excess of 50% of the applicable spending limit increases the spending limit for all other candidates in the race to 150% of the original limit and triggers other high-spending opponent provisions.[11]	None	Yes[12]
Oakland, CA	Opponent expenditures or receipt of contributions in excess of 50% of the applicable spending limit eliminates the spending limit for all other candidates in the race.[13]	If an IE committee spends more than $15,000 on a district city council or school board race, or spends more than $70,000 on any other race, the spending limits are no longer binding on any candidate running for the office.[13]	No[14]
Portland, OR	Opponent expenditures or receipt of contributions in excess of the applicable spending limits eliminates the spending limit for all other candidates in the race and makes participating candidates eligible to receive matching funds in an amount equal to the amount of contributions or expenditures by or on behalf of the nonparticipating candidate that exceeds the spending limits.[15]	If an IE committee supporting or opposing a candidate exceeds the applicable spending limit, the spending limits are no longer binding on any other candidates in the race and participating candidates become entitled to receive matching funds in an amount equal to the amount of independent expenditures that exceeds the spending limits.[16]	No
Richmond, CA	None	None	No
Sacramento, CA	Opponent expenditures in excess of 75% of the applicable spending limit eliminate the spending limit for all other candidates in the race.[17]	If an IE committee spends more than 50% of the applicable spending limit, the spending limits are no longer binding on any candidate running in the race.[17]	No
San Francisco, CA	Opponent expenditures or receipt of contributions in excess of the applicable spending limits eliminates the spending limits for all other candidates in the race.[18]	If an IE committee spends more than the applicable spending limits, the spending limits are no longer binding on any candidate in the race.[18]	Yes[19]
Suffolk County, NY	Opponent expenditures or receipt of contributions in excess of 50% of the applicable spending limits eliminates the spending limits for all other candidates in the race.[20]	None	No

State	High-Spending Opponent Trigger Provision	Independent Expenditure (IE) Trigger Provision	Debate Requirement[1]
Tucson, AZ	If an opponent makes expenditures or receives contributions in excess of $11,840, a participating candidate is no longer bound by state law contribution limits until the candidate raises an amount equal to the opponent personal wealth expenditures. Instead, such candidate will be bound by the less stringent Tucson Charter contribution limits ($500 from individuals and $1,000 from PACs) during this period.[21]	None	No

Source: Center for Governmental Studies, Los Angeles, California.

[1] Some jurisdictions require candidates who participate in the public financing program to also participate in a set number of public debates with their opponents.

[2] Opposing funds used against a participating candidate are calculated by totaling (1) the expenditures made by the opponent who has the highest total of expenditures and supportive independent expenditures, (2) the amount spent on independent expenditures in support of that candidate, and (3) the amount spent on independent expenditures in opposition to the participating candidate.

[3] Austin, TX, Code at § 2-2-12.

[4] *Id.* at § 2-2-12(C).

[5] *Id.* at § 2-9-35.

[6] Chapel Hill Town Ordinance § 2-95.

[7] Chapel Hill Town Ordinance § 2-99.

[8] Los Angeles, CA. Municipal Code §§ 49.7.14 and 49.7.22.

[9] *Id.* at § 49.7.19(C).

[10] New Haven, CT, Code of Ordinances, Title II, Special Laws, Article 18, § 2-249.

[11] New York City, NY, Administrative Code § 3-706(3).

[12] *Id.* at § 3-709.5.

[13] Oakland, CA. Municipal Code § 3.12.220 (2005).

[14] While receipt of public funds is not conditioned on participation in a debate, candidates are strongly encouraged to take part in at least one nonpartisan debate. *Id.* at § 3.13.170.

[15] Portland, OR, City Code §§ 2.10.150 (A) and (D) (2005).

[16] *Id.* at §§ 2.10.150(B) and (D).

[17] Sacramento, CA, City Code § 2.14.060.

[18] San Francisco, CA, Campaign and Governmental Conduct Code § 1.146(a) (2005).

[19] *Id.* at § 1.140(a) (5) (D).

[20] Suffolk County, NY, Charter § C41-5(D) (2005).

[21] Arizona Revised Statutes § 16-905(F) (2005). See also Tucson, AZ, City Charter, Chapter 16, Subchapter A. § 2 (2005).

4

⬦ ⬦ ⬦

Public Attitudes toward Publicly Financed Elections, 1972–2008

Stephen R. Weissman and Ruth A. Hassan
(with assistance from Jack Santucci)

Public financing for U.S. presidential elections is in crisis. Both the Republican and Democratic nominees rejected primary financing in 2004 and 2008. And Democrat Barack Obama became the first major party candidate since the system began in 1976 to spurn public financing for the general election campaign. Reform groups and their congressional allies have introduced legislation to modernize the system, making it more attractive to candidates and more supportive of small donors. But critics assert that the decline in participation in the voluntary federal tax form checkoff that funds the current system—a decline from 29 percent of eligible taxpayers in 1978 to 9 percent in 2006—proves that the American people oppose public financing of all federal elections (Internal Revenue Service 2006). This chapter explores the issue of popular attitudes toward public financing of elections—and the meaning of the checkoff decline—through an analysis of the results of major national opinion polls over more than three decades.

Since the inception of the public financing system for presidential candidates, various polls have been conducted in an effort to gauge public support for the current program and its proposed extension to congressional elections. On the basis of a survey and analysis of all major polls from 1972 to the present, with an emphasis on post-1990 data, we reach the following conclusions:

- Support or opposition regarding public financing of presidential and other federal elections varies greatly depending on the language used in the actual question(s), and on the context and tone of previous questions. It also appears to vary somewhat according to the political circumstances of the time.

- Where the prior context and tone are relatively neutral, and the question emphasizes the basic rules of the public financing program— such as limits on both private contributions and government funding for candidates (with resulting ceilings on candidate spending)— there is substantial support for public financing, generally in the 50 percent to 65 percent range. Such rules-oriented questions leave it to the respondent to consider the possible benefits or costs of the system (or these are sometimes elaborated in a subsequent question).

- Where the prior context and tone include statements highlighting the role of money or the influence of "special interests" in the political process, support for public financing is relatively high, generally at the 60 percent to 70 percent level.

- Where the prior context is neutral but the question emphasizes the cost of the system to individual taxpayers, such as referring to "using taxpayer dollars to pay for political campaigns" rather than to "public financing" or "voluntary taxpayer designations of funds that do not increase their personal taxes," support for programs is relatively low, generally under 20 percent. Yet where the question refers to "public financing" but omits any reference to limits on either private contributions or public subsidization for candidates, support rises to approximately 40 percent.

- No matter what the question is, support for public financing is far higher than the percentage of eligible taxpayers who check the box on their tax returns. Polling suggests that a major reason for this disparity is that perhaps a third of these taxpayers are not familiar with the Presidential Election Campaign Fund. Other reasons include popular cynicism about the political system generally and the unique attention of the tax form to a single government program.

- The analysis concludes with specific suggestions for improved survey questions regarding public financing of elections.

Positive Findings on Public Financing: Gallup Polls, 1972–1996

One polling firm, the Gallup Organization, asked a standard, relatively neutral question recurrently over a long period of time. Other firms have also employed this question. The question is "It has been suggested the Federal Government provide a fixed amount of money for the election campaigns of candidates [for the presidency and] for Congress and that all private contributions from other sources should be prohibited. Do you think this is a good idea?" It contained two basic concepts, a fixed amount of public financing and the prohibition of all private contributions, which entail limits on candidate spending. Gallup has posed this question within broader polls concerning a variety of issues, so the answers have not been affected by prior questions related to campaign finance. The results (Table 4.1) suggest fairly strong and consistent support—between 50 percent and 65 percent—for full public financing of federal elections. (All questions have covered Congress and some have also included the presidency.) While that support has varied—it reached its peak in the aftermath of the Nixon and Clinton administration campaign finance scandals—Gallup has never found a majority opposed to public financing.

The Gallup question does have some weaknesses. It makes no specific reference to the way in which the proposal would be financed and the extent to which this would involve tax money—even in the form of a voluntary taxpayer designation that involves no personal cost, as with the presidential election. Also, the question offers no indication that the costs have been relatively low—about $60 million a year for the 2000 presidential election including full public financing for the general election and partial public financing for

TABLE 4.1.   GALLUP ORGANIZATION

It has been suggested the federal government provide a fixed amount of money for the election campaigns of candidates for Congress and that all private contributions from other sources should be prohibited. Do you think this is a good idea or a poor idea?

	Good Idea (%)	Poor Idea (%)	No Opinion (%)	N
June 1972*	56	28	16	1,560
Sept. 1973*	65	24	11	1,502
Aug. 1974*	67	24	9	1,590
March 1977	57	32	11	1,550
Feb. 1979	57	30	13	1,512
Aug. 1982	55	31	14	1,514
Aug. 1982*	55	31	14	1,543
July 1984	52	36	13	1,523
March 1987	50	42	8	1,015
Oct. 1996	59	32	9	1,043
Oct. 1996*	64	26	9	1,043
Oct. 1996	64	28	8	1,264
Oct. 1996*	65	27	8	1,264

*It has been suggested the federal government provide a fixed amount of money for the election campaigns of candidates for the Presidency and for Congress and that all private contributions from other sources should be prohibited. Do you think this is a good idea or a poor idea?

the primaries. More generally, there is no reference to the benefits and costs of the proposal. On the one hand, it would reduce candidates' dependence on large private contributions; on the other hand, it would limit individuals' freedom to support candidates financially and incur some expense.

Even More Positive Results:
The Mellman Group Reports, 1995–2000

The Mellman Group (MG) conducted a series of surveys over this recent period for groups advocating campaign finance reform. The central questions posed strongly resembled those posed by Gallup except as follows:

- They usually discussed the prohibition or limitation of private contributions *before* mentioning public financing.
- They stated somewhat more explicitly than Gallup that candidates would be subject to spending limits (Gallup referred to "fixed" government funding).
- They usually included follow-up questions presenting pro and con arguments to see if these would affect opinions.

While Mellman's results are similar to Gallup's, they generally tend to show higher support for public financing plans.

Mellman's public financing questions have always been preceded by questions that invited respondents to focus on the role of special interests and their political contributions. This contextual element, in addition to the ordering and precision of the question itself, could help account for the fact that Mellman's results are, on balance, even more positive for public financing than Gallup's.

Mellman and Public Opinion Strategies (POS) conducted a survey on behalf of Campaign for America (CA) in July 1995. This survey clearly primes respondents to view the reform of public financing in a positive manner. It begins by having respondents focus on areas of the current political system that they are unhappy with, and raising the issue of lobbying reform. It then specifically refers to the problem of "special interests" in the first of a series of questions on public financing. (Table 4.2 presents the questions in order.)

Alone among the Mellman surveys, this one did not show a *decisively* positive response to its central question, "It has been proposed that spending by candidates in political campaigns be limited, that candidates be required to raise some of their campaign money themselves, and that they receive some money from the federal government treasury for their campaigns. Do you favor or oppose this proposal or don't you have an opinion on this?" (48

TABLE 4.2.   MG/POS FOR CA (SEPTEMBER 1995)

Do you strongly favor or oppose limiting the influence of special interests by using public funds to help pay for campaigns?

Favor	50%
Oppose	43%
Don't know	7%
N	1,007

It has been proposed that spending by candidates in political campaigns be limited, that candidates be required to raise some of their campaign money themselves, and that they receive some money from the federal government treasury for their campaigns. Do you favor or oppose this proposal or don't you have an opinion on this?

Favor	48%
Oppose	40%
Don't know	12%
N	1,007

Public finance mechanisms: Eliminate tax deductions for lobbying

Favor	58%
Oppose	34%
N	1,007

Public finance mechanisms: Increase voluntary checkoff to $5

Favor	48%
Oppose	40%
N	1,007

Public finance mechanisms: National lottery

Favor	37%
Oppose	58%
N	1,007

Public finance mechanisms: Free broadcast time/free postage

Favor	35%
Oppose	62%
N	1,007

Public finance mechanisms: Willingness to use increased checkoff
If the voluntary checkoff were increased to 5 dollars with the additional money used to provide public financing of congressional and senate campaigns, how likely do you think you would be to check off that box on your income tax return and allocate 5 dollars to public financing of congressional and senate campaigns?

Favor	42%
Oppose	54%
N	1,007

CA, Campaign for America; MG, Mellman Group; POS, public opinion strategies.

percent "favor," 40 percent "opposed," 12 percent "don't know"). This result may have occurred because the question differs from those used by Mellman in subsequent polls: It does not prohibit private contributions or envision full public financing. Also, it was posed at a time when confidence in Congress and its use of public resources was even lower than usual (see later discussion).

The poll also inquired into various public financing mechanisms including the voluntary tax checkoff (Table 4.3; see also Table 4.2).

The Mellman survey for the Center for Responsive Politics (CRP) in August 1996 again began with a series of questions regarding special-interest influence. However, this time a full public financing proposal for Senate and House candidates—modeled after a Maine ballot initiative—was presented. As previously discussed, the typical Mellman proposal differed from Gallup's question in that it began with the prohibition on private contributions and explicitly stated that candidate spending would be limited to a set amount of public financing.

The result (68 percent "favor," 23 percent "oppose," 9 percent "don't know") contained a 45 percent margin of positive over negative responses, one larger than Gallup has ever found, even during the Watergate scandal. It is bigger than the 27–36 percent margins Gallup reported in two polls regarding public financing of congressional elections during October 1996, just two months after the Mellman poll. It seems apparent that the less neutral context and modified question form of the Mellman poll helped produce a more favorable response.

Exposure to well-constructed and fairly presented arguments for and against the Mellman proposal produced little change of heart: 65 percent of respondents remained in favor, with 25 percent opposing.

A Mellman poll for Public Campaign (PC) in March 2000 was similar to that conducted for the CRP in 1996. Again it found robust support for full public financing. The survey tested a full public financing proposal modeled

---

TABLE 4.3.   MG FOR CRP (AUGUST 1996)

Under this proposal, candidates would no longer raise money from private sources. Instead each candidate would receive a set amount of money from a publicly financed election fund. Spending by candidates would be limited to the amount they receive from the fund. Do you favor or oppose this proposal?

Favor	68%
Oppose	23%
Don't know	9%
N	800

CRP, Center for Responsive Politics; MG, Mellman Group.

TABLE 4.4.   MG FOR PC (MARCH 2000)

Clean Money Proposal: Now I am going to read you a description of a specific proposal that some people say will change the way federal election campaigns are financed. Under this proposal, candidates would no longer raise money from private sources. Instead, each candidate would receive a set amount of money from a publicly financed election fund. Spending would be limited to the amount they receive from the fund. Generally speaking do you favor or oppose this proposal or don't you have an opinion on this?

Favor	68%
Oppose	19%
No opinion	13%
N	800

[Opponents' Argument]: Opponents say that public financing is like a welfare program for politicians. They say that making taxpayers pay for political campaigns will only lead to higher taxes and force further cutbacks in important programs like Medicare and education. Opponents also say that public financing will encourage candidates from fringe parties or organizations like the KKK and Communists to run for office and use tax dollars to spread their radical views. They say that special interests will always find loopholes to influence Congress anyway and that it makes no sense to spend taxpayers' money to help candidates run more negative ads.

[Supporters' Argument]: Supporters say campaign reform is an important first step toward restoring democracy to the American people. Right now, candidates are chosen on the basis of their bank accounts, not on the basis of their ideas. Politics has become such a big money game that only the rich or well-connected have a real chance to win. By eliminating private contributions and providing all qualified candidates with equal and limited amounts of public funding, this proposal will level the playing field so good people with good ideas can get elected, even if they don't have connections to the rich and powerful.

Favor	67%
Oppose	23%
No opinion	10%
N	800

MG, Mellman Group; PC, public campaign.

after "clean money" initiatives that had passed in four states (Maine, Arizona, Vermont, and Massachusetts). The question was virtually identical to that posed in 1996, as were the results: 68 percent of respondents favored the proposal, while 19 percent of respondents were opposed, a record positive margin of 49 percent. Again support of this full public financing system remained basically unchanged after the supporting and opposing arguments were presented, with 67 percent in favor and 23 percent in opposition (Table 4.4).

Other Surveys Indicating Majority Support for Public Financing, 1990–2006

The Analysis Group's (AG) survey of February 1990 did not "prep" the respondents in any way for the public financing question. The very first question (the same one that Gallup uses) established that 58 percent of respondents considered it a "good idea" that the federal government provide a fixed amount of money for the election campaigns of candidates for Congress and that all private contributions be prohibited (33 percent responded "poor idea," and 10 percent "did not know"). (See Table 4.5.)

The second question offered a neutral definition of a political action committee (PAC) and asked respondents whether or not PACs should be allowed to contribute financially to federal election campaigns for Congress and president. Fifty-seven percent of respondents felt that such contributions should not be allowed and 33 percent that they should be allowed; 10 percent did not know.

There followed four specific proposals for financing a public system, only one of which resembled the current presidential system and won a plurality of 49 percent support. (Two other funding mechanisms—tax credits for small givers and free TV time and reduced mailing fees—were more popular.)

The main subject of a November 1999 *Los Angeles Times* (LAT) survey was candidate preference in the impending 2000 presidential election. The poll did not appear to substantially bias the response to the public financing question by prior leading questions. (The three previous questions did concern campaign financing. But the first was rather neutral, "Would you say that the way Congressional and presidential candidates raise money for their campaigns is basically sound or not. . . ." And the other two questions discussed a subject other than presidential financing, namely, what priority should be given to the reduction of unlimited soft money contributions to political parties and whether or not a presidential candidate's refusal to accept party soft money would influence respondents' presidential choices.)

Interestingly, this survey is the only one we found that specifically addresses federal matching funds for private contributions in the *presidential primary system*. The question was rather neutral and detailed, focusing on the system's rules regarding the threshold level of private fund-raising required for eligibility for public matching funds, candidate spending caps, and voluntary taxpayer financing through the checkoff. Even though it lacked any explicit reference to the objective of limiting private contributions and did not specify that the voluntary tax checkoff would not increase any individual's taxes, the question revealed a margin of support for the system: 49 percent approved, 42 percent disapproved, and 9 percent did not know (Table 4.6).

More recently, an April 2006 Greenberg, Quinlan, Rossner Research poll conducted for the Brennan Center for Justice (BCJ) at New York University focused on the checkoff box for the Presidential Election Campaign Fund on the Internal Revenue Service's Form 1040 tax return. After several queries probing respondents' knowledge concerning the fund and reasons for checking or not checking the box, the poll presented two questions regarding public financing of presidential and congressional elections. The first,

TABLE 4.5.   AG FOR AI, ARCA, PAW, PC (FEBRUARY 1990)

It has been suggested that the federal government provide a fixed amount of money for the election campaigns of candidates for Congress and that all private contributions be prohibited. Do you think this is a good idea or a poor idea?

Good idea	58%
Poor idea	33%
Don't know	10%
N	900

A political action committee or PAC is composed of individuals who contribute funds to support candidates as a committee and may be composed, for example, of union members, corporation employees, or citizens concerned about a particular cause or issue. Do you agree or disagree: Political action committees or PACs should be allowed to contribute financially to federal election campaigns for Congress and President?

Agree	33%
Disagree	57%
Don't know	10%
N	900

It has been suggested that campaign finance reform include the following changes: a cap on campaign spending and severe restrictions on PAC contributions. The new system could permit a number of new ways to pay for campaigns. Please tell me whether you favor or oppose each of these proposals . . .
(a) Encouraging small contributions by reducing the taxes of small givers, dollar for dollar, for their contributions up to $100

Favor	72%
Oppose	23%
Don't know	6%
N	900

(b) Instead of giving campaigns money, provide them with a fixed amount of free TV time and reduced mailing rates to reduce the cost of campaigns

Favor	69%
Oppose	25%
Don't know	6%
N	900

(c) A federal program to give greater weight to small contributors by offering federal matching funds for small, in-state donations

Favor	49%
Oppose	40%
Don't know	11%
N	900

(d) Instituting a national lottery every two years to pay for campaigns and bar all other contributions

Favor	39%
Oppose	56%
Don't know	6%
N	900

AG, Analysis Group; AI, Advocacy Institute; ARCA, A.R.C.A. Foundation; PAW, People for the American Way; PC, public campaign.

TABLE 4.6.   LAT (NOVEMBER 1999)

Presidential candidates are eligible for federal matching funds, which are financed solely by a voluntary checkoff on income tax returns. In order to receive matching funds, candidates must raise five thousand dollars in each of twenty states and at least ten million dollars for the entire primary season and abide by certain rules, such as spending caps in each primary. Do you approve or disapprove of candidates receiving matching funds?

Approve	49%
Disapprove	42%
Don't know	9%
N	1,800

LAT, *Los Angeles Times.*

offered in three slightly different variations to portions of the overall sample, was based on the IRS's own description of the presidential fund. This question described the fund as helping pay for presidential campaigns in order to reduce candidates' dependence on large contributions and place the candidates on an equal footing in the general election and noted that checking off would not increase "your tax or refund." Those responding that the fund was "a good idea" ranged from 45 percent to 51 percent, while those seeing it as "a bad idea" ranged from 31 percent to 37 percent. The rest fell into the category, "Don't know/refused." (One of the three polls is presented in Table 4.7.)

The second question concerned public financing of congressional elections. It was largely based on the historical Gallup question. It stated that the federal government would provide a fixed amount of money and that contributions from other sources would be prohibited. It was more explicit than Gallup in stating that spending would be limited. Beyond the Gallup formulation, this question also referred to benefits (as per the IRS description) and budgetary costs ($10 per year per taxpayer) of the proposal. Among the respondents, 52 percent were favorable to such a system, 41 percent were opposed, and 8 percent were characterized as "Don't know/refused" (see Table 4.7).

Polls with Negative Findings on Public Financing, 1993–2008

Many polls since the 1970s have shown majorities opposed to public financing proposals. A number of these, all taken in the last decade, were cited by John Samples in a 2003 paper published by the Cato Institute. The most negative polls have included questions that alert respondents to the costs of the system—including potential personal financial costs—but *not* to its other primary elements or to its possible benefits. Such questions produce the lowest amount of support for public financing. For example, three questions

TABLE 4.7.   GREENBERG, QUINLAN, ROSSNER RESEARCH FOR BCJ (APRIL 2006)

As you may have gathered from the previous questions, there is a box at the top of your individual tax return form that allows you to direct $3 to go to the Presidential Election Campaign Fund. I am going to read you a description of the Presidential Election Campaign Fund.

This fund helps pay for presidential election campaigns by providing public funds to participating candidates. The fund reduces candidates' dependence on large contributions from individuals and groups and places the candidates on an equal financial footing in the general election. If you check a box, your tax or refund will not change.

Having heard this, do you think the Presidential Election Campaign Fund is a good or a bad idea?

Good idea, strongly	22%
Good idea, not so strongly	26%
Bad idea, not so strongly	11%
Bad idea, strongly	26%
Don't know/refused	15%
Total good idea	48%
Total bad idea	37%
N	177

Thinking about a different subject, there is currently a debate about how political campaigns should be paid for, not just campaigns for president but for Congress as well. It has been suggested the federal government provide a fixed amount of money for campaigns for Congress that would reduce their dependence on large private donations and level the playing field for candidates. Candidates taking part in this system would not be allowed to accept campaign contributions from individuals, groups or any other sources. This could cost about $10 a year per taxpayer and would limit the amount of campaign spending done by candidates. Generally speaking, would you favor or oppose such a system?

Strongly favor	30%
Somewhat favor	22%
Somewhat oppose	12%
Strongly oppose	29%
Don't know/refused	8%
N	811

BCJ, Brennan Center for Justice.

from 1993, 1997, and 2000 polls, cited by Samples, show less than 20 percent support for public funding of congressional elections or political campaigns. Each question emphasizes the use of "taxpayer dollars" but fails to offer the alternative of a *voluntary* checkoff that limits personal costs (Tables 4.8 and 4.9). None of the questions indicate the other rules, including limiting campaign spending and private contributions, or describe the benefits of public funding such as lessening dependence on large donors and promoting competition among candidates. Interestingly, Gallup/CNN/*USA Today* came up with somewhat similar results in a March 1997 poll reporting that only 30 percent of respondents were "personally" willing to pay "more in taxes to help fund the election campaigns of candidates for president and Congress—if those candidates agreed to federal restrictions on the amount of money they could spend on their campaigns." As in the three aforementioned polls, the Gallup question highlighted costs and contained no specific discussion of a voluntary checkoff or the actual cost of the subsidy. But, unlike the others, it did point to one purpose or possible benefit of a tax increase: limiting spending on campaigns. That may account for the increased support for public financing in the Gallup/CNN/*USA Today* response (Table 4.10).

TABLE 4.8.   TG/MLL FOR USNWR (JUNE 1993)

Thinking now about how the issues of public funding of congressional elections—do you favor or oppose using taxpayer dollars to pay for the political campaigns of candidates running for Congress?

Favor	18%
Oppose	77%
Unsure	5%
N	1,000

MLL, Mellman, Lazarus and Lake; TG, Tarrance Group; USNWR, *US News and World Report*.

TABLE 4.9.   CBS/NYT

Some people have proposed public financing of political campaigns—that is, using only tax money to pay for political campaigns. Would you favor or oppose public financing to pay for political campaigns?

	April 1997	February 2000
Favor	18%	20%
Oppose	78%	75%
Don't know	4%	5%
N	1,347	1,225

Do you think public financing of political campaigns would reduce the influence of special interests and large contributors, or not?

	April 1997
Would	50%
Would not	43%
Don't know	7%
N	1,347

CBS, Columbia Broadcasting System; NYT, *New York Times*.

TABLE 4.10.   GALLUP FOR CNN, USAT (MARCH 1997)

Would you, personally, be willing to pay more in taxes to help fund the election campaigns of candidates for President and Congress—if those candidates agreed to federal restrictions on the amount of money they could spend on their campaigns?

Yes	30%
No	67%
Depends	2%
Don't know	2%
N	1,009

CNN, Cable Network News; Gallup, Gallup Organization; USAT, *USA Today*.

How such cost-emphasizing questions may produce a somewhat misleading portrait of public opinion is indicated in the April 1997 CBS–*New York Times* poll results presented in Table 4.9. The question emphasizing tax money, revealing only 18 percent in favor of public financing, is directly followed by another asking, "Do you think public financing of political campaigns would reduce the influence of special interests and large contributors or not?" Now 50 percent of respondents say it would and 43 percent say it would not. The two responses, negative and positive, strongly suggest that there might be considerably more support for public financing if its benefits were described and its impact on individual taxes were shown to be limited.

In a similar vein, another CBS News survey (July 1999) cited by Samples adds "using tax money" (again with no reference to a voluntary checkoff) and "prohibiting large donations from individuals and special interest groups" to the description. Where this purpose or benefit is injected, even without any reference to a voluntary checkoff or limitation on candidate spending, approximately twice as many people—37 percent—say they favor public financing, although a majority remains opposed (Table 4.11).

Finally, Samples highlights a September 1994 CBS–*New York Times* survey of public financing of congressional campaigns that does *not* mention tax money and includes references to reducing contributions from special interests, but still shows a majority of 54 percent "opposed" to public financing, with a substantial 38 percent in "favor" and 8 percent "don't know" (Table 4.12). Again the result is significantly more positive than when use of tax money is emphasized.

While this result is significantly less supportive of public financing than the relatively neutral Gallup and Analysis Group polls from various years reviewed previously, the question fails to include limiting the amount of funds candidates may spend in campaigns. The question is also different from the Gallup and Analysis Group ones in that it proposes only to "reduce" special-interest contributions rather than replace them. Finally, it is quite possible that the response was affected by contemporary political circumstances. Var-

TABLE 4.11.   CBS (JULY 1999)

Public financing of political campaigns—that is, using tax money to pay for campaigns and prohibiting large donations from individuals and special interest groups—do you favor or oppose that?

Favor	37%
Oppose	58%
Don't know	5%
N	722

CBS, Columbia Broadcasting System.

TABLE 4.12.   CBS/NYT (SEPTEMBER 1994)

In order to reduce congressional campaign contributions from special interests, would you favor or oppose public financing to help congressional candidates in their campaigns?

Favor	38%
Oppose	54%
Don't know	8%
N	1,161

CBS, Columbia Broadcasting System; NYT, *New York Times*.

ious congressional scandals involving misuse of public resources during the early 1990s caused "support for the national legislature to reach an all-time low prior to the 1994 elections" (Hermson 1998, 24). (As discussed earlier, a July 1995 Mellman poll may have reflected unusually low support for public financing around the time.)

Further light on the subject is provided by a April 1993 NBC News/*Wall Street Journal* poll that utilized a similar question—"Do you favor or oppose using public funds to finance campaigns for Congress, in exchange for limits on contributions from individuals and PACs?"—and obtained similar results; 53 percent "opposed," 38 percent in "favor," and 9 percent "not sure." But when two subsequent questions raised the issues of "how much influence" people "who make large contributions" or "lobbyists" have in "determining what Congress and the President do," and the 62 percent of respondents who were opposed to or unsure about public financing were asked again if they would favor or oppose public financing "if money were made available by eliminating the tax deduction that allows corporations to avoid taxes on lobbying expenses," 24 percent of this group pronounced themselves favorable while 13 percent said they were unsure (Table 4.13).

And two recent polls show that when "public financing" is coupled with spending limits, even though there is no specific mention of limiting private or special interest donations, around 40 percent of those questioned favor the public program. A Gallup–*USA Today* poll in April 2007 inquired, "What do you think [presidential] candidates should do—agree to take public financing and accept spending limits, or opt not to take public financing and spend whatever money they can raise on their own?" The response was: 39 percent agree versus 56 percent opt out (Table 4.14). And a CBS–*New York Times* poll of July 2008 asked, "Do you favor or oppose using public financing to help pay for the fall presidential election campaign in exchange for restrictions on the amount the candidates can spend?" In favor of public financing were 43 percent; opposed were 46 percent (Table 4.15).

TABLE 4.13.   H&T FOR NBC, WSJ (APRIL 1993)

Do you favor or oppose making public funds available to finance campaigns for Congress, in exchange for limits on contributions from individuals and political action committees?

Favor	38%
Oppose	53%
Not sure	9%
N	1,004

How much influence to do you think lobbyists have in determining what Congress and the President do—a great deal, just some, or very little influence?

A great deal of influence	69%
Just some influence	19%
Very little influence	8%
Not sure	2%
N	1,004

How much influence do you think people and organizations who make large campaign contributions have in determining what Congress and the President do—a great deal, just some, or very little influence?

A great deal of influence	69%
Just some influence	21%
Very little influence	8%
Not sure	2%
N	1,004

If money were made available by eliminating the tax deduction that allows corporations to avoid taxes on lobbying expenses, would you favor or oppose public funding of congressional campaigns?

Favor if corporate lobbying deduction is eliminated	24%
Oppose even if corporate lobbying deduction is eliminated	61%
Favor eliminating corporate lobbying deduction but should not be used for campaign funds	2%
Not sure	13%
N	622*

H&T, Hart and Teeter Research Companies; NBC, National Broadcasting Company; WSJ, *Wall Street Journal.*

*This question was asked of those who do not favor and are not sure of public funding for Congress in exchange for limits on contributions—62 percent of the 1,004 respondents.

What is most important, we think, in this variety of negative polls is that nearly 40 percent of those polled favor public financing of elections as soon as the issue of *either* limiting donations or special interest contributions *or* mandating candidate spending limits is introduced—even if the use of tax money is specifically mentioned and the voluntary checkoff is ignored.

TABLE 4.14.   GALLUP/USAT (APRIL 2007)

As you may know, to fund their (election) campaigns, candidates for president can receive public financing from the federal government if they agree to limits on spending, or they can opt not to take pubic financing and spend whatever money they can raise on their own. What do you think candidates should do—agree and take public financing and accept spending limits, or opt not to take public financing and spend whatever money they can raise on their own?

Agree to take public financing	39%
Opt not to take public financing	56%
No opinion	4%
N	1,007

Gallup, Gallup Organization; USAT, *USA Today.*

TABLE 4.15.   CBS/NYT (JULY 2008)

Do you favor or oppose using public financing to help pay for the fall (2008) presidential election campaign in exchange for restrictions on the amount the candidates can spend?

Favor	43%
Oppose	46%
Don't know/no answer	11%
N	1,796

CBS, Columbia Broadcasting System; NYT, *New York Times.*

Why Americans Don't Check Off

The limited available polling information suggests that a large part of the population is uninformed about the presidential public financing system and that this is a major factor in the weak response to the checkoff. In two 1996 polls, about a fifth of the people in the sample stated that they were unaware that presidential candidates receive funds from the federal government, and another tenth had no opinion on the matter (Table 4.16). More recently, an April 2006 Greenberg, Quinlan, Rossner Research poll for the Brennan Center for Justice found that 28 percent of taxpayers did not "remember seeing or hearing about" a checkoff box for the Presidential Election Campaign Fund on the IRS tax return. Indeed 32 percent described themselves as "not at all familiar" with the fund. When the 72 percent of the sample that remembered not checking the box were asked why they had made their choice, 17 percent gave responses grouped by the pollsters as "lack of awareness" (such as "Was unaware of checkoff," "Didn't pay attention," "Lack of understanding," and "Tax preparer didn't ask me"); another 8 percent mistakenly thought that the checkoff would increase their taxes; and 10 percent either replied "Don't know" or refused to answer—so up to 35 percent demonstrated considerable ignorance of the presidential fund. (This result is

TABLE 4.16.   WP FOR KAISER, HARVARD

To the best of your knowledge, do presidential candidates receive campaign funds from the federal government?

	September 1996	November 1996
Yes	67%	70%
No	22%	19%
No opinion	10%	11%
N	1,144	1,205

Harvard, Harvard University; Kaiser, Henry J. Kaiser Family Foundation; WP, *Washington Post.*

hardly surprising, as there has been virtually no public education concerning this program since it went into effect in 1976, thirty-four years ago [see "Participation, Competition, Engagement" 2003, 54–58].) The poll suggested that one factor helping to account for this ignorance was that two-thirds of taxpayers used third parties to prepare their returns and a plurality of these said the preparer had not asked them directly about whether they wanted $3 to be designated for the Presidential Election Campaign Fund. It also seems significant that many of the other reasons given for not checking off the box do not indicate belief in the superiority of private financing of democratic elections or an unwillingness to fund candidates with whom the respondent disagrees. Rather, their reasons—which include "Don't trust where money is going/corruption," "Too much money already spent on elections," and "They/Campaigns don't need it"—express cynicism about the political system in general. The poll presents some interesting evidence that some of this cynicism might be overcome with further information about the purpose and operation of the program. After hearing the IRS rationale for the fund, a quarter of the opponents of the checkoff indicated they would probably check off if they had to do it over again (Table 4.17).

Finally, it should be remembered that this is the only federal government program for which the taxpayer is asked to personally designate funds, and it is one that does not directly satisfy material needs or interests. Implicit in this format is that the taxpayer is not being asked to help fund other more tangible and better known initiatives. One wonders how many other existing government programs would pass this test with a majority vote.

Conclusion: A Proposal for Pollsters

This analysis has shown that there is no completely objective set of findings from previous polling on public financing of federal elections. However, it has indicated that there are better and worse methods of gauging contemporary

TABLE 4.17.   GREENBERG, QUINLAN, ROSSNER RESEARCH FOR BCJ (APRIL 2006)

Do you remember seeing or hearing about a checkoff box on the IRS tax return form for the Presidential Election Campaign Fund?

Yes	63%
No	28%
Did not personally prepare taxes	5%
Don't know/refused	4%
N	811

I am going to ask you some questions about the Presidential Election Campaign Fund. First, how familiar are you with this fund, would you say you are very familiar, somewhat familiar, not very familiar or not at all familiar?

Very familiar	6%
Somewhat familiar	27%
Not very familiar	34%
Not at all familiar	32%
Don't know/refused	1%
N	811

(If accountant or family member/friend/financial advisor/commercial preparer on "Filing 2") Did the person or people who helped you with your taxes ask you directly about whether you wanted $3 to go to the Presidential Election Campaign Fund?

Yes	40%
No	46%
Don't know/refused	14%
N	543

(If "no" on checkoff) Can you tell me why you did not check the box on your IRS tax return form and did not allow money to go to the Presidential Election Campaign Fund?

Opposed the fund/idea	35%
Didn't want to donate	16%
Don't trust where the money is going/Corruption	6%
Don't like idea	5%
Don't like President/Don't like candidates	5%
Waste of money/Pointless	2%
Don't think it will do any good	1%
Funding sources	17%
They/Campaigns don't need it	11%
Too much money already spent on elections	4%
Campaigns should be privately financed	3%
Private funds are available	0%
Lack of awareness	15%
Was unaware of the check off/Didn't pay attention/	
Unaware of option	8%
Lack of understanding	3%
Spouse/someone else fills out taxes	2%
Tax preparer didn't ask me	1%
Increase taxes/Affordability	8%
Can't afford it	5%
Taxes already too high	2%
Would increase my taxes/fees	0%

(continued on next page)

TABLE 4.17. *Continued*

(If "no" on checkoff) (continued)

Money spent elsewhere	7%
Want money going to candidates/parties I support	5%
Prefer money goes to other things	2%
Other	16%
Other	6%
Don't know/refused	10%
N	585

BCJ, Brennan Center for Justice.

public opinion. Prior questions should not "prime" the respondents to be either favorably or unfavorably disposed toward the public funding query.

In our view, an improved central question—which has not yet been constructed—would indicate to the respondent that there is debate over how election campaigns are funded, then spell out the main elements or rules of the major public financing proposals under discussion (complete or substantial public, rather than private, funding for campaigns, candidate spending limits, a voluntary checkoff of a certain amount of money that does not itself increase an individual's taxes).

A follow-up question would present in neutral form the main *benefits* (reduction of dependence on large private donations, a more level playing field for candidate competition) and *costs* (increased government spending with an indication of the estimated cost to the median or average taxpayer, limits on individuals' freedom to contribute to candidates). It would then ask respondents if they still favored or opposed public financing. A good example of such a follow-up is found in the Henry J. Kaiser Family Foundation's June 2000 polling on the proposed federal patients' bill of rights. While 81 percent favored the proposal (and 12 percent were opposed), support slipped to 58 percent if "you heard it would increase the cost of health insurance premiums usually shared by employers and workers by about 20 dollars per month for a typical family." However, half the opponents changed their mind to favor the bill when presented with the argument that the bill might make health plans less likely to deny coverage for needed services (Henry J. Kaiser Family Foundation 2001).

Methodology

The survey data utilized in this chapter were compiled through searches on the Roper Center for Public Opinion Research database formerly maintained by Lexis-Nexus Academic Universe and now available through the

Roper Center's iPoll Web site. The file includes sources in opinion polling such as Gallup, Harris, and Roper; ABC, CBS, CNN, and NBC; and the *Los Angeles Times, New York Times, USA Today,* and *Wall Street Journal.* The file is maintained by the Roper Center for Public Opinion Research, a nonprofit education and research organization in the field of public opinion and public policy. Searches were conducted for information compiled between January 1972 and August 2008; various strings of the following search terms were employed: public financing, campaign, election, reform, tax, checkoff, matching, and funds. In addition, Mellman Group polls and press releases were obtained from Public Campaign, which sponsored some of the polling. The Greenberg, Quinlan, Rossner poll was obtained from the sponsoring Brennan Center for Justice at New York University.

While we do not discuss every poll we surveyed, those cited reflect the general tendencies revealed by polling and the variety of questions posed, and the contexts in which they appeared.

REFERENCES

Henry J. Kaiser Family Foundation. 2001. "Kaiser Public Opinion Update: The Public, Managed Care, and Consumer Protections." Available at http://www.kff.org/insurance/loader.cfm?url=/commonspot/security/getfile.cfm&PageID=14910.

Hermson, Paul S. 1998. *Congressional Elections: Campaigning at Home and in Washington,* 2nd ed. Washington, DC: CQ Press.

Internal Revenue Service. 2006. "Tax Year 2006: Taxpayer Usage Study Internal Revenue Service Report No. 15." Available at http://www.irs.gov/taxstats.

"Participation, Competition, Engagement: How to Revive and Improve Public Funding for Presidential Nomination Politics." 2003. Report of the Campaign Finance Institute Task Force on Presidential Nomination Financing. Washington, DC: Campaign Finance Institute. Available at http://www.cfinst.org/presidential/report/pdf/CFI_Chapter4.pdf.

Samples, John. 2003. "Policy Analysis: The Failures of Taxpayer Financing of Presidential Campaigns." *Cato Institute,* November 25.

II

The Consequences
of Public Financing

5

◇ ◇ ◇

Campaign Finance Reform Reconsidered

New York City's Public Finance Program
at Twenty

JEFFREY KRAUS

For two decades, municipal elections in New York City have been contested on what might be termed a "level" playing field. The New York City Campaign Finance Act, which became law in 1988, provided for partial public financing of campaigns for local office.[1] Today, twenty-seven states and fourteen local governments have instituted public financing for at least some of the political offices or political parties under their jurisdiction.

Brecher and colleagues (1993, 113–119) examined the program's impact on the 1989 election and concluded that the city's campaign finance reform program had partially met its goals, but recommended that some changes in the law mandating debates, access to broadcast and cable television, and limitations on the gathering of contributions by intermediaries be considered.

I evaluated the program's impact after four elections (in Scheele 1999, 82–100) and concluded that the program had slowed the growth of spending in citywide contests and forced candidates to broaden their fund-raising efforts. However, I also found that the program had not increased electoral competition or voter turnout, and that the program "does not neutralize incumbency or the candidate who wishes to 'buy' a council seat" (95).

Ryan (2003) suggested that the program's reporting requirements and contribution limits be extended to all candidates, whether or not they participated in the public finance program (ix). He also proposed that the program be modified to increase the additional funds received by program participants facing high-spending opponents, distribute public funds to candidates earlier in the election cycle, and limit campaign fund-raising to specified time periods (ix).

In 2006, I reviewed the first six cycles and concluded that not much had changed concerning the program's operation (Kraus 2006).

Here we briefly review the circumstances that led to the law's passage, outline its key provisions and objectives, and (based on the outcomes of seven election cycles) make some observations about the statute's effectiveness. The 2001 election is of particular interest because it was the first election where term limits forced a large number of officeholders from office and because of the presence of billionaire Michael Bloomberg, a candidate for mayor who opted out of the voluntary program in order to self-finance his campaign. Finally, we examine the recent changes in the law that have taken effect for the 2009 election cycle. The changes were intended to address problems encountered by the Campaign Finance Board as it administered one of the more comprehensive systems of public finance in the United States.

The Path to Public Financing of Campaigns in New York

New York's program was developed in response to growing concern about the influence of major donors in local politics and the political scandals that tarnished Mayor Edward I. Koch's third term.[2] State Senator Franz Leichter (1985) found that sixteen of the twenty-five largest campaign contributors had some matter before the city government between 1981 and 1985. Leichter found at least ten instances where donors significantly increased their financial support when they had matters pending before the Board of Estimate.[3]

Another concern was the escalating cost of political campaigns. In 1985, Mayor Koch spent nearly $6.3 million; Council President Andrew Stein $3 million, and Comptroller Harrison J. Goldin $1.3 million (Brecher et al. 1993, 126). Only Stein faced serious opposition. Spending was a factor in contested elections, where incumbent borough presidents outspent their opponents. In Brooklyn, the borough president spent $1.3 million, while his two Democratic primary opponents' combined expenditures were $500,000 (New York Public Interest Research Group 1987). In the Bronx, the borough president outspent his opponent by nearly four to one (ibid.).

The spiral of expenditure was fueled by large donations. According to Leichter (1986), the five largest donors between 1981 and 1986 had given more than $1.5 million to members of the Board of Estimate and the five Democratic county committees.[4] He concluded that "the line between a bribe and a contribution is almost invisible" (quoted in Barbanel 1985). Mayor Koch countered that there was nothing "immoral" about the contributions (ibid.).

A number of public finance bills were introduced in the city council in 1986, although none were passed. In September 1987 a campaign finance reform bill was introduced by Councilmembers Arthur Katzman, Ruth Messinger, and Stanley Michels. Mayor Koch signed the bill into law on February 9, 1988 (Local Law No. 8 of 1988).

The 1988 New York City Campaign Finance Act: Key Provisions and Objectives

In enacting the statute, the City Council declared that it sought to "ensure that citizens[—]regardless of their personal wealth, [or] access to large contributors or other financial connections[—]are enabled and encouraged to compete effectively for public office" (New York City CFB 1990). The law was intended to limit the size of campaign contributions, control campaign spending, increase competition for elective office, and provide voters with more information about the candidates and their finances.[5] A five-member board was established to oversee the program.[6]

Contribution Limits

Academic studies and journalistic accounts suggest that large donations made by individuals and PACs are intended to influence the votes of legislators on matters of interest (Adamany and Agree 1975; Frendreis and Waterman 1985; Wilhite and Theilmann 1987). Donors and recipients deny that contributions "buy" votes. Rather, they contend, funds are directed to those already supporting the donor's position. This view is supported by studies which conclude that there is no conclusive proof that PACs are able to "buy" votes (Chappell 1982; Welch 1982; Alexander and Haggerty 1984; Sorauf 1984; Wright 1985; Grenzke 1989; Sabato 1989). However, the perception that contributions "buy" influence persists. Chartock observed that "while most lobbyists claim their PACs have little clout, their proliferation suggests otherwise" (quoted in Sabato 1989, 240).

The Campaign Finance Act established contribution limits. While limits existed under state law, the local law imposed substantially lower limits. At the time, state law permitted individuals to give up to $50,000 per election (primary, runoff, and general) to candidates for citywide office.

The campaign finance law limited participating candidates for citywide office to $3,000 per election (New York City CFB 1990). Candidates for city council were allowed to accept no more than $2,000 per election. Another distinction between state law and the city program is that since 1998 participating candidates have been prohibited from accepting corporate contributions.[7] Nonparticipating candidates may accept corporate contributions.

Expenditure Limits

The act set spending limits for primary, runoff, and general elections, as well as for the three years preceding the election. The limits cover virtually all expenditures made to advance a candidate's campaign or in furtherance of his or her opponent's defeat.

Certain expenditures were exempt from the limits. These included costs required to comply with the Campaign Finance Act or the state election law. Of particular significance was the exemption of costs related to challenging or defending designating petitions.[8]

The limits were intended to slow the rate of increase of campaign expenditure and to reduce the fund-raising advantage that some candidates (particularly incumbents) enjoyed, with the ultimate aim of making races more competitive (Table 5.1).

Increased Competition

Another objective of the legislation was to encourage greater competition for local office. This was to be accomplished through the aforementioned contribution and spending caps, as well as the system of partial public financing. As the Campaign Finance Board's first report explained:

> To restrict the influence of money on electoral campaigns, the Campaign Finance Program sets limits on contributions and expendi-

TABLE 5.1. EXPENDITURE LIMITS UNDER THE CAMPAIGN FINANCE ACT, 1989–2009 (PER ELECTION)

Year	Mayor	Comptroller and Public Advocate	Borough President	City Council
1989	$3,000,000	$1,750,000	$625,000	$60,000
1991	N/A	N/A	N/A	$105,000
1993	$4,000,000	$2,500,000	$900,000	$105,000
1997	$4,732,000	$2,958,000	$1,065,000	$124,000
2001	$5,231,000	$3,270,000	$1,177,000	$137,000
2003	N/A	N/A	N/A	$150,000
2005	$5,728,000	$3,581,000	$1,289,000	$150,000
2009	$6,158,000	$3,850,000	$1,386,000	$161,000

tures and also imposes strict requirements for disclosure of campaign finances. By providing matching public funds to candidates who agree to observe these limits and requirements and who reach certain threshold levels in fundraising, the Program also intends to "level the playing field" for all candidates, whether or not they have access to substantial wealth. In this way, wider participation in the electoral process by both candidates and voters can be encouraged. (New York City CFB 1990, ix)

Pursuant to the U.S. Supreme Court's decision in *Buckley v. Valeo* (1976), the program is voluntary. Candidates "opt in" to the program.[9] Participating candidates must meet financial "threshold requirements" before they receive funds. The requirements vary, depending on the office being sought, but are based on the premise that candidates must demonstrate "public support" by gathering small contributions from donors in order to draw public monies.

From the program's beginning until 1997, candidates meeting the threshold were eligible for a dollar-for-dollar match of contributions, with the match increasing to two to one if the participating candidate was in a contest with a nonparticipant.[10] In October 1998 the City Council voted to increase the match to four to one for candidates who would forgo corporate contributions. Participants who did not take corporate contributions and ran against high-spending nonparticipants would be eligible for a five-to-one match.[11] Candidates accepting donations from corporations would still receive the one-to-one match.

Subsequently, the voters approved a revision to the New York City Charter that prohibited all candidates in the campaign finance program from accepting corporate contributions.

After the charter revision was approved, Mayor Rudolph Giuliani attempted to nullify the four-to-one match, since the purpose of the two-tiered system was to compensate participating candidates who agreed to the new limitation.[12] Giuliani asserted that the four-to-one match was nullified by the ban on corporate contributions to program participants.

In 1999 this issue came to a head when the New York City Office of Management and Budget (OMB) notified candidates in a special election (the first since the charter revision) that the four-to-one rule was illegal and that no public funds would be paid until the CFB changed its position. The board ignored OMB and paid candidates at the four-to-one ratio from funds left over from the 1997 election cycle (New York City CFB 2002, 5). When the Giluiani administration challenged the board in court, the City

Council enacted Local Law 21 of 2001 (over the mayor's veto) approving the four-to-one match, with a five-to-one match for those candidates competing against nonparticipating candidates. The council's action rendered the lawsuit moot.[13]

In 2004 the City Council enacted a change in matching funds, establishing a new six-to-one match for participating mayoral candidates who run against a nonparticipant who spends more than $17 million. The law targeted Mayor Bloomberg, over whose veto the legislation was enacted. City Council Deputy Majority Leader Bill Perkins, who sponsored the legislation, was obviously speaking of the mayor when he said:

> Clearly, we can't stop someone that is threatening to break the bank to win an election, someone who instead of running on his record is going to run on his dollars. . . . But we can make sure that the bullies in the schoolyard that do not play by the rules do not go unpunished, that those who play by the rules will be given an extra benefit against those who don't. (McIntire 2004)

For the 2009 elections, participating candidates received a six-to-one match, with a maximum of $175 in eligible contributions being matched with $1,050 in public funds. The law limits the use of public funds to "qualified campaign Expenditures." These include those made to educate the public about the candidate and the issues in the election. Proscribed uses of public funds include payments to a candidate or the candidate's family or business, cash payments, petition challenges or defense, entertainment, and the salaries of campaign workers (although consultants' fees can be paid). Any surplus funds remaining after the election are to be returned to the city.

Public Disclosure

Participants in the program are required to submit financial disclosure reports. While such documentation has been required by state law since 1974 (all candidates for municipal office are required to file periodic reports with the Board of Elections), the local law, modeled on the federal disclosure rules, requires a more detailed divulgence of campaign finances.

The board's more rigorous disclosure requirements were extended to nonparticipating candidates in 2004. Now, all candidates for municipal office must file disclosure statements with the board, adhere to the contribution limits (unless they are self-financed) established by the board, and be subject to audits by the Campaign Finance Board staff.

Taken together, the New York City Campaign Finance Act and the subsequent charter revision constitute probably one of the more ambitious and comprehensive electoral reform measures ever enacted in the United States.

The Public Finance Program after Eight Election Cycles

While the law has had some impact on elections, loopholes have been found and exploited. At the time of its enactment, a major loophole was evident: that the program was voluntary. Other flaws emerged over time. In some instances, the law's provisions have not had the desired impact.

Contribution Limits

One of the program's goals was to eliminate large contributions so as to end the perception that major donors had a disproportionate degree of influence in the political process. For instance, in the 1985 election cycle, $3.3 million (47 percent) of the funds raised by Mayor Koch's campaign committee came from 453 benefactors who gave at least $5,000 (New York State Commission on Government Integrity 1988). Comptroller Goldin (64 percent) and City Council President Stein (66 percent) raised even greater proportions of their campaign treasuries from donors who gave at least $5,000 (ibid.). The public finance program's lower contribution limits have had some impact on large contributors.

The 1989 election cycle provides an interesting contrast between "pre-" and "postreform" fund-raising. The campaign finance law took effect February 29, 1988, and different patterns were evident. Koch and Goldin had both historically relied on major donors. According to the New York City CFB (1990, 53), between July 12, 1983, and February 28, 1988, 20.4 percent of Koch's monetary contributions were in excess of $6,000 (the limits for both a primary and general election). For the same period, 28.6 percent of Goldin's receipts were in the form of gifts greater than $6,000. After February 29, 1988, Koch's receipt of donations in the $3,000-and-under range increased from 55 percent to 86 percent of the total collected. For Goldin, the increase was from 28 percent to 96 percent of his contributions. In 1989 the

TABLE 5.2.   TYPES OF CONTRIBUTIONS TO CANDIDATES, 1989–2005 (PERCENTAGE)

Type	1989	1991	1993	1997	2001	2003	2005
Corporations	16	11	14.7	26.58	0.8	0	0
PACs	4	10	9	5.49	4.6	14.7	7.1
Employee organizations	2	6	4.8	2.34	1.4	4.1	2.6
Partnerships	3	1	1.1	2.2	3.8	4.2	6.2
Individuals	75	68	64.07	61.47	86.7	75.3	84.5
Other	1	4	2.51	1.35	3.4	1.8	0
Unknown	0	0	3.4	0.55	0	0	0

Source: New York City Campaign Finance Board.

law appeared to have an impact on the amount of money raised: The victorious Democratic candidates for mayor and comptroller spent less than their counterparts had four years earlier (Brecher et al. 1993, 130–131). Therefore, the measure did control costs, at least at first.

Perhaps the most significant development related to contribution limits has been the creation of new fund-raising sources, strategies, and techniques. Where candidates once relied on real estate developers, lawyers, lobbyists, bankers, and businesspeople to capitalize their campaigns, they now needed to broaden their donor base. Donations from individuals constitute the largest category of contributions to participating candidates.

Where corporations once were a significant source of contributions to candidates in the program, their prohibition has resulted in a reliance on individual contributions to finance campaigns (Table 5.2).

Intermediaries: The Substitute for the "Big Donor"

Since the introduction of public financing, candidates for citywide office have made extensive use of "bundling," where intermediaries collect contributions and turn them over to candidates. In four of the five mayoral elections since the law took effect, "intermediaries" have played a significant role. In 1989, 19 percent of the monies raised by the participating mayoral candidates came through 391 intermediaries. It should be noted that the number of intermediaries is very close to the 453 contributors who gave more than $6,000 to Koch's 1985 race. In contrast, intermediaries accounted for 0.6 and 1.8 percent of the funds raised, respectively, by candidates for borough president and city council in 1989. Republican Rudolph Giuliani's campaign raised almost 45 percent of its funds through 252 intermediaries, the greatest reported utilization of intermediaries by any candidate in that cycle (New York City CFB 1990, 73).[14]

In the 1993 mayoral election, intermediaries again were significant. The New York Public Interest Research Group (1993, 5), analyzing CFB data, determined that intermediaries who delivered more than $10,000 played major roles in both mayoral campaigns. Through October 25, 1993, the David Dinkins campaign had raised 20 percent of its $9.2 million war chest through 58 intermediaries; Giuliani, one-third of his $7.8 million campaign fund through 32 bundlers.

In 1997 intermediaries accounted for 22 percent of the funds contributed to mayoral campaigns (New York City CFB 1998b, 38). In 2001, 25 percent of all contributions made to participating mayoral candidates were intermediated (New York City CFB 2002, 61). As Lawrence A. Mandelker observed, "by virtue of bundling, special interests still have the same influence" (quoted in Lynn 1989b).

Bundling declined in 2005 when only three of the mayoral candidates— Fernando Ferrer (22 percent); Gifford Miller (6.5 percent), and Anthony Weiner (5.85 percent)—collected significant sums through intermediaries. The decline in bundling extended to other contests as well. According to the Campaign Finance Board, intermediated contributions accounted for 5.5 percent of all contributions during the 2005 election cycle (New York City CFB 2006, 51). This figure compares with 17 percent in 2001 and 13 percent in 1997 (ibid., 51–52). The decline in bundling in 2005 is consistent with the 35 percent drop in contributions between the 2001 and 2005 election cycles (ibid., 33), a decline that can be explained by the paucity of "open seats" in 2005 (seven council seats and one borough presidency) as compared to 2001 (forty-four council seats, four borough presidencies, and all three citywide offices). Incumbency discouraged competition, thus reducing the need for fund-raising and bundling.

The aforementioned prohibition on corporate contributions had a significant impact on council campaigns. In 1997 corporate contributions accounted for 20 percent of the funds donated to candidates for the City Council (ibid., 52). In 2001, with the prohibition on corporate contributions in effect, the percentage of funds raised by council candidates from individuals increased from 61 percent (in 1997) to 83 percent of total contributions (ibid., 53).

However, the law's effect on contributions to municipal campaigns is limited to the extent that nonparticipating candidates are subject to the state law's more generous contribution limits and to the extent that wealthy candidates who are willing to self-finance their campaigns are not subject to any limits under state law.

Wealthy individuals, or those with access to money, can use their assets to their advantage. In 1989, Ronald Lauder, a wealthy businessman who was seeking the Republican mayoral nomination, spent almost $12.3 million, most of it his own (Brecher et al. 1993, 132). By not taking public funds, he was able to spend his own money without restraint, since donations by candidates or their spouses are exempt from even the loose limits of the state law (New York State Board of Elections 1988, 11).

In both 1989 and 1993, Andrew Stein declined public financing, declaring that it was "almost unconscionable . . . that while people are dying in city hospitals for lack of care, this money should be used to pay for TV commercials and shopping bags" (quoted in Lynn 1989c).

In 2001 billionaire businessman Michael Bloomberg declined to participate in the program, spending $75 million of his fortune on his campaign for mayor (Berkey-Gerard 2003).

In contrast, the seventeen mayoral candidates who participated during the primary and general elections collectively expended $38,980,000 (New York City CFB 2002, 70). In winning reelection in 2005, Bloomberg spent $84,587,319 (New York City CFB 2006, C-1). In contrast his Democratic opponent Fernando Ferrer, who participated in the program, expended $9,165,301 (ibid.). In 2009, Bloomberg spent $108,371,688 on his reelection campaign (New York City CFB 2010). His Democratic opponent, City Comptroller William Thompson, Jr., $9,374,826 (ibid.). Bloomberg, the wealthiest man in New York City, self-financed his campaign while Thompson participated in the city's public finance program. Despite outspending Thompson by more than eleven to one, Bloomberg was reelected by less than five percentage points (New York City Board of Elections 2009).

Affluent candidates have also run for the council. In a 1993 special election, Andrew S. Eristoff, a descendant of industrialist Henry Phipps, spent $343,711 ($256,000 of which was in the form of a personal loan he made to his campaign) to defeat Jane Crotty by 57 votes (McKinley 1993b). Eristoff outspent Crotty by almost $100,000 and conceded that he would not have won without his $256,000 loan, since it paid for cable television and radio advertising (rare in city council races at that time) and for ten mass mailings, including a decisive posting of sixteen thousand absentee ballot applications to Republicans (Eristoff was the only Republican in a seven-candidate field). Eristoff defended his outlay, saying that he didn't "owe anything to any union or to any leadership person in the Council" (McKinley 1993b). Chris Meyer of NYPIRG viewed it differently, suggesting that Eristoff's victory meant "that if you are rich enough in this town you can win an election with your own money" (ibid.). Eristoff would repeat the feat eight months later, spending almost $600,000 in winning a full term.

In the 1993 mayoral election, large contributions resurfaced. While contributions to participating candidates are limited, donations of up to $62,500 can still be made under state law by individual contributors to party organizations, which can then use the funds for so-called independent campaign efforts. Independent spending has been upheld by the courts, on First Amendment grounds.[15] While some concern was raised about such expenditures in 1989, the magnitude of these independent campaigns attracted greater attention four years later.

In 1993 the CFB for the first time had to adjudicate claims that "independent" expenditures were, in fact, coordinated with candidate committees and should be charged against their spending limit. Under pressure from the CFB, the Dinkins campaign voluntarily reimbursed the State Democratic Committee $226,000 for mail that the Giuliani campaign alleged was an attempt to circumvent the spending cap (McKinley 1993c). A Dinkins campaign counterclaim that a $750,000 election day operation financed by the Republican State Committee should be charged to the Giuliani campaign was dismissed by the CFB.

Allegations of coordinated independent expenditures continue to occur. In 2003, Service Employees International Union Local 1199 was charged with helping one of its former employees, Annabel Palma, in her successful race for a City Council seat. During the 2005 election cycle, formal complaints were brought against the campaigns of Melissa Mark-Viverito, a candidate for the City Council, who was alleged to have received assistance (mainly in the form of phone banking) from Local 1199 (Hicks 2005b), and Scott Stringer, a candidate for Manhattan borough president, who was the beneficiary of literature and recorded phone calls made on his behalf by the Working Families Party (Hicks 2005a). In October 2007, the CFB assessed a fine of $30,000 against Palma's campaign. The board found that Local 1199 did coordinate with the Palma campaign, and that Palma's campaign has misrepresented 1199's role in the campaign (Seifman 2007). In early 2008, the CFB dismissed the complaint against Mark-Viverito, concluding that their investigation "did not uncover sufficient evidence to substantiate the complaint" (New York City CFB 2008, 1). The board acknowledged that "expenditures made by an 'independent' entity in coordination with a participating campaign represent another threat to the integrity of Program spending limits" (New York City CFB 2006, 69).

Therefore, while large contributions to individual campaigns have been scaled back, bundling, the inability to regulate contributions to nonparticipating candidates, and expenditures by independent campaigns remain problems.

Limiting Campaign Expenditures

A second objective of the statute was to contain expenditures by imposing campaign spending limits. Once again, the program has achieved partial success. In 1985, the last mayoral campaign before regulation, Mayor Koch's campaign spent $7.1 million in what were lightly contested primary and general election campaigns (New York City CFB 1990, 84).

In subsequent mayoral elections, spending did level off among program participants. Despite the intense competition in 1993, no participant exceeded Koch's 1985 spending. In 1993 both campaigns increased their outlays, with Dinkins spending $10.9 million (primary and general election) and Giuliani $8.7 million (general election) (McKinley 1993d). In 1997, Giuliani spent $11.8 million, and Ruth Messinger, his Democratic opponent in the general election, $6.1 million (New York City CFB 1998b, 1). However, in both cases the spending was within the CFB's limits. In 2001, with the mayoralty open because of term limits, $38,980,000 was spent by the seventeen candidates who participated in the program, which included spending during the Democratic runoff primary (New York City CFB 2002, 70). These expenditures were eclipsed by the more than $75 million spent by Bloomberg. The program's accomplishments in slowing the growth of campaign expenditure can be ascribed to its willingness to sanction those exceeding the limit.[16]

In City Council races, public financing seems to have actually increased spending (Table 5.3). In 1985, eight candidates spent in excess of $100,000 in the Democratic primary.[17] Since then, fueled by public funds, candidates participating in the program have typically spent more than candidates who ran for office prior to the advent of the program.

The significant increase in spending in 2001 can be attributed to the implementation of the four-to-one match (and five-to-one bonus for participants who are running against nonparticipants) and an increase in the amount of public funds available to each candidate. The board itself acknowledged the increase in spending, calling the 2001 election "the most expensive elections in New York City history" (2002, 67). It is clear that the increased availability of public campaign funds has encouraged City Council candidates to spend more than ever before. It has also encouraged them to spend money on new campaign tactics. For example, in 2001, a number of City Council candidates spent money on cable television advertising. Considering that such advertising is expensive and wasteful, in that it reaches many viewers who cannot vote for the candidate, its use can be explained only by the "easy money" that public financing makes available

TABLE 5.3. EXPENDITURES BY PARTICIPATING CITY COUNCIL CANDIDATES, 1989–2009

Election	Number of Participating Candidates	Total Expenditures	Average Expenditures
1989	33	$2,740,000	$83,030
1991	135	$7,600,000	$56,296
1993	112	$4,480,000	$40,000
1997	109	$7,210,000	$66,146
2001	301	$26,220,000	$87,043
2003	106	$10,466,354	$98,739
2005	138	$15,771,951	$114,289
2009	170	$21,439,333	$126,113

Sources: For 1989–2001, New York City Campaign Finance Board 2002, 71. For 2003, CFB disclosure data submitted by candidates. For 2005, New York City CFB 2006, I-10. For 2009, New York City CFB 2010.

to campaigns that would otherwise be more careful about the use of their resources.

One criticism of public financing after the 1989 election was that the spending limits for City Council candidates were too low, making it difficult for nonincumbents, who must mount credible campaigns against well-known officeholders, to take part in the program.[18] The expenditure limit was increased 75 percent ($60,000 to $105,000 for each election, primary and general) for the 1991 and 1993 council elections. The spending limit was increased in subsequent election years to $124,000 (1997), $137,000 (2001), and $150,000 (2003). For the 2009 election cycle, the expenditure limit for council races has been set at $161,000 for each election.

Increases in the expenditure limits were intended to make challengers more competitive with incumbents. However, the increases in the expenditure limit have benefited incumbents, who have generally raised and spent more than challengers (Table 5.4).

The fund-raising advantages enjoyed by incumbents have actually increased during the life of the program. In 1989 incumbents outraised their opponents by a ratio of 2.28 to one. In the most recent election cycle, incumbents raised an average of $5.19 for every dollar raised by their challengers. In discussing the 2005 City Council elections, the Campaign Finance Board found:

> With 44 incumbents running for reelection in 51 districts, the uphill battle for challengers proved virtually insurmountable. Of the $9.8 million in total contributions raised by 126 participating Council

TABLE 5.4.   AVERAGE TOTAL CONTRIBUTIONS TO CITY COUNCIL
CANDIDATES, 1989–2009

Year	Incumbents	Nonincumbents*
1989	$100,532	$43,921
1991	$57,557	$15,084
1993	$62,239	$29,334
1997	$99,548	$23,654
2001	$92,272	$37,011
2003	$109,119	$24,410
2005	$160,727	$30,927
2009	$97,295	$37,488

Source: New York City Campaign Finance Board and New York City Board of Elections.

* Nonincumbents in contests against incumbents. Does not include candidates in open seats.

candidates in 2005, over half—$5.5 million—was raised by the 38 incumbents who joined the Program. In other words, the incumbents, who comprise 30 percent of the Program's participants, raised well over half (56 percent) of the total contributions by participants at the Council level. (2006, 37)

In 2009, while the fund-raising edge enjoyed by incumbents narrowed, there was still a better than two-to-one edge for incumbents.

Another weakness of the program was that, in some cases, the public finance program allowed candidates facing token opposition to spend public funds. In 1989, Ruth Messinger, a candidate for Manhattan borough president, spent $1.6 million (including $600,714 in public funds) although she had no serious opposition (New York City CFB 1990, J-1).[19] Messinger testified at the CFB's 1989 public hearing that she spent the funds because they were "an entitlement to a candidate, not a revocable gift" (Lynn 1989a).

Four years later, Messinger, Fernando Ferrer (the Bronx borough president) and Charles Millard (a Manhattan councilman) made large expenditures in the general election despite token opposition.[20] In 1997, Council Speaker Peter Vallone spent over $231,000 even though his opponent was a minor party candidate who polled 761 votes out of almost 13,000 cast (New York City CFB 1998b). In 2001, the *New York Daily News* editorialized that "self control and selflessness would be welcome from . . . other politicians. Doing the right thing has its own rewards."

Such expenditures serve one of two purposes. First, by increasing turnout, they may help candidates in other races (and amount to an "independent expenditure" on their behalf). They may also help candidates who expend the funds by increasing their name recognition for a subsequent election.[21]

For the 2003 City Council elections the Campaign Finance Board implemented a new local law limiting candidates to receipt of one-quarter of the maximum amount of public funds available for the office being sought where the participating candidate faced nominal opposition.[22] Under this rule, four city council candidates were limited to receiving $20,625.[23]

However, the rule did not deter all from seeking full payment. Candidates could still seek the full public funds payment by submitting a written statement to the Campaign Finance Board.

Fourteen candidates submitted these statements for the primary, and seven candidates did so for the general election. For example, Councilmember Michael Nelson requested additional funds (and received the maximum of $82,500) because, as he wrote, "I am opposed on the ballot in the general election" (Nelson 2003). The opposition referred to by Nelson was the candidate of the Conservative Party, a third party (who polled 515 votes to Nelson's 7,495).

Another candidate, Councilmember Charles Barron, wrote that his campaign's "budget forecast included receiving the maximum amount of public matching funds" (Barron 2003). Barron, who would receive $66,304 in public funds, received 84 percent of the vote in the primary. Of the fourteen candidates who sought extra funds during the primary, three ultimately did not have a primary, eight won, and three lost. In the general election, all seven candidates who sought additional funding were elected, and none received less than 76 percent of the vote.

In 2005, five candidates for the council requested a full public funds payment despite token opposition, and ten did so for the general election. Councilman Barron again requested additional funding, citing as the first reason for this need "to meet contractual obligations to campaign consultants, landlord of headquarters, online communications systems, and wages to campaign staff workers" (Barron 2005). Barron would receive $141,077 in public funds during the primary and general elections (New York City CFB 2005, C-17). Barron's opponent in the primary and general election, John Whitehead, failed to qualify for matching funds, and Barron won 84 percent of the vote in the primary and 89 percent of the vote in the general election. The additional funds provided Barron amounted to nothing more than New York City taxpayers subsidizing political consultants, landlords, and campaign workers—not exactly furthering the cause of free elections. In 2009, eleven candidates filed statements of need during the primary, and three did so for the general election (New York City CFB 2009b).

It seems that the board's efforts to limit the use of public funds in one-sided campaigns was not all that successful during the first two election cycles where these lower public-funds payment limits were in effect. The board acknowledged this failure, noting that

> the Board does not have the power under law to evaluate or contradict the "Statements of Need" submitted by the candidates, but it was hoped that the public posting of the letters would discourage candidates from seeking additional public funding unless there was a true need for it. The new law did not, however, significantly lower public funds payments in noncompetitive races. (New York City CFB 2004, 2)

Increased Competition

Another aim of public financing is to increase the level of competition for public office. The New York program has not had the desired effect. There were fewer citywide candidates in the 1997 Democratic Primary than in 1985. Data for the City Council show that the law has not led to an increase in the number of office seekers. In 1989, the first year of public financing, there were fewer candidates in both the Democratic primary and the general election than in 1985. While the number of candidates increased fivefold in the 1991 Democratic primary, there were ten fewer candidates in 1993 than in 1985. In 1997 the number of council hopefuls increased by 30 percent. In 2001, when thirty-seven of the fifty-one incumbent City Council members were forced to leave office because of term limits, there were 202 Democratic hopefuls. In 2003 and 2005, when most council seats were occupied by incumbents, the numbers of Democratic City Council candidates were sixty (2003) and eighty-five (2005).

The 1991 increase can be attributed to the creation of sixteen "open seats" by the expansion of the council from thirty-five to fifty-one. Of the 162 Democratic primary candidates, 100 (61.7 percent) were in the contests where there was no Democratic incumbent. The remaining 62 (38.3 percent) competed in the nineteen districts in which a Democrat was seeking reelection. There were twelve districts where no Democratic primary was held (in eleven there were Democratic incumbents, while the remaining seat was held by a Republican). In the twenty open seats there was an average of 5.0 candidates; in the thirty-one seats contested by incumbents, the average number of candidates was 2.38. In 1997 there were primaries in eight seats where no Democratic incumbent was seeking reelection (compared to two seats four years earlier). The average number of candidates in the open-seat primaries was 3.75. In the fifteen primaries where Democratic incumbents sought renomination the average was 2.66.

A number of factors contributed to the 150 percent increase in Democratic City Council candidates in 2001. First, term limits forced thirty-seven council members to leave office. Another factor was the change in the public-funds marching ratio from a one-to-one ratio to a four-to-one match, as well as the increase in the maximum matching funds payment from $40,000 to $82,500 per election. Once again, open seats drew the most candidates. In the thirty-six open seats there was an average of 4.80 candidates in Democratic primaries. In the fifteen seats where there were incumbents, the average number of candidates was 1.53.

In 2003 there were two open seats.[24] In the eighteen Democratic primaries involving incumbents, the average number of candidates was 2.61. In six primaries where there was no Democratic incumbent, there were 2.16 candidates. However, if one factors in the contests where the Democratic incumbent was not challenged, the average number of candidates in districts where incumbent Democrats sought reelection was 1.69.

In 2005 there were eight open seats. In the open-seat races, there was an average of 5.3 candidates. Where an incumbent was seeking reelection, the average number of candidates was 1.59.

For the 2009 election cycle, initially 294 candidates filed with the New York City Campaign Finance Board and/or the Board of Elections as candidates for the City Council. However, following the enactment of Local Law 51 of 2008, which allowed the mayor and other municipal officials elected in 2001 and reelected in 2005 to seek a third term, the number of the candidates running for the City Council dropped significantly. Many term-limited council members who were planning to seek higher office dropped back to run for council, and many of those planning to retire decided to seek a third term. There were Democratic primaries in thirty-two of the fifty-one council districts, with a total of 137 candidates making the ballot; nineteen council members had no primary (compared with twenty-seven in 2005). Council members in twenty-four districts faced opposition (with an average of 3.9 candidates in the primary). There were primaries in eight open seats, with an average of 5.3 candidates per contest. Therefore, as in earlier cycles, open seats attracted more competitors.

However, there were some interesting developments during the last cycle. Five Democratic incumbents were defeated in primaries (a 79 percent reelection rate); four of the defeated council members had voted to extend term limits. While most incumbents still prevailed, the average margin of victory (29 percent) was nearly 20 points lower (48 percent) in 2005 (Fauss 2009). However, while the average margin of victory may have been lower, it still constituted a "landslide" in a year when voter anger against incumbents in New York City probably reached new heights.

It appears that incumbency and the higher costs faced by insurgents (as well as the fund-raising advantages enjoyed by incumbents) are considerations that prospective candidates take into account. In 1991, 1997, and 2001, the unusually large number of open seats attracted many candidates. In 1993, with only two open seats, the number of candidates declined precipitously.[25] In 2003 and 2005, with few open seats, the number of candidates declined. These results clearly demonstrate that incumbency is a formidable barrier to competition, regardless of whether or not public funds are available to subsidize candidates.

While public financing may mitigate the cost factor, it does not address incumbency. Competition tends to occur where open seats exist, independent of the availability of public funds.

A second area to examine is the degree of competition in an election. Has campaign finance reform in New York resulted in core competitive elections?

It appears that campaign finance reform has had little bearing on the "competitiveness" of elections (Table 5.5). City Council Democratic prima-

TABLE 5.5.   NUMBER OF CANDIDATES FOR CITYWIDE OFFICES, BOROUGH PRESIDENT, AND CITY COUNCIL IN DEMOCRATIC PRIMARIES, 1981–2009

Year	Mayor	Comptroller	Public Advocate	Borough President	City Council
1981	3	2	3	2	N/A
1982	N/A	N/A	N/A	N/A	47
1985	3	3	6	8	59
1989	4	5	3	2	30
1991	N/A	N/A	N/A	N/A	162
1993	3	3	6	2	49
1997	5	0	3	6	70
2001	5	2	7	9	202
2003	N/A	N/A	N/A	N/A	57
2005	6	0	6	9	85
2009	3	4	5	3	120

Sources: New York Times, September 23, 1981, B4; September 25, 1982, 33; September 11, 1985, B4; September 14, 1989, B2; September 15, 1993, B11. 1991 data from New York City CFB 1992, 108–135. Data for 1997, 2001, 2003, 2005, and 2009 from New York City Board of Elections, Statement and Return of the Votes for the aforementioned primaries.

ries offer the best opportunity for evaluating the competitive level of electoral contests. For purposes of this study, "competitive" elections are defined as those where the margin between the winning and second-place candidates is 10 percent or less.

In 1985, the last cycle prior to public financing, six of the twenty races were "competitive." Only 1991, a reapportionment year when the City Council's size was expanded from thirty-five to fifty-one, yielded a higher proportion of competitive races (41.5 percent). In 1989, 1993, 2003, and 2005, four cycles featuring few open seats, there was actually a smaller proportion of contested races than in 1985. In 1997, despite more open seats (eight), there were fewer competitive races than in 1993. As for the general election, the availability of public funds has not ended the Democratic Party's hegemony. There has not been more than one competitive council race in each of the last seven general elections (Table 5.6). One might believe that the public

TABLE 5.6.   "COMPETITIVE" CITY COUNCIL CONTESTS, DEMOCRATIC PRIMARIES, AND GENERAL ELECTIONS, 1985–2009

	Contested Seats	Competitive Seats
Primary election		
1985	20	6 (30%)
1989	12	2 (16.7%)
1991	36	15 (41.5%)
1993	19	5 (26.3%)
1997	23	4 (17.4%)
2001	45	8 (17.8%)
2003	23	1 (4.3%)
2005	24	1 (4.1%)
2009	31	11 (35.5%)
General election		
1985	35	1 (2.8%)
1989	35	0
1991	51	1 (1.9%)
1993	51	1 (1.9%)
1997	51	1 (1.9%)
2001	51	1 (1.9%)
2003	51	0
2005	51	0
2009	51	2 (3.9%)

Sources: New York Times, September 11, 1985, B4; November 7, 1985, B6; September 11, 1989, B2; November 9, 1989, B6; September 15, 1993, B11; November 3, 1993, B5. Data for 1991 from New York City CFB 1992, 108–135. Data for 1997 from the New York City Board of Elections. Data for 2001, 2003, 2005, and 2009 from the New York City Board of Elections, Statement and Return of Votes for the elections of the aforementioned year.

financing could result in more competitive general-election contests. That has not been the case.

In the 1993 election cycle, a new loophole was exploited. As noted earlier, a key provision of the statute mandated that participants received two dollars of public funds for every dollar they raise when a nonparticipant triggers the "bonus" by reaching specified thresholds. In addition, participants are then exempt from spending limits.

The two-for-one rule was put to the test in a Brooklyn council district where a nonparticipating candidate evaded the penalty by failing to file state-required financial reports. While it was obvious that the candidate had spent far more than the threshold amount, the participating candidate was denied the bonus because there was no proof that his opponent had exceeded the threshold. State law provides for less stringent reporting requirements and spending and contribution limits, and the penalties for noncompliance are trivial.[26] As a result, the CFB changed its policy. The board would "rely on other information to determine whether the double matching rate has been triggered" (New York City CFB 1997, 27).

In 2004 the City Council enacted Local Law Number 59, which requires nonparticipating candidates to comply with the Campaign Finance Board's requirements for campaign finance disclosure and to submit to audits of their accounts by the Campaign Finance Board. This law makes it possible for the Campaign Finance Board to determine when a nonparticipant triggers the thresholds for bonus matching funds. There are questions as to whether the program, which is essentially a spending program of the government of the City of New York, can impose requirements on nonparticipating candidates beyond those established in the New York State Election Law.

Public Education

The Campaign Finance Board publishes a voter guide for municipal elections, and citywide candidates who are participants in the program must participate in debates. There is no evidence that the voter guides, which contain one-page statements that are submitted by the candidates in the summer of the election year, have contributed to greater knowledge on the part of the electorate.

As for the mandated debates, it is not clear that they have any more of an impact on the electorate than the voter guides. Also, there have usually been other debates during the election season, giving the CFB-sponsored debates no great significance.

Changes for 2009

The City Council enacted a number of changes in the program for the 2009 election cycle, when all three citywide elected officials, four of the five borough presidents, and as many as thirty-six of the present council members would have been term-limited.[27]

Contributions from limited liability corporations (LLCs), limited liability partnerships (LLPs), and partnerships are prohibited after January 1, 2008. The definition of "intermediary" was broadened. Since the program's inception, the contribution had to be physically collected by the "bundler." Under the new statute, any individual who solicits money on behalf of a campaign with the campaign's knowledge shall be considered an intermediary. This redefinition eliminates a loophole whereby many bundlers could avoid identification by merely soliciting the contributions rather than gathering them.

The new legislation also addressed the issue of "pay to play"—that is, the perception that contributing to political campaigns facilitates doing business with the government. Under legislation that took effect on February 2, 2008, contributions from New York City residents who "do business" with the City of New York are no longer "matchable" for public-funds payments (Table 5.7). In addition, lower contribution limits apply to individuals who "do business." They are limited to contributions no greater than $400 to candidates for mayor, public advocate, and comptroller; $320 to candidates for borough president; and $250 to candidates for the City Council.

By sharply reducing the amount that those doing business with the city could give to candidates, as well as by making their contributions ineligible for match, the goal was to reduce the influence of these contributors to candidates for municipal office.

TABLE 5.7.   CONTRIBUTIONS FROM DONORS DOING BUSINESS WITH THE CITY OF NEW YORK, 2009

Office	Number of Candidates Receiving Donations	Number of Contributors Doing Business Transactions	Amount Contributed by Those Doing Business	Amount Refunded	Average Contribution
Mayor	3	234	$69,044	$21,180	$205
Public advocate	5	525	$152,600	$42,465	$209
Comptroller	5	485	$198,844	$81,150	$243
Borough president	10	381	$111,021	$15,086	$252
City council	138	2,086	$414,797	$92,235	$155

Source: New York City Campaign Finance Board, 2010. Doing Business Contributions Summary, February 9, 2010.

Conclusion

The Campaign Finance Act, regarded as a landmark in election law reform, is an ambitious and comprehensive statute. The law limits contributions and expenditures, requires greater financial disclosure, and encourages participation. Like most ambitious reforms, there has been some success, some failure, some change, and some unintended outcomes.

Campaign finance reform has slowed the growth of expenditure in citywide races and forced candidates to broaden their fund-raising efforts. The days when citywide candidates could rely on a small coterie of lawyers, lobbyists, and real estate developers to directly finance their campaigns are over. However, "bundling" of campaign contributions by intermediaries and "independent expenditures" by state party organizations prove that "big money" is still part the process. The statute's disclosure requirements, more detailed than those of the state law, offer great insight into the financing of political campaigns. The extension of the requirements to nonparticipants in 2005 offers the electorate a more comprehensive picture of campaign finance in New York's municipal elections.

The program has flaws. The voluntary nature of the program offers an escape hatch to well-off candidates and those willing to raise large sums of money. A public finance act cannot stop candidates from spending their personal fortunes. While the *New York Times* has used its editorial columns to urge participation, calling the program a "commitment to cleaner politics" in its April 30, 1993, edition, not all are attracted by the siren song of political reform.

Nonparticipating candidates, "bundlers," and the financial backers of noncoordinated independent campaigns have all found ways to skirt the limits in the act. In some cases, candidates without significant opposition actually spend more, since they are using public funds to do so. These expenditures allow them to help other candidates or generate higher levels of name recognition for future campaigns. The framers of the legislation surely did not have this result in mind when they crafted the bill. Subsequent efforts to limit spending by candidates with token opposition by requiring them to write a letter seeking the funds have not been a meaningful deterrent.

It would be difficult to assert that the program has increased competition. There were actually fewer city council candidates and a smaller proportion of "competitive" council seats in 2003 than in 1985. The law cannot control for the advantage of incumbency. Indeed, it is difficult to ascertain, as far as City Council elections are concerned, whether the problems the program addresses are real. Few candidates (including incumbents) spent anywhere near the amounts allowed under the program in the years prior to its creation. Indeed, the increased availability of public funds has fueled the increase in spending by council candidates since the program's establishment.

Candidates had become increasingly willing to forgo the program, concluding that the program's requirements and compliance efforts were not worth the money. As a result, the council amended the Campaign Finance Act to require, beginning in 2005, nonparticipants to comply with the program's disclosure and audit requirements.

Other nonparticipants have opted out of the program for strategic reasons. While their opponent might receive "bonus" funding, they still must raise funds in conformance with the statute. They must also spend money in conformance with the more rigorous local law. Public financing may make some candidates viable, but it does not neutralize incumbency or a self-financed nonparticipant, as Michael Bloomberg proved in 2001, 2005, and 2009. Given the existing political environment (the incumbency advantage, dominance by the Democratic Party in council elections, ballot access requirements, the complications of an urban setting), it seems unlikely that public funds alone will smash the barriers to political participation.

While enhanced financial disclosure provides the electorate with more information about the candidates, there is no empirical evidence that this has resulted in a more aware electorate. Levels of competition and the efforts of the candidates seem to be the more important variables that influence voter turnout.

As for the CFB, it is threatened with entanglement in what is often the contact sport of New York City politics. Mayor Giuliani's effort to appoint one of his supporters to the CFB on the morning when the body was considering sanctioning the mayor's campaign is an example of how the board can be politicized.[28] Councilmember Kenneth Fisher, in testimony before the CFB, warned, "there's no guarantee . . . that every decision for all time is going to be made on the merits" (New York City CFB 1991b, 117).

Political candidates now see the CFB as another arena in which to challenge their opponents. Complaints for violations of the Campaign Finance Act have become more commonplace. Even when complaints are groundless, they serve as a diversion, as staff and funds are expended to respond to the complaint, and serve to delay the receipt of public funds (since the CFB will not disburse funds until complaints are adjudicated). Here, participants are at a disadvantage; nonparticipants, while not required to adhere to the act, can initiate actions against candidates who are in the program. Public financing, while "leveling" the playing field in some areas, has created new hazards in the political landscape.

The city's program demonstrates the limits of campaign finance reform. Some reform objectives will remain beyond reach simply because finances, while important, may be only one of a number of factors affecting the outcome. Even where finances are decisive, until meaningful reform takes place at the state level, the dual system of campaign finance in New York City reduces participation in public finance to a strategic political decision based more on candidates' ability to raise money (or be willing to self-finance) than on their commitment to "cleaner" politics.

Self-financed candidates, like Mayor Bloomberg, demonstrate the inherent weakness of the program. The changes implemented in 2009 address the important issues of "bundling" and "pay to play." How effective these changes will be in the long term remains to be seen.

After eight cycles, New York's experiment in campaign finance reform is a cautionary tale for those who believe that reducing the influence of money will transform the political process.

NOTES

1. Local Law No. 8 of 1988.

2. For more on Koch era scandals, see Newfield and Barrett (1988).

3. Leichter found that New York's real estate boom of the mid-1980s had an impact on campaign contributions made to members of the City's Board of Estimate (the mayor, City Council president, comptroller, and the five borough presidents), which had final authority on land use matters. The donors Leichter cited were 60 Hudson Street Associates (the board approved a $40 million lease of this property by the Department of Correction in November 1985); Morgan Stanley, Forest City Associates, Ian Bruce Eichner, and Barney's (recipients of zoning variances for projects in 1985); William Zeckendorf (given approval to build a mixed-use project in Union Square in January 1985); Jack and Burton Resnick (beneficiaries of modifications in the Lower Manhattan Mixed Use Zone, where they constructed an office tower); Shearson Lehman–American Express (in June 1984 the board authorized the sale of city-owned land to the firm for the construction of a computer facility); Olympia and York (the board gave the firm approval to sell individual structures in its World Financial Center complex); and George Klein, Michael Lazar, Larry Silverstein, Nederlander Theaters, and Jujcamyn Theaters (players in the Times Square Redevelopment Project).

4. The five were Donald Trump ($350,000), Gerald Guterman ($349,000), Robert Brennan ($310,000), Seymour Cohn ($297,000), and Bear, Stearns and Company ($268,000) (Leichter 1986).

5. A brief history of the statute can be found in New York City CFB 1990, 9–12.

6. Two members are mayoral appointees and must not be members of the same political party. The city council speaker appoints two members who cannot belong to the same party. The mayor, in consultation with the speaker, selects the chairperson. Members serve staggered five-year terms and can be removed only for cause. CFB members must be registered voters in the city of New York, and cannot take part in any campaign under the panel's jurisdiction.

7. The City Charter was revised to bar participating candidates from accepting corporate contributions.

8. For a discussion of New York's ballot access laws, considered the most byzantine in the United States, see Scarrow (1983).

9. From the program's inception, candidates had to sign up no later than the thirtieth day before the first day to submit designating petitions, or, if petitions are not filed, within seven days after nomination.

10. Contributions were originally matched to a maximum of $1,000 per donor. When the match was increased to a four-to-one ratio, the first $250 contributed was matched. With the increase in the match to six to one for the 2009 municipal elections, the first $175 contributed is matched.

11. Mayor Giuliani had proposed a complete ban on corporate contributions. The City Council, which was divided on the question, adopted a two-tiered structure. The purpose of the enhanced match was to offer an incentive to candidates to forgo corporate contributions. Candidates who continued accepting corporate contributions would receive matching public funds at the existing one-to-one ratio.

12. The mayor's position was supported by an opinion issued by the Corporation Counsel, the city's law department. Opinion of the Corporation Counsel 1-98 (December 29, 1998). The Corporation Counsel is appointed by, and serves at the pleasure of, the mayor.

13. *City of New York v. The New York City Campaign Finance Board*, Index No. 400550/01 Sup. Ct. N.Y. Cty., February 20, 2001.

14. The proportion of funds raised by intermediaries may actually have been underreported. A bundler could encourage those solicited to make their contributions directly to the campaign, instead of giving their check to the intermediary. This practice would not be considered, by the CFB's definition, bundling. Local Law 34 of 2007 makes solicitation, even if the contribution is submitted directly to the campaign, bundling if the solicitation is undertaken with the knowledge of the campaign.

15. The U. S. Supreme Court, in *Buckley v. Valeo*, ruled that restrictions on "independent expenditures" were unconstitutional as long as there is no coordination between a candidate and the independent effort.

16. In 1991 the CFB fined Mayor Koch's campaign committee $35,000 for violating limits on contributions and expenditures in the 1989 campaign. The agency's auditors found that Koch's campaign spent $84,785 more than permitted (Strom 1991). In 1993 the Dinkins campaign was fined $320,000 for overspending during the 1993 primary (McKinley 1993a).

17. The leading spender was David Rothenberg, who spent $258,368 (source: campaign disclosure filed with the New York City Board of Elections).

18. Thomas Duane, a candidate who spent $163,000, testified that he decided not to participate in the program because the spending limit was "not a realistic amount of money" (New York City CFB 1991a, 6).

19. Messinger polled 84.4 percent in the primary and 83.1 percent in the general election. (New York City Board of Elections 2005).

20. According to disclosure statements furnished by their committees for the 1993 election cycle, Messinger spent $732,159; Ferrer, $1,319,932, and Millard, $229,389.

21. In 1993, Messinger sent out mail urging Mayor Dinkins's reelection, and Millard distributed literature featuring Mr. Giuliani. Millard was an unsuccessful congressional candidate in 1996, and Peter Vallone was a candidate for governor in 1998. Ferrer and

Messinger ran for mayor in 1997 (Ferrer withdrew before the primary to run for reelection as Bronx borough president).

22. New York City Administrative Code 3-705(7)(c). Candidates could still seek the maximum amount of public funds if they were opposed by a participating candidate who had qualified for public funds, if the Campaign Finance Board had determined that a participating candidate was opposed by a candidate who had raised or spent more than one-fifth of the program's expenditure limit for the office being contested, or if a candidate submitted a written statement requested the additional funds and the reasons that such funds were required.

23. The four candidates were Yvette Clarke, Helen Diane Foster, Oliver Koppell, and Christine Quinn.

24. Actually, at the beginning of the designating petition process there were no open seats. Pedro Espada, Jr., who represented the Parkchester, Castle Hill, and Soundview neighborhoods of the Bronx, announced that he would not seek reelection and would substitute his son, Pedro G. Espada, on the Democratic Primary Ballot (Kappstatter 2003). On July 23, 2003, City Councilman James Davis was assassinated in City Hall by one of his political opponents, Othniel Askew. Davis's brother, Geoffrey Davis, replaced him as the Democratic Party candidate.

25. In 1993 only two incumbents, Susan Alter and Sam Horowitz, chose not to run for reelection. Alter gave up her seat to run as Giuliani's "fusion" running mate for public advocate. After losing the Democratic primary, she ran as the Republican-Liberal candidate. She was defeated in the general election by Mark Green, the Democrat. Horowitz, who had served for two decades, retired.

26. Section 14-126 (1) of the State Election Law provides that the maximum penalty for failing to file a financial statement is $100 (New York State Board of Elections 1988a, 27).

27. Intro. No. 586-A was introduced by the speaker of the council, Christine Quinn, and was cosponsored by twenty-five members and Public Advocate Betsy Gotbaum, in conjunction with Mayor Bloomberg. It was enacted as Local Law 34 of 2007 on June 27, 2007, and was signed by Mayor Bloomberg on July 3, 2007.

28. The mayor attempted to appoint Joseph Erazo to the CFB as the body was considering sanctioning the Giuliani campaign for accepting illegal contributions. Erazo was not permitted to sit because the Department of Investigation had not completed its background investigation.

REFERENCES

Adamany, David W., and George E. Agree. 1975. *Political Money: A Strategy for Campaign Financing in America*. Baltimore: Johns Hopkins University Press.

Alexander, Herbert E. 1991. *Reform and Reality: The Financing of State and Local Campaigns*. New York: Twentieth Century Press.

Alexander, Herbert E., and Brian A. Haggerty. 1984. *PACs and Parties: Relationships and Interrelationships*. Los Angeles: Citizen's Research Foundation, University of Southern California.

Barbanel, Josh. 1985. "Leichter Says Builders Gave Most to Members of Board of Estimate." *New York Times*, November 27, p. B4.

Barron, Charles. 2003. Letter to the Campaign Finance Board, dated August 6.

———. 2005. Letter to the Campaign Finance Board, dated August 9.

Berkey-Gerard, Mark. 2003. "Campaign War Chests." *Gotham Gazette*, November 3. Available at http://www.gothamgazette.com/article/2003-11-03.00:00:00/202/617.

Brecher, Charles, and Raymond D. Horton (with Robert A. Cropf and Dean Michael Mead). 1993. *Power Failure: New York City Politics and Policy since 1960*. New York: Oxford University Press.

Buckley v. Valeo. 1976. 424 U. S. 1.

Chappell, Henry W., Jr. 1982. "Campaign Contributions and Congressional Voting: A Simultaneous Probit-Tobit Model." *Review of Economics and Statistics* 64 (February): 77–83.

Editorial. 2001. *New York Daily News*, October 29, p. 40.

Fauss, Rachael. 2009. "New York City Council Races Get More Competitive." *Gotham Gazette* (December). Available at http://www.gothamgazette.com/article/governing/20091216/17/3127.

Frendreis, John P., and Richard W. Waterman. 1985. "PAC Contributions and Legislative Behavior: Senate Voting on Trucking Deregulation." *Social Science Quarterly* 66 (June): 401–412.

Grenzke, Janet M. 1989. "PACs and the Congressional Supermarket: The Currency Is Complex." *American Journal of Political Science* 33 (February): 1–24.

Hicks, Jonathan P. 2005a. "Finance Rule Violation Charged in Manhattan Borough Race." *New York Times*, September 12, p. 49

———. 2005b. "Tie to Labor Called a Plus, But Is It an Unfair Edge?" *New York Times*, August 27.

Kappstatter, Bob. 2003. "Espada Rules Out New Run—Puts Son on Dem Primary Ballot." *New York Daily News*, July 16.

Kraus, Jeffrey. 1999. "Public Funding and Political Campaigns in New York City: The Limits of Reform." In Paul E. Scheele, *"We Get What We Vote For . . . Or Do We?" The Impact of Elections on Governing*, 82–100. Westport, CT: Praeger.

———. 2006. "Campaign Finance Reform Reconsidered: New York City's Public Finance Program after 15 Years." *The Forum* 3, no. 4, art. 6. Available at http://www.bepress.com/forum/vol3/iss4/art6.

Leichter, Franz S. 1985. "Study of Campaign Contributions by State Senator Franz Leichter."

———. 1986. "Campaign Contributions to Members of the Board of Estimate and the Democratic County Committees, 1981–1986." A Report by State Senator Franz Leichter, 28th Senate District, Manhattan.

Lynn, Frank. 1989a. "Candidates Ask for More Public Campaign Money." *New York Times*, December 14, p. B2.

———. 1989b "Finance Law Called a Partial Success." *New York Times*, November 12, p. 42.

———. 1989c. "Stein Attacked on Campaign Finance Refusal." *New York Times*, January 25, p. B3.

Mayhew, David R. 1974. *Congress: The Electoral Connection*. New Haven, CT: Yale University Press.

McIntire, Mike. 2004. "Council Defeats Veto of Increase in Public Funds for Some Races." *New York Times*, December 16, p. A1.

McKinley, James C., Jr. 1993a. "Campaign Finance Board Fines Dinkins over Spending." *New York Times*, October 21, p. 1.

———. 1993b. "A Costly Council Victory ($70 a Vote to Be Precise)." *New York Times*, March 27, p. 24.

————. 1993c. "Dinkins Campaign to Pay Party Panel for Some Ads." *New York Times*, October 20, p. B2.

————. 1993d. "Steering around the New York City Campaign Finance Law." *New York Times*, December 26, p. 33.

Nelson, Michael. 2003. Letter to the New York City Campaign Finance Board, dated September 18.

Newfield, Jack, and Wayne Barrett. 1988. *City for Sale: Ed Koch and the Betrayal of New York*. New York: Harper and Row.

New York City Board of Elections. 1998. "1997 Annual Report of the Board of Elections in the City of New York." January.

————. 2001. "Statement and Return of the Votes for Various Offices."

————. 2002. "2001 Annual Report of the Board of Elections in the City of New York." January.

————. 2009. "Statement and Return Report for Certification General Election 2009—11/03/2009 Crossover—All Parties and Independent Bodies: Mayor, Citywide, Vote for 1." November 24.

New York City Campaign Finance Board (CFB). 1990. "Dollars and Disclosure: Campaign Finance Reform in New York City," September.

————. 1991a. "1991 Post-Election Public Hearings," Transcript. December 11. Carol Mele and Catherine M. Donohue, reporters.

————. 1991b. "1991 Post-Election Public Hearings," Transcript. December 12. Carol Mele and Catherine M. Donohue, reporters.

————. 1992. "Windows of Opportunity: Campaign Finance Reform and the New City Council," July.

————. 1993. "New York City Campaign Finance Board Holds Public Hearings Today and Tomorrow Following the 1993 Elections." Press release. December 8.

————. 1994. "Types of Contributors." Data as of April 5 (draft).

————. 1997. "Campaign Finance Handbook." January.

————. 1998a."A Decade of Reform: 1988–1998." September.

————. 1998b. "2001 Disclosure Guide." March.

————. 2002. "An Election Interrupted: The Campaign Finance Program and the 2001 New York City Elections." September.

————. 2004. "Campaign Finance Handbook."

————. 2006. "Public Dollars for the Public Good: A Report on the 2005 Elections." September.

————. 2008. "CFB Assesses Penalties against Two Campaigns." Press release. January 17.

————. 2009a. "Certified Statements of Need (General)." Available at http://www.nyccfb. info/reports/stnp_09.htm?sm=press.

————. 2009b. "Certified Statements of Need (Primary)." Available at http://www.nyccfb. info/reports/stnp_09.htm?sm=press.

————. 2010. "Campaign Finance Summary: 2009 Citywide Elections. Available at http:// www.nyccfb.info/VSApps/WebForm_Finance_Summary.aspx?as_election_cycle =2009&sm=press_&sm=candidates_cfs.

New York 1. 2005. "Road to City Hall." Television program. March 28. New York: New York 1 News.

New York Public Interest Research Group. 1987. "Wanted: A Government That Money Can't Buy."

————. 1993. "Testimony of Neal Rosenstein and Gene Russianoff, Government Reform Coordinator and Senior Attorney, New York Public Interest Research Group, Inc.

before the New York City Campaign Finance Board hearing on Impact of Campaign Finance Program and Voter Guide on 1993 City Elections." December 8.

New York State Board of Elections. 1988. "Guide to Campaign Financial Disclosure."

New York State Commission on Government Integrity. 1988. "Unfinished Business."

Phillips, Kevin, and Paul Blackman. 1975. *Electoral Reform and Voter Participation*. Stanford, CA: American Enterprise System.

Piven, Frances Fox, and Richard Cloward. 1988. *Why Americans Don't Vote*. New York: Pantheon.

Ryan, Paul. 2003. *A Statute of Liberty: How New York City's Campaign Finance Law Is Changing the Face of Local Elections*. Los Angeles: Center for Governmental Studies.

Sabato, Larry. 1989. *Paying for Elections: The Campaign Finance Thicket*. New York: Priority Press Publications.

Scarrow, Howard A. 1983. *Parties, Elections, and Representation in the State of New York*. New York: New York University Press.

Scheele, Paul E., ed. 1999. *"We Get What We Vote For . . . Or Do We?" The Impact of Elections on Governing*. Westport, CT: Praeger.

Seifman, David. 2007. "Haul of Shame Game." *New York Post*, October 13.

Sorauf, Frank. 1984. *What Price PACs? Report of the Twentieth Century Fund Task Force on Political Action Committees*. New York: Twentieth Century Fund.

Strom, Stephanie. 1991. "Koch's Campaign Panel Fined $35,000 for '89 Race." *New York Times*, May 22, p. B3.

Welch, William P. 1982. "Campaign Contributions and Legislative Voting: Milk Money and Dairy Price Supports." *Western Political Quarterly* 35 (December): 478–495.

Wilhite, Allen, and John Theilmann. 1987. "Labor PAC Contributions and Labor Legislation: A Simultaneous Logit Approach." *Public Choice* 53:267–276.

Wolfinger, Raymond, and Steven Rosenstone. 1980. *Who Votes?* New Haven, CT: Yale University Press.

Wright, John R. 1985. "PACs, Contributions, and Roll Calls: An Organizational Perspective." *American Political Science Review* 79 (June): 400–414.

6

◇ ◇ ◇

Leveling the Playing Field

Publicly Financed Campaigns
and Electoral Competition

COSTAS PANAGOPOULOS

imited electoral competition is a key feature of contemporary elections in the United States for all levels of office (McDonald and
Samples 2006; Panagopoulos and Green 2008b). High—and mount-
ing—incumbent reelection rates alarm critics who believe officeholders have
become impervious to serious challenges, potentially diminishing responsiveness to public preferences, enhancing the prospects for corruption, and
compromising the very nature of democracy and representation.

In the face of such disquieting possibilities, reformers in recent decades
have renewed calls to identify policy solutions designed to promote competition in elections. Proposals considered in jurisdictions across the country, as
well as in the U.S. Congress, include the adoption of term limits for elected
officials and redistricting reform to protect against brazen gerrymandering.
In addition, a series of campaign finance reform measures have been con-
templated, or adopted, to the same end, including campaign contribution
and spending limits and regulated advertising. Within the category of such
campaign finance reform schemes, activists have endorsed public financing
of campaigns as an effective policy response to declining competition and
mounted nationwide efforts to promote the adoption of public financing policies. As other chapters in this volume note, the "clean elections" movement
has succeeded in passing public financing policies in several states across
the country.

Advocates commonly promote clean elections proposals on the grounds
that publicly financed campaigns enhance electoral competition. They argue

that public financing reduces fund-raising advantages that incumbents, in particular, routinely enjoy over challengers, thereby leveling the playing field and reducing the number of lopsided election results (Mayer, Werner, and Williams 2006). Public financing would also enable challengers to overcome barriers to entry by providing reliable sources of funding (Basham and Polhill 2005).

Opponents of public financing are skeptical about these claims. Critics argue that public finance programs masquerade as political reform while they are actually designed to protect incumbents (Wallison and Gora 2009, 55). Among other problematic aspects, critics believe spending or expenditure limits typically associated with participation in public financing programs are "inevitably and invariably protective of incumbents" (ibid., 63). They assert that "in the real world . . . incumbents will not enact public financing programs unless they contain various limitations that protect them against well-funded challengers" (ibid., 70). In some respects, these arguments accord with scholarly research which finds that election outcomes are influenced significantly by levels of challenger spending but not necessarily by incumbent spending (Jacobson 1978, 1990; Abramowitz 1991; Gerber 2004). Thus efforts to limit campaign expenditures may indeed prove disproportionately beneficial to incumbents. Moreover, some contend that aspects of clean elections measures are actually unconstitutional. A report critical of public funding initiatives issued by the Center for Competitive Politics summarizes its view as follows: "Government-financed elections are the ultimate fool's gold of campaign finance regulation . . . [and] a poor use of taxpayer dollars" (quoted in Wallison and Gora 2009, 78).

The impact of other, standard elements of public financing programs—evenhanded grants or subsidies to all participating candidates, for example—on electoral outcomes is also an open question. Empirical assessments of these claims are linked to the long-standing, unsettled debate among political scientists about campaign spending effects. While some believe spending by challengers is more effective than spending by incumbents, perhaps reflecting challengers' relative obscurity (Jacobson 1978, 1990; Abramowitz 1991; Gerber 2004), others find incumbent and challenger spending effects to be similar (Green and Krasno 1988, 1990; Levitt 1994; Erikson and Palfrey 2000), with challengers enjoying a smaller edge in spending efficiency than suggested by early studies. All these studies, however, imply that policies that grant resources to both incumbents and challengers will advantage challengers because of diminishing marginal returns. The average incumbent outspends the average challenger, so an equal grant to both candidates should work to the challenger's advantage. In this regard, public finance programs designed to provide such evenhanded support should render elections more competitive.

Researchers have devoted considerable attention to examining the empirical evidence about the impact of public financing programs on electoral competition, relying almost exclusively on observational approaches, but mixed and inconclusive findings have only exacerbated the tension between advocates and opponents of these reforms. In a study of state-level public financing efforts, Malbin and Gais (1998, 137) concluded, "There is no evidence to support the claim that programs combining public funding with spending limits have leveled the playing field, countered the effects of incumbency, and made elections more competitive." Similarly, a recent examination of gubernatorial races from 1978 to 2004 conducted by Primo, Milyo, and Groseclose reveals "no statistically or substantively significant impact of public funding on electoral competitiveness" (2006, 280). By contrast, Mayer, Werner, and Williams argue that there is "compelling evidence that Arizona and Maine have become much more competitive states in the wake of the 1998 clean elections programs" (2006, 263), but public financing programs have had only minimal impact on competition in Minnesota, Hawaii, and Wisconsin. Still, the authors assert, "there is no merit in the argument that public funding programs amount to an incumbent-protection act" (Mayer, Werner, and Williams 2006, 264).

As this brief summary of recent scholarship suggests, the impact of public financing on electoral competition remains disputable. In this chapter, I turn to available field experimental evidence to investigate this matter further. Bringing evidence from randomized experiments to bear on this enduring question overcomes many of the challenges associated with observational studies, facilitating reliable causal inference that can shed light on the debate over the impact of aspects of public funding programs.

The ideal randomized field experiment to test the impact of varying funding levels on election outcomes would assign fund allocations to actual candidates at random. While it would be infeasible in practice to design such a study, a series of randomized field experiments conducted recently by Panagopoulos and Green (2008a, 2008b) are instructive. The experiments, conducted in 2005 and 2006, assigned voters in randomly selected jurisdictions to be exposed to nonpartisan radio advertising campaigns in the week leading up to the November general elections. (See next section for treatment details.) The advertisements reminded voters about the upcoming elections and provided minimal information about the main candidates. In each case, the names of both incumbents and challengers were provided to voters. As such, the radio advertising intervention can be viewed as a publicity outlay of equal value to both candidates in a race, thereby simulating a scenario in which both candidates (incumbent and challenger) receive funds in a manner that approximates the design of some public funding programs. Since randomization ensures that treatment and control groups are balanced in terms of expected vote-share outcomes as well as other observable and unobservable covariates (candidate spending, media attention, election salience, and competitiveness, for instance), any differences in the observed outcomes would be a function of the intervention—in this case, a radio campaign designed to imitate a grant of equal size to candidates in the race. Summaries of the experimental procedures and results follow.

The 2005 Mayoral Experiment and 2006 Replication

The first two experiments, which are described in this section, were conducted in the context of mayoral elections taking place in 2005 and 2006. The basic experimental procedures followed a matched-pair design. From the population of municipalities holding mayoral elections in November 2005, Panagopoulos and Green (2008a) identified twenty-eight pairs of cities that were balanced based on matching criteria thought to affect electoral competition, including voter turnout in the previous mayoral election, incumbent vote share in the previous mayoral election, whether mayoral elections are partisan or nonpartisan, and whether the 2005 mayoral election was contested. All the cities and towns included in the final sample were municipalities in which the local executive is selected by popular vote (as opposed to appointment by the city or town council). The matching exercise was conducted to ensure that the treatment and control groups were as similar as possible in terms of observable characteristics. Once completed, one city in each pair was randomly assigned to be treated with the radio campaign, while voters in the control cities were not exposed to any advertisements. Depending on costs associated with radio advertising in each locality, voters in treatment cities were exposed to 50, 70, or 90 gross-ratings points (GRPs) of radio advertising. In 2006 identical procedures were used to conduct a smaller-scale replication involving eleven matched pairs of cities holding mayoral elections.[1]

Following is the sample radio script that was used for Syracuse, New York:

> Many people don't realize how important local government is. But think about it. Your local government is in charge of things that affect your life every day: police protection, transportation, garbage

collection, tax assessment. From fire departments to libraries to safe drinking water—it's all part of local government.

Here's where you come in: Voting. If you're a registered voter in SYRACUSE, you have an opportunity to shape the direction of your city by electing the mayor and other local officials. On Tuesday, November 8th residents of SYRACUSE will vote to decide whether to RE-elect Democratic MAYOR MATTHEW DRISCOLL or to support his opponent Republican JOANNIE MAHONEY.

Take part in shaping your city's future. Be sure to vote on November 8th.

Paid for by the Institution for Social and Policy Studies, a non-partisan organization that encourages citizens to take an active role in their communities.

Mayoral races involved contested incumbents in forty-nine (out of seventy-eight) cases in the combined (2005 and 2006) experiments. Following the elections, candidate vote shares were obtained and analyzed to determine the impact of the intervention. Restricting the analysis to the cases with contested incumbents, the most conservative experimental results described in Panagopoulos and Green (2008a) suggest that 100 GRPs of radio advertising *lowered* incumbent vote shares by 7.8 percentage points on average. At an average cost of $75 per GRP of radio advertising, the intervention can be viewed as providing a $7,500 name recognition-enhancing grant in an even-handed fashion to both challengers and incumbents in these contests. All else equal, the evidence suggests such an intervention would raise challenger performance substantially. Consistent with claims about campaign spending effects, and based on these results, we conclude public finance laws that allocate resources evenly to incumbents and challengers will likely enhance electoral competitiveness.

The 2006 Congressional Experiment Targeting Latino Voters with Spanish-Language Radio Advertisements

The initial, field experimental results reported in Panagopoulos and Green (2008a) suggested that the radio intervention stimulated electoral competition in mayoral races. The task remained to examine whether or not such an intervention would operate similarly in different electoral contexts or targeting select voter populations. To investigate these questions, we conducted a parallel, large-scale field experimental extension in the November 2006 congressional elections targeting Latino voters with Spanish-language radio advertisements. In this experiment, 206 congressional districts across the United States that featured minimally contested incumbents were randomly assigned to be exposed to 50, 75, or 100 GRPs of radio advertising, depending on advertising costs in treatment districts. Overall, thirty-six districts were assigned to the treatment group, as the experiment was not a matched-pair design. The content of the radio appeal was similar to that used in the mayoral experiments, with the identification of the incumbents and challengers as the key ingredient.[2] Following is the English-language translation of the script used in Florida's Twenty-fourth Congressional District:

> Many people don't realize how important the upcoming congressional election is. But think about it. Our representative in Congress deals with the biggest issues confronting our country: immigration, taxes, education, war—it's all part of what makes Congress so important.
>
> Here's where you come in: voting. If you're a registered voter, you have an opportunity to shape the direction of your country by electing your member of Congress. On Tuesday, November 7th people in Florida's Twenty-fourth Congressional District will vote to decide whether to reelect Republican Congressman Tom Feeney or to support his opponent Democrat Clint Curtis.
>
> Take part in shaping your country's future. Be sure to vote on November 7th.
>
> Paid for by the Institution for Social and Policy Studies, a nonpartisan organization that encourages citizens to participate in public affairs.

The outcome measures necessary to estimate treatment effects in this experiment were congressional-district vote data among Latino voters. Since these data are not readily available, we gathered vote data for high-density Latino precincts (precincts in which a majority of voters were Hispanic) in order to gauge how Latinos voted in the elections. Reliable vote data for majority-Latino precincts were obtained for a total of eighty-three congressional districts, and these data were analyzed to estimate treatment effects. Consistent with the findings in the mayoral experiments, our most conservative estimates suggested that 100 GRPs of radio advertising lowered congressional incumbents' vote shares by 6.1 percentage points on average among Latino voters targeted in this experiment.

The comparability of the treatment effects detected for both general and targeted (Latino) audiences and in different (mayoral and congressional) electoral conditions suggests that the radio intervention likely operates similarly across varying settings and can be generalized in a variety of contexts.

Conclusion

Taken together, the evidence yielded by the field experiments described in this chapter bolsters the long-standing argument that evenhanded campaign finance laws can elevate electoral competitiveness. Given the limitations associated with observational studies, it may take years before newly enacted public funding laws generate statistically reliable changes in the electoral competitiveness of legislative elections. In the meantime, experimental evidence of the sort summarized in this chapter offers some useful insights about the likely impact of certain types of public funding initiatives. Moreover, the magnitude of the experimental effects is worth underscoring. From a practical perspective, reducing incumbent vote shares by 6–8 percentage points with such a modest intervention may not reverse many election outcomes, but it would certainly render contests more competitive. Consider that the intervention would shrink an incumbent victory margin of 40 percentage points (such outcomes are not uncommon in the United States) by over one-third, to 28 or 24 percentage points. In closer contests, the impact could be consequential. Of course, by themselves, the experimental results described are not conclusive and are subject, as all experimental findings are, to confirmation, updating, and revision. Moreover, the manners in which elements of public financing programs (evenhanded grants, for example) interact with other features (such as spending limits) remain open questions worthy of deeper inquiry. Nevertheless, the findings provide additional support for claims that electoral competition can be enhanced by public funding programs.

NOTES

1. The description of the experiments presented here is only a summary. Readers are directed to Panagopoulos and Green 2008a for complete details about the experimental protocols.

2. See Panagopoulos and Green 2008b for complete details about the experiment.

REFERENCES

Abramowitz, Alan I. 1991. "Incumbency, Campaign Spending, and the Decline of Competition in U.S. House Elections." *Journal of Politics* 53 (1): 34–56.

Basham, Patrick, and Dennis Polhill. 2005. "Uncompetitive Elections and the American Political System." *Policy Analysis* 547:1–20. CATO Institute. June 30. Available at http://www.cato.org/pubs/pas/pa547.pdf (accessed June 22, 2009).

Erikson, Robert S., and Thomas R. Palfrey. 2000. "Equilibria in Campaign Spending Games: Theory and Data." *American Political Science Review* 94 (3): 595–603.

Gerber, Alan. 2004. "Does Campaign Spending Work?" *American Behavioral Scientist*, 47 (5): 541–574.

Green, Donald P., and Jonathan Krasno. 1988. "Salvation for the Spendthrift Incumbent: Reestimating the Effects of Campaign Spending in House Elections." *American Journal of Political Science* 32 (4): 884–907.

———. 1990. "Rebuttal to Jacobson's 'New Evidence for Old Arguments.'" *American Journal of Political Science* 34 (2): 363–372.

Jacobson, Gary C. 1978. "The Effect of Campaign Spending in Congressional Elections." *American Political Science Review* 72 (1): 469–491.

———. 1990. "The Effects of Campaign Spending in House Elections: New Evidence for Old Arguments." *American Journal of Political Science* 34 (2): 334–362.

Levitt, Steven D. 1994. "Using Repeat Challengers to Estimate the Effect of Campaign Spending on Election Outcomes in the U.S. House." *Journal of Political Economy* 102 (4): 777–798.

Malbin, Michael, and Thomas L. Gais. 1998. *The Day after Reform: Sobering Campaign Finance Lessons from the American States*. Albany, NY: Rockefeller Institute Press.

Mayer, Kenneth, Timonthy Werner, and Amanda Williams. 2006. "Do Public Funding Programs Enhance Electoral Competition?" In *The Marketplace of Democracy: Electoral Competition and American Politics*, ed. Michael McDonald and John Sample. Washington DC: Brookings Institution Press.

McDonald, Michael, and John Samples. 2006. "The Marketplace of Democracy: Normative and Empirical Issues." In *The Marketplace of Democracy: Electoral Competition and American Politics*, ed. Michael McDonald and John Samples. Washington, DC: Brookings Institution Press.

Panagopoulos, Costas, and Donald Green. 2008a. "Field Experiments Testing the Impact of Radio Advertisements on Electoral Competition." *American Journal of Political Science* 52 (1): 156–168.

———. 2008b. "Name Recognition and Incumbency Advantage: Evidence from a Mass Media Field Experiment Targeting Latino Voters." Paper presented at the annual meeting, American Political Science Association, Boston, September.

Primo, David, Jeffrey Milyo, and Tim Groseclose. 2006. "State Campaign Finance Reform, Competitiveness and Party Advantage in Gubernatorial Elections." In *The Marketplace of Democracy: Electoral Competition and American Politics*, ed. Michael McDonald and John Sample. Washington DC: Brookings Institution Press.

Wallison, Peter, and Joel Gora. 2009. *Better Parties, Better Government: A Realistic Program for Campaign Finance Reform*. Washington, DC: American Enterprise Institute Press.

7

✧ ✧ ✧

Public Financing and Candidate Participation in Gubernatorial Elections

Conor Dowling

In recent years, since the advent of full public funding of elections in Maine and Arizona in 2000, public financing of elections has received increased scholarly and media attention. Since the implementation of these new public funding systems, there has been no shortage of studies examining their effects on electoral competition (e.g., Government Accountability Office 2003; Malhotra 2008; Mayer, Werner, and Williams 2006). Like studies of the effects of public financing systems more generally (e.g., Adams 2007; Bardwell 2002; Hamm and Hogan 2008; La Raja 2007; Mayer and Wood 1995), however, no clear determination of the effect of public financing on candidate entry has been made.

In this chapter, I make three contributions to the study of the effects of public financing on candidate entry. First, I include a more complete candidate typology. In particular, I examine the effect of public funding on candidate entry to open seats, not just incumbent-defended seats, which have been the focus of previous research. I also distinguish between candidates that have held previous elective office ("experienced candidates") and those who have not ("amateur candidates"), as there is some reason to believe experienced (or "quality") candidates are more likely to be enticed by public funding. Second, I provide a theoretical framework within which the public funding of candidates is expected to operate, situating its potential effect in the standard decision-making calculus of a potential candidate for elective office (e.g., Black 1972). Third, my results suggest that under specific circumstances public financing may encourage greater candidate participation, but that on the whole public funding does not appear to be increasing the number of candidates competing in elections, at least gubernatorial elections.

The chapter proceeds in the following fashion. In the next section I present Black's (1972) decision-making calculus of potential candidates for office and discuss how public funding systems might affect this calculus. Then, I present the data on gubernatorial elections from 1980 to 1998 used to test the theoretical expectations laid out in the preceding section. Next, I present and discuss my results, and then conclude.

Public Funding of Candidates and Candidate Entry

The decision a potential candidate for office faces is relatively straightforward: If the benefits of office (discounted by the probability of victory) are greater than the costs of running for office, then the potential candidate declares candidacy. Formally, the standard decision-making calculus (Black 1972, 146) is

$$u(O) = (P \times B) - C$$

where

$u(O)$ = the utility of the target office O

P = the potential candidate's estimate of her probability of victory

B = the benefit she receives from attaining the target office

C = the costs required to obtain the target office

An ever-growing body of evidence supports the use of this calculus. Most notably, perhaps, is that the probability of winning affects candidate entry (e.g., Canon 1990; Jacobson 1989; Jacobson and Kernell 1981; Lazarus 2008a; Maestas et al. 2006; Maisel 1982; Maisel and Stone 1997; Squire 1989). Additionally, there is some evidence that the benefits from attaining office affect the willingness of candidates to enter the electoral fray (Stone, Maisel, and Maestas 2004). In terms of the costs of running for office, there is evidence that "personal" costs (e.g., Maestas et al. 2006; Stone, Maisel, and Maestas 2004) and the risk of losing her existing seat (e.g., Rohde 1979) factor into a candidate's decision-making calculus. Electoral laws (or, more broadly, institutions), such as the public funding of candidates, may also factor into a candidate's decision-making calculus by shaping the costs of running for office, but as of yet have been overlooked.

I distinguish between personal and institutional factors that may affect the costs of running for office, and focus on institutional costs (also see Black 1972; Schlesinger 1966). To do so, I modify the decision-making calculus of a potential candidate in the following fashion:

$$u(O) = (P \times B) - (C_{pers} + C_{inst})$$

where

C_{pers} = the personal cost required during a campaign
to obtain the target office

C_{inst} = the institutional impediments that need to be met
in order to obtain the target office

Modified in this fashion, the decision to enter a race occurs when the value (B) of the target office (O) in combination with the probability (P) of victory is greater than both the *personal* and *institutional* costs ($C_{pers} + C_{inst}$) of running for the target office. In other words, institutional costs may have a systematic effect on the expected utility of those considering running for office.[1]

Previous research suggests that the public funding of candidates has the capacity to assuage some of the costs associated with running for office. Such funding may make becoming a candidate less costly because it alleviates some of the burden normally placed on the candidate. For example, using a nationwide sample of candidates who ran for state legislature from 1998 to 2000, Francia and Herrnson (2003) find that publicly funded candidates spend less time over the course of their campaign devoted to fund-raising. Miller (2009) confirms the Francia and Herrnson finding, and also finds that fully funded candidates have much greater time flexibility, devoting significantly more time to voter mobilization efforts.

Thus offices in which candidates receive public funding could, in theory, alleviate part of the cost associated with becoming a candidate, which in turn increases the expected utility a potential candidate has for becoming an actual candidate. Put differently, offices that do not allow for public funding of candidates may limit candidate entry. If potential candidates consider this possibility when deciding if they should contest an election, then public funding of candidates should have a positive effect on candidate entry, resulting in more candidates contesting elections.

As public funding laws are typically enacted at the state level, we can think about how a prospective candidate's decision-making calculus looks different in those states with public funding of candidates compared to those states that do not publicly fund candidates.[2] For those states with public funding of candidates we expect

$$u(O) = (P \times B) - (C_{pers} - C_{PF})$$

where C_{PF} = the presence of public funding for candidates.

The availability of public financing lowers the overall costs of the campaign for a candidate. Conversely, assuming no other institutional costs on candidate entry, in states without the public funding of candidates we would expect

$$u(O) = (P \times B) - (C_{pers} - 0)$$

and there is no effect of public financing on candidate entry.

Previous work on public funding of candidates and candidate entry has yielded mixed results (e.g., Adams 2007; Bardwell 2002; Hamm and Hogan 2008; La Raja 2007; Mayer and Wood 1995). Recent survey evidence from potential state legislative candidates in Connecticut, Massachusetts, and Rhode Island suggests public funding may encourage certain types of candidates (e.g., low income, those who dislike fund-raising) to run in state legislative contests (La Raja 2007), but does not say anything about the probability of an incumbent receiving a challenge or the number of candidates entering in specific races. Work that has been done in this vein has generally found that public funding of candidates does not increase the probability of an incumbent's being challenged (e.g., Adams 2007 on city council elections in New York and Los Angeles; Bardwell 2002 on gubernatorial primary elections; Mayer and Wood 1995 on state legislative elections in Wisconsin), but does narrow the spending gap between incumbents and challengers (Bardwell 2003; Mayer and Wood 1995). Most recently, however, Hamm and Hogan (2008) find that public funding of state legislative candidates increases the chances of an incumbent's being challenged using data from three election cycles (1994, 1996, 1998) and twenty-five states. In all these works, however, the full range of candidates has not been analyzed.

This chapter aims to improve on these works by extending them in three ways. First, I examine open-seat gubernatorial contests, in addition to incumbent contests, which have been the focus of previous research (Bardwell 2002; Hamm and Hogan 2008). Open-seat contests may be more likely to permit public funding to boost candidate entry than incumbent elections because the incumbent is not there as a deterrent. In other words, when there is an incumbent running for reelection, the costs of running for office for a prospective candidate must be lowered to a greater extent (because the probability of winning [i.e., defeating an incumbent] is lower) compared to when there is an open seat for the taking.

Second, like Bardwell (2002), I focus on gubernatorial elections because more states make public funding available to statewide candidates than they do lower-level state candidates (e.g., state legislative races). In so doing, I have more variation across the states on my independent variable of interest and avoid some of the pitfalls that led Hamm and Hogan to be wary of some of their results concerning public funding and challenger entry in state legislative contests. The authors note, "Caution must be exercised in interpreting the results for the public financing variable, given that only three of the states examined employ public financing of legislative elections" (2008, 464n10). The fact that twelve states (i.e., the full sample of states), and nearly 20 percent of elections, in my data set operate under public funding systems allows me to be much more confident in my results concerning the effect of the public funding of candidates on candidate entry.

Third, it may be the case that by not separating candidates by quality (i.e., into experienced and amateur candidates) previous studies have been unable to observe the influence of public funding. Because public funding systems are very intricate in nature,[3] it may take an "experienced" candidate to be able to take advantage of them. In other words, the null finding for the effect of public funding on candidate entry from previous research could be the result of the inclusion of amateur candidates washing out the effect for experienced candidates.

Studying Candidate Entry with a More Complete Candidate Typology

While we might expect potential candidates of all stripes to be influenced by the possibility of public funding, it is likely to affect the entry decisions of some more than others. In terms of the experienced/amateur candidate dichotomy mentioned previously (see, e.g., Jacobson 1989), while amateur candidates might need the money that public funding provides, experienced candidates are probably better able to meet the criteria to receive public funding. Experienced candidates should have an easier time raising the requisite amount of seed money and subsequently filing the necessary paperwork to qualify for public funding with the proper federal or state agencies. Additionally, there is some survey evidence that public funding may encourage high-quality candidates—those that say they have been contacted by a group about running for office—to run for state legislative seats (La Raja 2007). Therefore, I expect experienced candidates to be more likely to take advantage of public funding than amateur candidates.

The effect of public funding on candidate entry is probably a bit more nuanced; the amateur/experienced distinction is probably not sufficient to fully appreciate how public funding relates to candidate entry. Specifically, we might expect candidates for open seats to take advantage of public funding more than candidates contesting incumbents. This expectation arises because, assuming the incumbent has a significant war chest and is not suffering from extremely low job approval ratings, a real chance at defeating the incumbent oftentimes requires more money than public funding allots. Put differently, public funding is not likely to systematically decrease the costs of running for office so that they are less than the probability of winning (i.e., defeating the incumbent) times the benefit of office.

In open seats, however, the incumbent is not there as a deterrent, so public funding may result in more candidates deciding to contest office. This occurs only if public funding systematically decreases the costs of running for office to the point that they are lower than the probability of winning times the benefit of the office for a given candidate. In other words, public funding may be enough to entice a candidate who is on the fence about running to contest the open seat, whereas the arduous task of having to finance one's own campaign may be enough to dissuade the same candidate.

A final distinction that I make, following Lazarus (2008a, 2008b), is between candidates of the out party (i.e., those in the opposite party of the incumbent) and incumbent party (i.e., those in the same party as the incumbent). However, it is not entirely clear which type of candidate would be more likely to accept public funding. For instance, there may be no difference if all that matters is whether or not an incumbent runs for reelection—that is, both out- and incumbent-party candidates are equally likely to decline public funding because they face the prospect of having to defeat the incumbent. In this case, the occupied and open-seat distinction would be sufficient.

To summarize, in general I expect public financing to increase the number of candidates contesting elections, but that certain types of candidates may be more likely to take advantage of such funding. Specifically, experienced candidates should be more likely to take advantage of public funding than amateur candidates; open-seat candidates should be more likely to take advantage of public funding than occupied-seat candidates; and any differences between out-party and incumbent-party candidates are not readily apparent.

Research Design and Data

Gubernatorial elections offer an ideal setting to test for the effects of public funding on candidate entry because they provide substantial variation on the main independent variable of interest. Furthermore, gubernatorial elections should provide a demanding test for the proposed effects because governorships are highly regarded and valued political offices, so often the decision for a potential candidate is less about *whether* to run and more about *when* to run.[4] In other words, in many cases potential gubernatorial candidates have made up their mind that they will run—they are just waiting for their probability of winning to increase (e.g., for an open seat), and public funding may make no difference to them.

In addition, unlike state legislatures, most cross-sectional office-specific differences (e.g., salary and professionalism of the office), which several scholars (see McCormick and Tollison 1978; Fiorina 1994; Hibbing 1999) point to as increasing the propensity of individuals to run for a given office (because the *B* term in the decision-making calculus increases), tend to be relatively small when comparing governorships. Therefore, the number of candidates in each state may be more directly comparable prima facie. In fact, when a control for gubernatorial salary is included in the estimations of candidate entry, I find that it does not contribute to the entry of any of the eight candidate types.

The methodology I follow to test for the effect of public financing on gubernatorial candidate entry is fairly straightforward (also see Lazarus 2008b). I use counts of eight different types of candidates divided by quality (experienced from amateur), seat type (open from occupied), and party (incumbent from out), leaving me with the eight candidate types outlined in Table 7.1. The candidate quality data come from *Congressional Quarterly Weekly Report*, which reported whether a candidate previously held elective office with its listing of primary election results from 1980 to 1998.[5] As the eight dependent variables are count data (with one exception), I use Poisson and, when overdispersion is present, negative binomial regression to model the effect of public funding on candidate entry. The lone exception is experienced incumbent-party challengers for occupied seats. I use logistic regression analysis to estimate entry for this candidate type, as only two of the 138 elections of this variety saw more than one experienced challenger, and their count was two—Maryland (1982) and West Virginia (1992). Consequently, interpretation of the results is confined to the *likelihood* a candidate will run, not how many of this type runs.

TABLE 7.1   TYPOLOGY OF CANDIDATES FOR ELECTIVE OFFICE

	Occupied Seats	Open Seats
Experienced candidates	Out party	Out party
	Incumbent party	Incumbent party
Amateur candidates	Out party	Out party
	Incumbent party	Incumbent party

Note: As described in the text, "experienced" candidates are those who have held previous elective office, while "amateur" candidates are those who have not.

States with Public Funding of Gubernatorial Candidates, 1980–1998

For the time period under study in this chapter (1980–1998), twelve states offered public funding to candidates in gubernatorial elections (see Feigenbaum and Palmer 2000; Malbin and Gais 1998), affecting 47 of the 263 elections (18 percent). While Kentucky is the most recent state to offer public funding to gubernatorial candidates in the data set, beginning with its 1995 election (the only election in the data set where public funding is available in Kentucky), three other states began their programs in the 1990s as well—Florida (1990), North Carolina (1992), and Rhode Island (1990). Half of the states, however, had public funding systems for the duration of the period under study—Maryland and Montana being the other two exceptions (Table 7.2).

TABLE 7.2.   STATES WITH PUBLIC FINANCING FOR GUBERNATORIAL CANDIDATES, 1980–1998

State	Election Years	Number of Elections
Florida	1990–1998	3
Hawaii	1982–1998	5
Kentucky	1995–1998	1
Maryland	1986–1998	4
Massachusetts	1982–1998	5
Michigan	1982–1998	5
Minnesota	1982–1998	5
Montana	1984–1998	3
New Jersey	1981–1998	5
North Carolina*	1992–1998	2
Rhode Island*†	1990–1998	4
Wisconsin*	1982–1998	5

Note: Except where noted, gubernatorial elections occur every four years. Vermont's public financing system, although passed in 1997, did not become available to candidates until the 2006 election.

*Public financing only for general election candidates. All other states make public financing available for both the primary and general elections.

†Rhode Island had elections every two years until 1994, when it switched to every four years.

Of the twelve states, nine have public funding of candidates in both the primary and general election; conversely, North Carolina, Rhode Island, and Wisconsin publicly fund only their general-election candidates. Even though my statistical analyses include the full array of primary candidates, I include North Carolina, Rhode Island, and Wisconsin because the prospect of public funding in the general election may be enough to engender more candidates, even without the availability of public funds in the primary election.

In the quantitative analyses that follow, I eliminate gubernatorial contests (eleven in all) in which the incumbent governor was an independent or a member of a third party, as those races most likely have very different dynamics than the more typical races involving gubernatorial offices held by one of the two major parties. This restriction leaves 26 of 138 occupied-seat elections (nearly 19 percent) and 17 of 114 open-seat elections (nearly 15 percent) with public funding available as an option to their candidates. The only state systematically (nearly) eliminated by leaving out these contests is Minnesota, as only its 1994 election, in which incumbent governor Arne Carlson ran for reelection, remains in the data set for analysis.

Empirically, I measure the public funding of gubernatorial candidates with a dichotomous indicator scored one (1) for those states that allow for such funding, and zero (0) for those that do not, which is consistent with recent work employing it as an independent variable in models estimating challenger entry (Bardwell 2002; Hamm and Hogan 2008). Accordingly, a positive coefficient is expected in the analyses; however, there may be differences across candidate types. In particular, I expect open seats to be more amenable to public funding having a positive impact on candidate entry, and experienced candidates to be more capable of navigating and making use of public funding systems.

Control Variables

Another institutional factor that is likely to factor into the decision-making calculus of potential gubernatorial candidates is the state's ballot access laws. In particular, the filing fee and petition requirements the state has in place may affect candidate entry in gubernatorial elections (Dowling 2008; Dowling and Lem 2009). I measure the effect of these ballot access laws on candidate entry by including four variables, two for each type of ballot access requirement. First, I include dichotomous variables indicating whether each requirement is present in the state ("Fee Dummy" and "Sig. Dummy"), scored one (1) if there is a requirement, otherwise zero (0). Next, I include a continuous measure for each requirement: the filing fee requirement in hundreds of dollars ("Fee Req. [in $100]")[6] and the number of signatures, also in hundreds. For the signature requirement, I first calculated the actual number of signatures required by electoral law by using the election code references and election results as reported by *The Book of the States* (Council of State Governments, various years). Then, to make this variable comparable across states, the number of signatures was divided by the total population. This new measure ("Sig. Req. [percent of pop., in 100s]") reflects the percentage of people needed to sign a petition in order for a candidate to be placed on the ballot, thereby making the measure comparable across states as it controls for state size.

The various legal requirements and election code references were obtained from Richard Winger (personal correspondence), editor of *Ballot Access News*.[7] A negative coefficient is expected for the ballot access measures because, as these requirements increase, the process of becoming a candidate becomes progressively more difficult, and should result in fewer candidates running for office—although these results may also differ across candidate types (Dowling 2008).

Another institutional factor I control for is whether a state allows for preprimary party endorsements of candidates. In gubernatorial elections specifically, the preprimary endorsement of candidates by state parties has been found to decrease the likelihood that an incumbent is challenged in her party's primary (Bardwell 2002). Here, I test to see if this finding extends to open seats, and whether politically experienced candidates or amateurs (or both) are kept out by party endorsement systems. Preprimary party endorsement is measured by a dichotomous variable ("Party Endorse") scored one (1) if a state permits such endorsements and zero (0) if the state does not.[8] Thus the coefficient for "Party Endorse" should be negative as it restricts candidate entry.

A final institutional factor I control for is whether the state has term limits for its governors. I measure the potential effect of term limits on candidate entry with a dichotomous variable scored one (1) for states that have term limits for their governors and zero (0) for those that do not. It could be the case that the use of term limits makes prospective candidates more willing to wait for an open seat and less willing to challenge an incumbent. Thus I expect term limits to have a negative coefficient for incumbent-defended seats because in the subsequent election (assuming a limit of two terms) the seat will be open, meaning an incumbent will not be there as a deterrent, which would presumably lower a prospective candidate's probability of winning.

In order to control for the probability of winning office, I include measures that have been found to influence gubernatorial candidate entry (e.g.,

Brown and Jacobson 2008; Lazarus 2008b) and that serve as proxies for a candidate's perceived probability of winning. Specifically, I control for (1) the lagged two-party vote share of the incumbent's party ("Lagged Vote Share of Inc."), (2) the percentage change in the nation's gross domestic product from two to one year prior to the election (i.e., $GDP_{t-1} - GDP_{t-2}$) ("Δ in GDP"), (3) presidential approval one year prior to the election ("Presidential Approval"), and (4) the statewide two-party vote share of the incumbent party's presidential candidate in the most recent election ("Presidential Vote Share"). I also include one indicator of the state economy, the percentage change in the state's real personal income from two years to one year prior to the election (i.e., $RPI_{t-1} - RPI_{t-2}$) ("Δ in State RPI").

In addition, consistent with the most recent treatment of gubernatorial candidate entry (Lazarus 2008a and b), I control for whether a state was a member of the confederacy ("South") and the party of the incumbent representative ("Democrat"). I also control for the potential dynamic aspect of amateur candidate entry by including a dummy variable ("Experienced Challenger") indicating whether or not an experienced challenger is running, but for only out-party amateurs. Last, I control for the size of the state. I do so because states with larger populations might naturally have more candidates than smaller states, as a consequence of their larger pool of potential candidates. "State size" is simply coded as the number of congressional districts in the state; the more districts, presumably the more candidates.[9]

Last, I include a time trend because there is some evidence that fewer experienced out-party challengers are running for governor for both open and occupied seats. The time trend ("Time") is simply an electoral sequence counter; it equals one (1) for the first election in the data set from that state, two (2) for the second, and so forth. When the eight candidate types are regressed on "Time" alone, experienced out-party challengers ex a negative trend, and experienced incumbent-party challengers into open seats are close to statistical significance (and also negative). Therefore, I include "Time" in the full model to observe whether the time trend maintains its statistical significance with the addition of the other independent variables.

Results and Discussion

Tables 7.3 (out-party challengers into occupied seats), 7.4 (incumbent-party challengers into occupied seats), 7.5 (out-party challengers into open seats), and 7.6 (incumbent-party challengers into open seats) present the results of the eight models estimating the various types of candidate entry in gubernatorial elections from 1980 to 1998. Each model is estimated without public

TABLE 7.3. ENTRY OF OUT-PARTY CHALLENGERS FOR GOVERNOR INTO OCCUPIED SEATS, 1980–1998

	Experienced Challengers		Amateur Challengers	
Public funding	—	.031 (.145)	—	-.027 (.169)
Fee dummy	-029 (.171)	-.024 (.172)	.106 (.193)	.103 (.190)
Sig. dummy	-.089 (.217)	-.096 (.219)	.599 (.209)[†]	.608 (.215)[†]
Fee req. (in \$100)	.008 (.006)	.008 (.006)	-.003 (.006)	-.003 (.006)
Sig. req. (% of pop., in 100s)	.923 (2.04)	.952 (2.03)	-7.06 (2.29)[‡]	-7.12 (2.29)[‡]
Experienced challenger	—	—	-.355 (.125)[†]	-.355 (.124)[†]
Lagged vote share of inc.	-.022 (.012)*	-.022 (.012)*	-.012 (.011)	-.012 (.011)
Δ in GDP	-.012 (.048)	-.012 (.048)	.031 (.054)	.030 (.055)
Presidential approval	.005 (.007)	.005 (.007)	-.005 (.006)	-.005 (.006)
Δ in state RPI	-.008 (.029)	-.008 (.029)	.002 (.038)	.002 (.038)
Presidential vote share	-.016 (.007)*	-.016 (.007)*	.001 (.009)	.001 (.009)
Democrat	-.272 (.148)*	-.274 (.147)*	.065 (.149)	.068 (.149)
State size	-.002 (.007)	-.002 (.007)	-.001 (.007)	-.001 (.007)
South	-.294 (.227)	-.289 (.228)	.218 (.168)	.212 (.168)
Party endorse	-.235 (.214)	-.231 (.215)	-.379 (.240)	-.380 (.238)
Term limits	.272 (.133)*	.272 (.133)*	.283 (.163)*	.285 (.164)*
Time	-.096 (.057)*	-.097 (.057)*	.010 (.058)*	.100 (.058)*
Constant	2.60 (.812)[‡]	2.58 (.813)[‡]	.747 (.791)	.760 (.791)
N (χ^2)	138 (34.4)	138 (34.3)	138 (59.1)	138 (60.0)

Note: Poisson regression estimates with robust standard errors in parentheses.

*$p \le .05$; [†]$p \le .01$; [‡]$p \le .001$. All significance tests are one-tailed.

TABLE 7.4. ENTRY OF INCUMBENT-PARTY CHALLENGERS FOR GOVERNOR INTO OCCUPIED SEATS, 1980–1998

	Experienced Challengers		Amateur Challengers	
Public funding	—	.378 (.802)	—	.159 (.224)
Fee dummy	.948 (.774)	.918 (.750)	.570 (.294)	.590 (.294)*
Sig. dummy	.401 (.744)	.298 (.787)	.004 (.303)	-.056 (.297)
Fee req. (in \$100)	.019 (.026)	.018 (.026)	.016 (.007)[†]	.015 (.007)*
Sig. req. (% of pop., in 100s)	10.66 (6.88)	11.03 (6.89)	-6.92 (3.77)*	-6.56 (3.69)*
Lagged vote share of inc.	.043 (.052)	.042 (.053)	-.041 (.020)*	-.041 (.019)*
Δ in GDP	.065 (.198)	.071 (.200)	.103 (.097)	.107 (.098)
Presidential approval	.001 (.025)	-.001 (.026)	.018 (.012)	.018 (.013)
Δ in state RPI	-.360 (.155)[†]	-.357 (.155)*	-.094 (.061)	-.094 (.061)
Presidential vote share	.071 (.038)*	.069 (.039)*	.029 (.010)*	.028 (.010)[†]
Democrat	.898 (.697)	.826 (.742)	.620 (.220)[†]	.588 (.216)[†]
State size	-.070 (.048)	-.075 (.054)	.002 (.011)	.003 (.011)
South	1.319 (.756)*	1.382 (.772)*	-.277 (.296)	-.253 (.308)
Party endorse	-.594 (.898)	-.581 (.902)	-1.304 (.561)[†]	-1.290 (.559)*
Term limits	.856 (.803)	.872 (.809)	.021 (.192)	.007 (.198)
Time	-.388 (.240)	-.377 (.245)	.015 (.097)	.016 (.096)
Constant	-6.70 (3.56)*	-6.48 (3.50)*	-.976 (1.06)	-.968 (1.06)
N (χ^2)	138 (22.3)	138 (22.9)	138 (68.5)	138 (71.4)

Note: Logistic (experienced) and Poisson (amateur) regression estimates with robust standard errors in parentheses.

*$p \le .05$; [†]$p \le .01$. All significance tests are one-tailed.

TABLE 7.5.   ENTRY OF OUT-PARTY CHALLENGERS FOR GOVERNOR INTO OPEN SEATS, 1980–1998

	Experienced Challengers		Amateur Challengers	
Public funding	—	.242 (.170)	—	−.083 (.212)
Fee dummy	−.346 (.196)*	−.316 (.184)*	.188 (.233)	.179 (.232)
Sig. dummy	−.018 (.243)	−.046 (.230)	−.192 (.279)	−.180 (.288)
Fee req. (in $100)	.001 (.009)	.001 (.009)	−.005 (.009)	−.004 (.009)
Sig. req. (% of pop., in 100s)	−1.41 (1.82)	−1.30 (1.62)	−4.37 (2.52)*	−4.43 (2.57)*
Experienced challenger	—	—	−.353 (.251)	−.354 (.252)
Lagged vote share of inc.	−.006 (.009)	−.006 (.009)	−.032 (.011)†	−.032 (.011)†
Δ in GDP	−.004 (.063)	.000 (.060)	−.121 (.057)*	−.123 (.058)*
Presidential approval	−.012 (.008)	−.011 (.008)	.015 (.009)*	.015 (.009)*
Δ in state RPI	−.024 (.040)	−.023 (.036)	.080 (.044)*	.080 (.044)*
Presidential vote share	−.011 (.009)	−.012 (.010)	.004 (.010)	.004 (.010)
Democrat	−.192 (.178)	−.224 (.179)	.009 (.172)	.014 (.170)
State size	.012 (.009)	.012 (.008)	.013 (.009)	.013 (.009)
South	−.122 (.179)	−.098 (.179)	−.352 (.202)*	−.358 (.202)*
Party endorse	−.310 (.279)	−.250 (.275)	−.582 (.511)	−.597 (.515)
Term limits	.262 (.177)	.290 (.179)	.015 (.204)	.010 (.205)
Time	−.119 (.073)	−.112 (.072)	−.101 (.070)	−.104 (.071)
Constant	2.78 (1.09)†	2.68 (1.00)†	2.59 (1.23)*	2.63 (1.25)*
Alpha	—	—	.138 (.093)*	.135 (.093)*
$N (\chi^2)$	114 (15.9)	114 (17.9)	114 (52.8)	114 (53.1)

Note: Poisson (experienced) and negative binomial (amateur) regression estimates with robust standard errors in parentheses.

*$p \leq .05$; †$p \leq .01$. All significance tests are one-tailed.

funding, as a baseline, and then with public funding. To facilitate discussion, I focus on the results of the electoral law variables (especially public funding), noting differences in their effects across the eight types of candidate entry.

Beginning with the public funding of candidates, there is one very interesting result. Specifically, more experienced challengers run for open seats in states with public funding, and this is statistically significant for those of the same party as the incumbent (see Table 7.6) and has a z-score of 1.42 for those of the opposite party of the incumbent (see Table 7.5). Thus there is some evidence that experienced politicians take advantage of public funding in open seats, a result not found before because focus had been limited to incumbent-defended seats (e.g., Bardwell 2002). On the whole, however, public funding of candidates does not appear to increase candidate participation all that much. I provide a more substantive interpretation of these results in the final section, after discussing some other noteworthy results.

With respect to ballot access laws, I find that the level of the signature requirement curbs amateur candidate entry for all types of seats—incum-

TABLE 7.6. ENTRY OF INCUMBENT-PARTY CHALLENGERS FOR GOVERNOR
INTO OPEN SEATS, 1980–1998

	Experienced Challengers		Amateur Challengers	
Public funding	—	.315 (.166)*	—	.009 (.203)
Fee dummy	-.196 (.195)	-.179 (.179)	.421 (.247)*	.421 (.247)*
Sig. dummy	-.007 (.233)	-.052 (.217)	.081 (.286)	.079 (.285)
Fee req. (in $100)	-.008 (.010)	-.009 (.010)	-.020 (.010)*	-.020 (.010)*
Sig. req. (% of pop., in 100s)	-1.08 (2.20)	-.936 (2.06)	-8.44 (3.18)†	-8.44 (3.16)†
Lagged vote share of inc.	.018 (.010)*	.018 (.010)*	.018 (.011)*	.018 (.011)*
Δ in GDP	-.005 (.051)	-.004 (.049)	.010 (.053)	.010 (.052)
Presidential approval	-.006 (.009)	-.005 (.008)	.009 (.010)	.009 (.010)
Δ in state RPI	-.040 (.041)	-.037 (.040)	-.005 (.039)	-.005 (.040)
Presidential vote share	.001 (.009)	-.002 (.009)	.021 (.010)*	.021 (.011)*
Democrat	.452 (.188)†	.397 (.197)*	.553 (.216)†	.553 (.219)†
State size	.013 (.008)	.013 (.008)*	.016 (.010)	.016 (.010)
South	.037 (.183)	.067 (.181)	.198 (.224)	.199 (.228)
Party endorse	-.186 (.374)	-.123 (.373)	-1.140 (.498)*	-1.139 (.499)*
Term limits	.255 (.203)	.291 (.206)	-.302 (.214)	-.302 (.213)
Time	-.068 (.069)	-.061 (.068)	.013 (.063)	.014 (.063)
Constant	-.155 (1.05)	-.160 (.970)	-2.37 (1.19)*	-2.37 (1.19)*
Alpha	—	—	.217 (.107)†	.218 (.107)†
N (χ^2)	114 (27.1)	114 (36.3)	114 (50.7)	114 (51.0)

Note: Poisson (experienced) and negative binomial (amateur) regression estimates with robust standard errors in parentheses.
*$p \le .05$; $^\dagger p \le .01$. All significance tests are one-tailed.

bent and out party, open and occupied. Conversely, no type of experienced candidate is influenced by the petition requirement. In fact, the only statistically significant result for experienced challengers is that the presence of a filing fee keeps the count of the out party down in open seats. Filing fees do not keep amateur candidates of any type from contesting office. Thus it appears to be the case that ballot access requirements are a more effective means of keeping amateur candidates from running for office than they are experienced candidates, and that for gubernatorial candidates the signature requirement is much more effectual than the filing fee.

Consistent with prior research on gubernatorial candidate entry (Bardwell 2002; Lazarus 2008a and b), preprimary party endorsements are found to limit the field of candidates, although not quite as consistently as signature requirements. In particular, party endorsements keep amateur candidates from contesting, but only amateurs of the same party as the incumbent (see Tables 7.4 and 7.6), although "Party Endorse" is close to statistical significance ($z = -1.60$) for amateurs of the out party in open seats (see Table 7.5) as well.

Other findings of note are that fewer amateur out-party challengers run when an experienced challenger emerges in *occupied* seats (see Table 7.3), but not *open* seats (see Table 7.5), a finding that is consistent with Banks and Kiewiet (1989). Also, for experienced challengers to occupied seats, the incumbent's previous vote share appears to matter for out-party challengers (see Table 7.3), while the change in the state's real personal income appears to matter for incumbent-party challengers (see Table 7.4); but the presidential vote share matters to each as one would expect—negative for the out party, positive for the incumbent party. Additionally, Democratic incumbents face fewer (experienced) out-party challengers (see Table 7.3), and more (amateur) incumbent-party challengers (see Table 7.4). Finally, "Term Limits" is uniformly positive for occupied seats, but statistically significant for only out-party challengers (see Table 7.3), suggesting that states with terms limits observe more (experienced and amateur) candidates than we would expect otherwise when an incumbent is running for reelection. This result is contrary to the notion that the use of term limits makes prospective candidates more willing to wait for an open seat and less willing to challenge an incumbent.

The Substantive Impact of Public Financing on Candidate Entry

This section provides more substantive interpretations of the results from the count models presented in the previous section. Specifically, I calculate the expected number of candidates when public funding is in effect and, for comparison, across the range of the two continuous ballot access measures (i.e., "Fee Req. [in $100]" and "Sig. Req. [percent of pop., in 100s]"). In order to do so, I hold all the other variables in the model constant at their means (continuous variables) or modes (discrete variables).

Table 7.7 displays the expected number of gubernatorial candidates (by candidate type) for five different scenarios. The first column, labeled "Baseline," displays the expected value for that candidate type when all the independent variables, including the public funding and ballot access measures, are set to their means (continuous variables) or modes (discrete). As only twelve states have public funding at any point in time from 1980 to 1998, the modal state does not have public funding of candidates, so "Public Funding" is set to zero (0) to calculate the baseline. As the modal state in the data set has a filing fee requirement (thirty-one states in all), but not a petition requirement (only twenty states), the ballot access dichotomous variables are set to one (1) for the filing fee requirement and zero (1) for the petition requirement. The continuous petition requirement measure is also set to zero (0), whereas the continuous filing fee requirement measure is set to its mean of $644 (which is approximately the filing fee in Nebraska and

TABLE 7.7.   EXPECTED NUMBER OF GUBERNATORIAL CANDIDATES BY BALLOT ACCESS
REQUIREMENT AND PUBLIC FUNDING, FOR EACH TYPE OF CANDIDATE

	Baseline*	Public Funding	No Ballot Access Require- ments	Filing Fee Maximum	Petition Maximum
Occupied seats					
Experienced					
Out party	1.44	1.49^{NS}	1.40	2.27^{NS}	1.54^{NS}
Inc. party[†]	0.15	0.20^{NS}	0.05	0.33^{NS}	0.44^{NS}
Amateur					
Out party	1.67	1.62^{NS}	1.53	1.43^{NS}	0.66
Inc. party	1.71	2.00^{NS}	0.86	3.96^{NS}	0.21
Open seats					
Experienced					
Out party	1.69	2.15^{NS}	2.30	1.75^{NS}	1.73^{NS}
Inc. party	1.81	2.48	2.30	1.15^{NS}	1.84^{NS}
Amateur					
Out party	2.65	2.44^{NS}	2.28	2.12^{NS}	0.84
Inc. party	2.80	2.82^{NS}	2.11	0.97	0.49

Note: Cell entries are the expected number of candidates for that type of candidate, except for incumbent-party experienced candidates in occupied seats (see [†] note). All other variables are held at their mean (continuous variables) or mode (discrete variables).

[NS] Coefficient was not statistically significant; all other coefficients significant.

*All variables set to their mean or mode to calculate the baseline expected number of candidates.

[†] The entries for experienced candidates of the incumbent party in occupied seats are predicted probabilities based on the logistic regression results reported in Table 7.4.

Utah). This baseline is used to help evaluate how much of an effect ballot access requirements and the public funding of candidates have on candidate entry in gubernatorial elections.

Is the lone statistically significant effect of public funding on candidate entry—experienced challengers of the incumbent party in open seats (see Table 7.6)—substantively important? In short, the effect of public funding on candidate entry amounts to a 37 percent increase in the number of experienced candidates of the incumbent party in open-seat gubernatorial elections; we move from 1.81 candidates to 2.48 candidates. In other words, for every ten open seat elections that have public financing, seven of them would end up with one more experienced incumbent-party challenger. Whether this is truly substantively important remains to be seen. While a few more experienced candidates should result in more competitive elections, gubernatorial elections are already fairly competitive, for the most part. Nevertheless, this finding does provide some evidence that public funding is not entirely inconsequential to candidate participation in gubernatorial elections.

To ascertain the substantive effect of ballot access requirements on candidate entry in gubernatorial elections, the last three columns of Table 7.7 report the expected number of candidates when (1) no ballot access requirements are in use, (2) the filing fee is at its maximum (but there is no petition requirement), and (3) the petition requirement is at its maximum (but there is no filing fee required). The expected numbers of candidates in Table 7.7 confirm what the results from Tables 7.3 to 7.6 suggested: Ballot access requirements (more precisely, the petition requirement) limit amateur candidate entry but have no real impact on experienced candidate entry in gubernatorial elections.

For instance, while there is a minimal impact of the *absence* of both ballot access requirements on experienced challenger entry in open seats, it amounts to the difference between having just under two experienced candidates and having just over two experienced candidates. Amateur candidates, on the other hand, are severely limited by the arduous task of collecting signatures. In incumbent-defended gubernatorial elections, the maximum petition requirement (0.2 percent of the population, South Dakota—1990) decreases the number of amateur out-party (incumbent-party) challengers by 61 percent (88 percent), moving from a baseline of 1.67 (1.71) candidates to 0.66 (0.21) candidates. In other words, one or more amateur candidates from both the incumbent and out party are deterred from running for gubernatorial office by the prospect of having to collect a significant amount of signatures when an incumbent is running for reelection.

In addition, the effect of the number of signatures needed in order to be put on the ballot on amateur candidate entry is just as substantial in open seats. Specifically, for *out*-party amateurs in open seats, when the petition requirement is at its maximum (as is the case in Virginia), the expected number of candidates *decreases* from 2.65 candidates to 0.84 candidates (a 68 percent decrease). Similarly, for *incumbent*-party amateurs in open seats, when the petition requirement is at its maximum, the expected number of candidates *decreases* from 2.80 candidates to 0.49 (an 83 percent decrease). Thus, even in open seats, the count of amateur candidates (both of the incumbent and out party) decreases by roughly two candidates when the petition requirement is at its most burdensome.

Conclusion

While the decision to become a gubernatorial candidate is ultimately an individual one, I have shown that it can be structured in important ways by the institutional environment within which the decision is made. In particular, the public funding of candidates is found to influence the entry of one of the eight candidate types—experienced incumbent-party challengers in open seats. This result provides some evidence that experienced politicians take advantage of public funding in open seats, a result not found in prior research because the focus had been on incumbent-defended seats and candidates had not been separated into amateur and experienced groups. Future research on the effects of public funding on candidate entry, or even public funding on electoral competition more broadly, should benefit from the examination of open seats in addition to incumbent-defended seats. In combination with Hamm and Hogan's (2008) finding that public funding contributes to challenger entry in state legislative elections, this result provides some preliminary evidence that public funding could be a means through which some of the costs of running for office, albeit not for all types of candidates, are offset, thereby increasing candidate participation and the probability of a contested election.

Another electoral law, however, is more pervasive in its effect on candidate participation in gubernatorial elections. Specifically, petition requirements limit the entry of amateur candidates (particularly to incumbent-defended seats), for both the incumbent and out parties. Thus we are left with the conclusion that ballot access requirements, especially petition requirements, are a more effective means of keeping amateur candidates from running for office than they are experienced candidates. Moreover, if policy makers or reformers seek an increase in candidate *participation* in elections, reducing ballot access requirements (in some states) is more likely to have that desired effect than instituting public funding systems—at least the types of systems that were in place during the 1980s and 1990s; whether full public funding will increase participation remains to be seen.

NOTES

1. See Dowling 2008 for a more complete theoretical account of how institutional factors may influence the costs of running for office.

2. For simplicity, I discuss public funding of candidates in terms of a simple dichotomy—either the state has such a system or it does not. Later, I measure and model the effect of the public funding of candidates in the same fashion, which is consistent and therefore directly comparable to previous work (Bardwell 2002; Hamm and Hogan 2008).

3. For example, Nebraska "had a public funding law on the books as of 1998, but funds are provided to candidates only if their opponent breaks the spending caps. No gubernatorial candidate has ever received funding under the Nebraska program" (Bardwell 2003, 815). See also Malbin and Gais 1998 for a thorough discussion of state public financing programs. Like Bardwell (2002, 2003), I do not consider Nebraska a public funding state in my empirical analyses.

4. See Maestas et al. 2006 for a thorough treatment of this two-stage decision-making process.

5. I thank Jeffrey Lazarus for generously sharing his candidate quality data with me (see Lazarus 2008b). Unfortunately, *CQWR* changed its reporting procedures after 1998, and the same information can no longer be gathered for all candidates from this source. The total count of major-party candidates obtained from *CQWR* is highly correlated ($r = .93$) with another source of data on gubernatorial candidates, Beyle and Jensen's *Gubernatorial Campaign Expenditures Database* (see Jensen and Beyle 2003). As this database includes any individual who spent some amount of money on a campaign, but did not necessarily end up on a primary ballot, it includes a few more candidates than *CQWR* reports.

6. In Alabama, Arkansas, Delaware, and South Carolina the parties set the filing fee. When this occurs I use the less stringent fee requirement, so that prospective candidates have to jump over only the lowest bar.

7. *Ballot Access News* can be found at http://www.ballot-access.org/.

8. Seven states allow for preprimary endorsement by the parties: Colorado, Connecticut, North Dakota, New York, New Mexico, Rhode Island, and Utah (Jewell and Morehouse 1996).

9. As states are larger entities than congressional districts, I also included other controls for the "pool of potential candidates." However, state population size, the number of statewide elected executive branch offices (other than the governor), and the size of the state legislature (lower and upper house) never achieve statistical significance and are therefore not included in the results presented here.

REFERENCES

Adams, Brian E. 2007. "The Impact of Public Financing Programs in Municipal Elections: Evidence from New York and Los Angeles." Paper presented at the *Annual Meeting of the American Political Science Association*, Chicago.

Banks, Jeffrey S., and D. Roderick Kiewiet. 1989. "Explaining Patterns of Candidate Competition in Congressional Elections." *American Journal of Political Science* 33 (4): 997–1015.

Bardwell, Kedron. 2002. "Money and Challenger Emergence in Gubernatorial Primaries." *Political Research Quarterly* 55 (3): 653–668.

———. 2003. "Campaign Finance Laws and the Competition for Spending in Gubernatorial Elections." *Social Science Quarterly* 84 (4): 811–825.

Black, Gordon S. 1972. "A Theory of Political Ambition: Career Choices and the Role of Structural Incentives." *American Political Science Review* 66 (1): 144–159.

Brown, Adam R., and Gary C. Jacobson. 2008. "Party, Performance, and Strategic Politicians: The Dynamics of Elections for Senator and Governor in 2006." *State Politics and Policy Quarterly* 8 (4): 384–409.

Canon, David T. 1990. *Actors, Athletes, and Astronauts: Political Amateurs in the United States Congress.* Chicago: University of Chicago Press.

Council of State Governments. Various years. *The Book of the States.* Lexington, KY: CSG.

Dowling, Conor M. 2008. "The Institutional Cost of Running for Office: How Electoral Campaign Laws Structure Candidate Entry in U.S. Elections." Ph.D. diss., Binghamton University (SUNY).

Dowling, Conor M., and Steve B. Lem. 2009. "Explaining Major and Third Party Candidate Entry in U.S. Gubernatorial Elections, 1980–2005." *State Politics and Policy Quarterly* 9 (1): 1–23.

Feigenbaum, Edward D., and James A. Palmer. 2000. "Campaign Finance Law 2000: A Summary of State Campaign Finance Laws with Quick Reference Charts." Edited by FEC. Washington, DC: Federal Election Commission.

Fiorina, Morris P. 1994. "Divided Government in the American States: A Byproduct of Legislative Professionalism." *American Political Science Review* 88 (2): 304–316.

Francia, P. L., and P. S. Herrnson. 2003. "The Impact of Public Finance Laws on Fundraising in State Legislative Elections." *American Politics Research* 31 (5): 520–539.

Government Accountability Office. 2003. "Campaign Finance Reform: Early Experiences of Two States That Offer Full Public Funding for Political Candidates." No. GAO-03-435. Washington, DC.

Hamm, Keith E., and Robert E. Hogan. 2008. "Campaign Finance Laws and Candidacy Decisions in State Legislative Elections." *Political Research Quarterly* 61 (3): 458–467.

Hibbing, John R. 1999. "Legislative Careers: Why and How We Should Study Them." *Legislative Studies Quarterly* 24 (2): 149–171.

Jacobson, Gary C. 1989. "Strategic Politicians and the Dynamics of U.S. House Elections, 1946–86." *American Political Science Review* 83 (3): 773–793.

Jacobson, Gary C., and Samuel Kernell. 1981. *Strategy and Choice in Congressional Elections*. New Haven, CT: Yale University Press.

Jensen, Jennifer M., and Thad Beyle. 2003. "Of Footnotes, Missing Data, and Lessons for 50-State Data Collection: The Gubernatorial Campaign Finance Project, 1977–2001." *State Politics and Policy Quarterly* 3 (2): 203–214.

Jewell, Malcolm E., and Sarah M. Morehouse. 1996. "What Are Party Endorsements Worth? A Study of Preprimary Gubernatorial Endorsements." *American Politics Quarterly* 24 (3): 338–362.

La Raja, Raymond J. 2007. "Candidate Emergence in State Legislative Elections: Does Public Funding Make a Difference." Paper presented at the *Annual Meeting of the American Political Science Association*, Chicago.

Lazarus, Jeffrey. 2008a. "Buying In: Testing the Rational Model of Candidate Entry." *Journal of Politics* 70 (3): 837–850.

———. 2008b. "Incumbent Vulnerability and Challenger Entry in Statewide Elections." *American Politics Research* 36 (1): 108–129.

Maestas, Cherie D., Sarah Fulton, L. Sandy Maisel, and Walter J. Stone. 2006. "When to Risk It? Institutions, Ambitions, and the Decision to Run for the U.S. House." *American Political Science Review* 100 (2): 195–208.

Maisel, L. Sandy. 1982. *From Obscurity to Oblivion: Running in the Congressional Primary*. Knoxville: University of Tennessee Press.

Maisel, L. Sandy, and Walter J. Stone. 1997. "Determinants of Candidate Emergence in U.S. House Elections: An Exploratory Study." *Legislative Studies Quarterly* 22 (1): 79–96.

Malbin, Michael J., and Thomas L. Gais. 1998. *The Day after Reform: Sobering Campaign Finance Lessons from the American States*. Albany, NY: Rockefeller Institute Press.

Malhotra, Neil. 2008. "The Impact of Public Financing on Electoral Competition: Evidence from Arizona and Maine." *State Politics and Policy Quarterly* 8 (3): 263–281.

Mayer, Kenneth R., Timothy Werner, and Amanda Williams. 2006. "Do Public Funding Programs Enhance Electoral Competition?" In *The Marketplace of Democracy: Electoral Competition and American Politics*, ed. M. P. McDonald and J. Samples. Washington, DC: Brookings Institution Press.

Mayer, Kenneth R., and John M. Wood. 1995. "The Impact of Public Financing on Electoral Competitiveness: Evidence from Wisconsin, 1964–1990." *Legislative Studies Quarterly* 20 (1): 69–88.

McCormick, Robert E., and Robert D. Tollison. 1978. "Legislatures as Unions." *Journal of Political Economy* 86 (1): 63–78.

Miller, Michael. 2009. "Public Election Funding, Candidate Time, and Citizen Engagement in American Elections." Typescript, Cornell University.

Rohde, David W. 1979. "Risk-Bearing and Progressive Ambition: The Case of Members of the United States House of Representatives." *American Journal of Political Science* 23 (1): 1–26.

Schlesinger, Joseph R. 1966. *Ambition and Politics: Political Careers in the United States.* Chicago: Rand McNally.

Squire, Peverill. 1989. "Challengers in U.S. Senate Elections." *Legislative Studies Quarterly* 14 (4): 531–547.

Stone, Walter J., L. Sandy Maisel, and Cherie D. Maestas. 2004. "Quality Counts: Extending the Strategic Politician Model of Incumbent Deterrence." *American Journal of Political Science* 48 (3): 479–495.

8

◇ ◇ ◇

Public Money, Candidate Time,
and Electoral Outcomes
in State Legislative Elections

MICHAEL G. MILLER

*The candidates that I knew this last election that ran traditional
were having fundraisers two or three times a week, while (publicly
funded candidates) were going out knocking on doors. That, I think,
is a big difference in how you spend your time. In an evening after
work, I can knock on fifty to seventy doors of people who will actually
go to the polls for me, as opposed to that candidate who has to go out
and raise and spend two, three hours with lobbyists who often don't
even live in their district. Yeah, they're going to get the money, but
I'm the one going out and meeting the voters.*

—ARIZONA LEGISLATOR

W hile money alone does not guarantee victory, its absence all but
ensures defeat for federal and state candidates alike (e.g., Caldeira and Patterson 1982; Giles and Pritchard 1985; Tucker and
Weber 1987; Green and Krasno 1990; Gierzynski and Breaux 1991, 1993;
Cassie and Breaux 1998). Thus, as races become more expensive, challengers
find themselves shut out of meaningful opportunities to compete. Advocates
of public election financing believe they hold the solution to this problem,
and their influence is growing. As of 2008, nearly half of the states will offer
some form of public funding in at least one election.[1] Most provide matching funds to candidates or parties, funded by tax checkoffs. Others utilize
various mechanisms of partial public financing, in which candidates receive
subsidies that comprise a percentage of campaign costs. However, full public financing has been employed in state elections since 2000, when Arizona

Earlier versions of this chapter were presented at meetings of the Northeastern, Midwest, and Great
Plains Political Science Associations and in research colloquia at Cornell University.

and Maine became the first states to offer subsidies equivalent to their spending limits (see the Appendix). Since then, full funding has become more common; it was expected to be offered in at least some elections in six state and two major metropolitan elections in 2008.

With mandated financial equality and the chore of fund-raising removed, supporters of public funding reason that the election can be won by the candidate who works the hardest to reach the largest number of voters. Francia and Herrnson (2003) confirmed that candidates who accept full public subsidies spend a significantly smaller percentage of their campaign time raising money than those in partially subsidized or traditional funding systems. If they spend less time on the money chase, candidates in fully subsidized systems should be expected to devote substantially greater effort to interaction with voters and groups. An important question therefore remains: What effect does the recapture of fund-raising time have on the campaigns of publicly funded candidates?

Public Funding: Toward Competitive Elections

The potential for enhanced competition has been the most studied aspect of public election finance. However, definitive conclusions remain elusive. It has been demonstrated that the spending caps associated with public financing can curb expenditures, in theory opening avenues for a greater number of viable challengers (Mayer and Wood 1995; Gross and Goidel 2003, 55), but partial subsidies have proven ineffective in reducing spending in New York City elections (Kraus 2006) and Minnesota state elections (Schultz 2002). Likewise, numerous studies have found little competitive change in partially subsidized elections (e.g., Jones and Borris 1985; Mayer and Wood 1995; Malbin and Gais 1998, 136), but there is some evidence of enhanced competition in Minnesota (Donnay and Ramsden 1995). Simulation studies have linked public money to enhanced electoral competition, with greater impact realized by higher subsidies (Goidel and Gross 1996). In Arizona and Maine, the only two states implementing full public election funding, higher levels of competition are beginning to become apparent (U.S. General Accounting Office 2003; Mayer, Werner, and Williams 2006).

The greater promise of full subsidies should come as no surprise. To gain standing against an incumbent, challengers in traditional funding systems must engage political elites by raising a substantial sum of money, but in terms of activating voters, candidate attributes and campaign activities are negated by incumbents' financial power (Howell 1982). Meanwhile, political campaigns have become increasingly important forces in voter mobilization (Rosenstone and Hansen 1993). Gerber (2004) finds that challengers reap the highest rewards, effectively translating their campaign efforts into votes. While radio advertising holds some promise in stimulating competition by bolstering challenger name recognition (Panagopoulos and Green 2008), face-to-face efforts appear to be the most effective voter mobilization tools, particularly when delivered on time to targeted populations (Kramer 1970; Gerber and Green 2000; Niven 2001, 2002; Green, Gerber, and Nickerson 2003; Hillygus 2005; Parry et al. 2008).

For challengers in state legislative elections, many of whom may harbor realistic expectations of knocking on a majority of their district's doors, these findings are promising. However, canvass-intensive campaign techniques require a large investment of candidate time. Time spent fund-raising reduces the number of hours that can be devoted to interaction with the electorate at large, and so challengers, who typically begin the campaign well behind in both funding and name recognition, face a paradox: To be viewed as viable by political elites, interest groups, and media, they must raise substantial sums of money. The time required to raise the requisite funds significantly limits candidates' ability to mobilize voters. Thus, when deciding how to use scarce time, challengers in particular must choose from options that are less than ideal.

If partial subsidies have not improved competition, this result is likely due to the inability of challengers to solve this problem. Even when the subsidy covers half of the funding level allowed under the spending cap, the challenger's strategic considerations relative to those in privately funded elections are largely unchanged, and a large spending gap between challengers and incumbents is likely to persist. As Table 8.1 illustrates, in all three partially financed states, legislative challengers must raise well more than half of the average expenditure level, and substantially more effort is required to reach financial parity with incumbents.[2] The practical result is that the day-to-day campaign in a partially funded system is little different from one in which all money comes from private sources. The challenger is always outspent, and the great fund-raising effort required to maintain competitive financial status constrains the challenger's choices of voter mobilization tactics. Combined, these circumstances diminish the impact of personal campaigning: The incumbent can exploit a financial advantage to counteract retail politics with mass advertising and mailings while the challenger campaigns around a fund-raising schedule.

The comparatively narrow gaps between challenger and incumbent spending in Arizona and Maine evident in Table 8.1 suggest the possibility of a different sort of campaign being waged in those states, where the equalization

TABLE 8.1.   AVERAGE SPENDING IN 2004 LOWER HOUSE ELECTIONS OF FIVE PUBLICLY
             FINANCED STATES

	Cost of Race (dollars)	Incumbent Spending (dollars)	Challenger Spending (dollars)	Gap (dollars)	Gap, Percentage of Total Average Cost
Arizona	27,835	29,641	26,752	2,889	10.4
Maine	4,587	4,946	4,389	557	12.1
Hawaii	30,911	45,929	19,617	26,312	85.1
Minnesota	23,668	35,226	15,770	19,456	82.2
Wisconsin	24,189	32,619	16,892	15,727	65.0

Source: Data in this table were obtained from the Wisconsin Campaign Finance Project, available at http://campfin. polisci.wisc.edu/Index.asp. As of this writing, 2004 is the most recent year for which the WCFP has full data.

Note: Cell entries reflect aggregate means for lower house candidates in the respective states, and are listed in 2004 dollars. Public subsidies in Arizona and Maine are 100 percent of spending limits. In Hawaii, they are capped at 15 percent, in Wisconsin, 45 percent, and in Minnesota, 50 percent. Through 2006, these states are the only ones employing public financing for legislative elections.

of challenger and incumbent funding levels may diminish the importance of political money, freeing candidates to choose how to plan their activities most effectively. Full public funding changes the power dynamic between challengers and incumbents. Traditionally financed challengers, who typically begin the campaign well behind in both funding and name recognition, find their options severely limited when it comes to getting out the vote. With the necessity of fund-raising eliminated, full financing creates a different kind of politics. Fully funded challengers in Arizona and Maine face not only financial competition with incumbents but also campaign finance regulations in the two states that preclude them from accepting any donations once they have qualified for the program.[3] Candidates in those states have more time to campaign door to door, telephone constituents, and post signs, all under the cover of "air support" provided by advertising and mailings purchased with public funds.

Enhanced competitiveness, if it exists, is a symptom of an electoral environment that is fundamentally transformed. The availability of funds is likely to draw more challengers to politics. These challengers will be strategically minded individuals who view public money as a mechanism to clear otherwise existent financial hurdles that would occlude their entry. If system-wide competition is enhanced, the presence of a greater number of challengers alone is likely the cause, but this outcome says little about the dynamics of the elections themselves. In publicly financed elections, candidates should, as Francia and Herrnson (2003) find, spend less time raising money. Consequently, they are likely to devote more effort to interacting with the public, media, and interest groups. With sufficient money to wage a strong campaign, challengers should find themselves empowered to optimize their political strategy, facilitating higher levels of voter mobilization and more votes in the election.

Data and Methodology

I construct three models associating candidate public interaction with electoral success, utilizing survey data obtained from 2006 lower-house legislative candidates in Arizona, Maine, and Maryland. Surveys were delivered in both electronic and paper form to all registered primary candidates.[4] Candidates were asked to quantify the devotion of their time to fund-raising, public speeches, field activity, electronic campaigning, media relations, research, strategy, and the courting of interest groups. Electronic messages were sent to available addresses, but paper surveys were mailed to the entire candidate population in all states, achieving redundant coverage for most candidates but at least some solicitation of all. The letters directed the respondents to the electronic survey, and they included prepaid return envelopes for completion of the paper version. There were 510 known candidates in Maryland, 386 in Maine, and 186 in Arizona. After a response window that lasted from early September through December 31, 2006, 346 responses were received, for an overall response rate of 32 percent.[5] This rate is lower than that of many general surveys but is consistent with previous polling of elite candidate populations (e.g., Francia and Herrnson 2003; Howell 1982). Candidate demographic proportions were comparable between samples, and the samples are reasonably representative of the candidate populations of each state (see Appendix Table 8.1).[6]

Responses from the individual time categories are reduced to two indices which take on a normal distribution while allowing for the use of fewer predictors in the model. The *public* index is an additive grouping of time, measured in raw weekly hours or fractions thereof devoted to the public solicitation of votes, either directly or indirectly. The public index includes candidate time allocations to field activity, electronic campaigning, media relations, public speaking, and interactions with groups. The *housekeeping* index encompasses tasks that are integral to the maintenance of a campaign but that are performed behind the scenes and do not involve voter mobilization. Fund-raising, policy research, and strategy meetings are included in the housekeeping index.

The inclusion of fund-raising in the housekeeping category is warranted here. The activities, goals, and strategy that accompany the search for cash are of a wholly different character than the environment in which a candidate seeks votes. While the candidate must interact with the public for fund-raising purposes, the fund-raising audience is a narrow sector of the electorate, and it is usually targeted because of well-known preferences favorable to the candidate. Funding lists typically target political elites who have demonstrated a capacity to give money, and there is little reason to believe that the act of contributing changes their political preferences (Wilcox 2001). In other cases, funds may be solicited from individuals who live outside the candidate's district or state, negating any potential electoral benefit from fund-raising activities. As Table 8.2 indicates, contributors represent less than 2 percent of the voting population in the three states, and any mobilization achieved through fund-raising efforts is likely negligible.

The addition of Maryland facilitates the modeling of campaign behavior in a privately financed state that is otherwise quite similar to Arizona. The states are comparable in population, and entering the 2006 election, both houses of each state's legislature were controlled by similar majorities of one party.[7] Maryland and Arizona also employ parallel electoral timelines, with multimember districts in the lower house and primaries on the same day in early September. Most important, the two states are positioned in close approximation within Squire's (2000) measure of legislative professionalization.[8] Their key difference is in campaign finance regulation: Maryland's election finance laws are more conventional than those of the other two states. While candidates on gubernatorial tickets are entitled to public funds, those for the Maryland General Assembly operate in a traditional, privately financed environment.[9] With no public funds available, Maryland's legislative candidates must self-fund or seek contributions from individuals and PACs. Maryland therefore adds value to this analysis by providing a basis for comparison between the states employing optional full funding and one that operates under more familiar traditional funding guidelines.

The entries in Table 8.3 confirm the similarities between the two states. Overall, candidates in Maryland and Arizona spend remarkably similar pro-

TABLE 8.2. CONTRIBUTIONS AS PERCENTAGE OF REGISTERED VOTERS, 2006 ELECTION

	Registered Voters	Contributions	Percentage
Arizona	2,568,401	39,651	1.5
Maine	993,748	14,012	1.4
Maryland	3,056,657	35,344	1.2

Source: National Institute for Money in State Politics, http://www.followthemoney.org.

Note: Different state reporting regulations lead to the availability of different information. The figures for Maryland reflect the number of individual contributions to candidates for state electoral office, while the figures for Arizona and Maine represent contributions from all entities except parties and the public fund. Thus, in all three cases, the actual number of voters who directly contribute to campaigns is inflated; individuals who donate to more than one campaign are counted each time, and in Arizona and Maine, PAC contributions are included in the tabulation.

TABLE 8.3.   TIME ALLOCATIONS OF 2006 CANDIDATES*

State	Average Weekly Campaign Hours	Fund-raising, Percentage of Time	Public Index, Percentage of Time	Housekeeping Index, Percentage of Time
Arizona	42.0[†]	7.5[†‡]	68.8[†]	31.2[†]
Maryland	48.7[†]	12.6[†‡]	69.9[†]	30.1[†]
Maine	34.75[†]	3.4[†]	81.5[†]	18.5[†]

*For the three-state comparison, means are tested with ANOVA and Kruskal-Wallis methods. Differences between Arizona and Maryland are examined with Tukey-Kramer tests.

[†] One-way ANOVA indicates at least one state is significantly different at $\alpha = .05$.

[‡] Arizona and Maryland are significantly different at $\alpha = .05$.

portions of their time engaged in public interaction and housekeeping activities. However, as Francia and Herrnson's (2003) finding would suggest, Marylanders overall spend a significantly greater proportion of their time on fund-raising than candidates in either Arizona or Maine. Despite this difference, candidates in Arizona and Maryland do not devote significantly different percentages of their time to either public interaction or housekeeping activities. Moreover, the candidates for Maine's nonprofessionalized legislature differ significantly from Maryland and Arizona in the expected direction. In short, Arizona and Maine, as the only two states offering full public funding in the 2006 election, provide a unique opportunity to measure the impact of public money on candidate time and electoral outcomes in very different environments.

Data are regressed from incumbent-contested elections for the lower house of each state. The dependent variable in the model is the respondents' general-election vote share. Model data include only candidates who ran in the general election and who responded to the time usage component of the survey. Primary losers and candidates who did not respond to questions regarding their time allocation were excluded, as were unopposed and weakly challenged incumbents.[10] The three states are modeled separately, and while the small sample in the case of Arizona ($N = 27$) presents some difficulty, I believe it preferable to the alternative of a pooled model that would group traditional candidates in Maine with those in Maryland, given substantial differences in professionalism and political culture between the two states.

The inclusion of Arizona and Maryland requires some modification to the data from those states. All candidates for the Arizona House of Representatives run in multimember districts. Voters choose two candidates on each ballot, and the top two vote recipients are elected to represent the district in tandem. Candidates for the Maryland House of Delegates run in one-, two-, or three-member districts with similar voting instructions. Because candidates in multimember districts are typically elected with between 25 percent and 35 percent of the overall votes cast, meaningful comparison of their vote percentage with the receipts of candidates in a conventional two-person race is difficult.

I address this issue with the correction first described by Niemi, Jackman, and Winsky (1991) and since employed effectively by others (e.g., Cox and Morgenstern 1993; Mayer, Werner, and Williams 2006). Using this method, the raw vote of the top recipient from one party in a multimember district is added to the lowest recipient of the other party, and percentages for each are calculated from the total. The same process is followed for the second-highest and second-lowest vote recipients, yielding "pseudo pairs" that approximate the dynamics of a traditional head-to-head race, allowing Arizona House candidates and those in multimember Maryland House of Delegates contests to be meaningfully compared to Maine and Maryland candidates running in single-member districts.

The number of hours each candidate devotes to public interaction and housekeeping activities is included as an independent variable. I expect that the financial parity present in most Arizona and Maine elections will diminish the relative importance of money, allowing candidates to drive voters to the polls with their field activity. In other words, greater public interaction efforts should result in higher levels of support on election day. I therefore anticipate public interaction activities to be positively associated with general-election vote percentage. Because time spent on housekeeping detracts from candidates' ability to spread their message, I anticipate those activities to display a negative correlation.

I do not expect candidate activity to be the sole determinant of electoral success. Accordingly, I add to the model a dummy variable reflecting candidate status as a challenger or incumbent, coded 0 for challengers and 1 for incumbents. I anticipate that the incumbency dummy will absorb not only the effects of incumbent advantage, including the inherent ability of incumbents to raise more money than challengers, but also the partisan preferences of voters in the district. Further, I expect the incumbency dummy to reflect differences in candidate experience. State house races are often entry-level contests; a dummy variable for challenger quality in this data set is highly collinear with a dichotomous measure of incumbency, rendering any potential control for challenger quality redundant.[11] In Maryland, the incumbency dummy is therefore the only predictor included in the model, aside from the public interaction and housekeeping variables.

TABLE 8.4.   TIME EXPENDITURES OF ARIZONA AND MAINE LOWER HOUSE
CANDIDATES, IN WEEKLY HOURS

	Clean Elections Status	Public Interaction	Housekeeping Activities
Overall			
Arizona	Opted out	20.3*	12.3
	Accepted	34.0*	13.6
Maine	Opted out	20.9*	7.1
	Accepted	31.4*	7.6
Incumbents			
Arizona	Opted out	22.5*	14.5
	Accepted	38.0*	11.2
Maine	Opted out	17.5*	6.9
	Accepted	29.0*	5.8
Challengers			
Arizona	Opted out	16.3*	10.2
	Accepted	33.1*	16.0
Maine	Opted out	13.4*	5.4
	Accepted	31.5*	7.8

*One-tailed tests, statistically significant at α = .05.

In all three states, I test the hypothesis of whether the number of hours a candidate devotes to public interaction and housekeeping is a significant predictor of candidate vote share. However, in Arizona and Maine, there are reasons to include additional regression terms. As Table 8.4 indicates, average hours devoted to behind-the-scenes tasks are remarkably similar between publicly financed candidates and those who run their campaigns with privately donated money, and when the groups are segmented into incumbents and challengers, there are no significant differences in housekeeping activities. Regardless of their clean elections status, candidates in Arizona and Maine recognize a need to perform basic maintenance. However, it is worth noting that the housekeeping hours of publicly funded candidates are almost certainly overstated, and the gap between them and traditional candidates is underreported, as a result of the wording of the survey question.[12]

The limitations of the questions have no bearing on the public interaction index, and publicly funded candidates in both Arizona and Maine spend significantly more time interacting with the public (see Table 8.4).[13] In Arizona, candidates in general spend nearly fourteen hours more per week engaged with voters or groups. In Maine, the disparity is almost eleven hours. The direction and size of the relationship is similar when the data are separated into challenger and incumbent groups. This consistent trend is indicative of a different sort of campaign when public money is involved: Publicly funded candidates in both states spend more time actively seeking votes.

However, while the entries in Table 8.4 demonstrate that candidates who accept public funds interact with the public to a greater extent, they also show that publicly funded candidates devote more time to their campaign in total, and that difference cannot be fully explained by the shift from fundraising to public interaction. There are a number of potential reasons for this difference: Traditional candidates may, for some reason, be inclined to campaign part-time. Publicly funded candidates may also possess traits that make them harder-working or more ambitious, or those who accept public funds may be less prone to burnout, allowing them to sustain higher levels of activity throughout their campaign.

Regardless of the reason, there is a difference in activity between the two groups. If publicly funded candidates tend to campaign more in general, it is reasonable to expect the effect of public interaction to differ between candidates in the two categories. I therefore add a dummy variable coded 0 for candidates who opt out of public funding and 1 for those who accept subsidies, and include an interaction term to arrive at the following model in publicly funded states:

$$Y = a + b_1 X_1 + b_2 X_2 + b_3 X_3 + b_4 X_4 + b_5 X_1 X_4$$

where

Y = vote percentage

X_1 = public interaction (mean centered)

X_2 = housekeeping

X_3 = a dummy variable for incumbency

X_4 = a dummy variable for publicly funded candidates

Because of the expected difference in the impact of public interaction between traditional and publicly funded groups, the interaction between the public funding dummy variable and the number of public interaction hours is the predictor of interest. I anticipate a positive, significant interaction coefficient in both Arizona and Maine, indicating a stronger effect of public interaction for publicly funded candidates. The candidate's number of weekly public interaction hours is centered based on a mean of 34.83 in Arizona and 30.23 in Maine. Centering allows for more meaningful interpretation of the coefficient for public interaction. The interaction component terms, in this case the public funding dummy variable and the public interaction variable, reflect the expected effect of those variables when the other equals zero. The coefficient for the public funding dummy in a model with a noncentered variable would be interpreted as the effect of moving from the privately financed to the fully funded category when the number of public interaction hours equals zero. Subtracting the mean from each data point in the public interaction variable allows for that effect to be measured when those hours are at their mean level instead of zero in the respective states. Since the candidate who spends zero hours devoted to public interaction is a rare animal, for the purposes of this question, mean centering produces a better interpretation.

Findings

The relationship between public interaction and general-election vote percentage is engaged with an OLS regression model for each state. The model includes a multiplicative interaction term reflecting the product of a dummy variable for publicly funded candidates and a mean-centered term for the number of weekly hours candidates devoted to public interaction. Regression coefficients, which are contained in Table 8.5, demonstrate that the relationship between public interaction and vote percentage, as mediated by status as a clean elections candidate, appears markedly different in Maine and Arizona. Despite no evidence of heteroscedasticity, I report robust standard errors to adjust for any nonrandom variance that may be present.[14]

With R^2 ranging from .43 to .84, the models in all three states demonstrate good predictive power. As expected, the dummy variables for incumbency are highly significant, with p-values approaching zero in all three cases: Not surprisingly, incumbents performed better in the general election. Moreover, in both Arizona and Maine, the models verify the existence

TABLE 8.5.   CAMPAIGN ACTIVITY AND VOTE PERCENTAGE, INCUMBENT-CHALLENGED RACES

	Arizona ($N = 27$, $R^2 = .84$)	Maine ($N = 72$, $R^2 = .48$)	Maryland ($N = 47$, $R^2 = .43$)
Constant	48.9* (.11)	40.04* (3.40)	45.4* (5.79)
Public index	.44* (.11)	−.06 (.10)	.07 (.10)
Housekeeping index	−.22* (.09)	−.30* (.12)	−.29 (.21)
Incumbency dummy	14.78* (1.78)	16.02* (2.05)	17.44* (3.42)
Public money dummy	−1.20 (2.21)	7.15* (3.01)	NA
Public dummy × public index	−.36* (.11)	.29* (.12)	NA

*Statistically significant $p \leq .05$. Ordinary least squares (OLS) regression. Robust standard errors in parentheses. Dependent variable is candidate general-election vote percentage.

of a time-opportunity cost when candidates perform housekeeping tasks. In other words, every hour that candidates in those two states devote to fund-raising, strategy meetings, and research detracts from their general election vote percentage. In Maryland, neither the housekeeping nor public interaction indices achieve significance, indicating that campaign activities matter little there: In the traditionally funded elections of Maryland, the power of candidates' activities pales in comparison to the effect of incumbency and the accompanying gaps in spending ability.

In the publicly funded states, the differences in campaign activity between publicly funded and traditional candidates necessitate the inclusion of an additional variable and interaction. The interaction term is significant in both Arizona and Maine, verifying that the effect of public interaction on general-election vote percentage is meditated by candidates' participation in the program. However, the models yield evidence of opposite effects for the two candidate groups in Arizona and Maine. The coefficients for the terms involved in the interaction are interpreted differently than they would be in a strictly additive linear model. Because public interaction is centered in this model, the coefficient of the predictor for the public funding dummy can be interpreted as the effect of public interaction at mean levels on general election vote percentage for all candidates in the sample. Thus on average a candidate in Maine who devotes approximately thirty hours per week to public interaction can expect a gain of 7.15 points. In Arizona, this term fails to achieve significance. In other words, on average, candidates in Arizona face conditions similar to those in Maryland: The hours that they devote to public interaction have no ultimate effect on their vote receipt.

The coefficient of the predictor for the public index reflects the effect of a one-hour increase in public interaction by traditionally funded candidates.[15] In Arizona traditional candidates can expect to gain nearly 0.5 percent in general-election vote total with a one-hour increase in the average devotion of their campaign time to public interaction. The positive significant coefficient of the public interaction index in Arizona indicates that while candidates overall reap little benefit from public interaction, traditionally financed candidates receive a bump of nearly 0.5 percent for every weekly public interaction hour. In Maine the opposite is true: The insignificance of the public index coefficient shows that traditional candidates receive no benefit from public interaction.

The coefficient for the interaction term can be interpreted as the difference in slopes between traditional candidates and those receiving public money. The model therefore predicts a coefficient for public interaction of publicly funded candidates in Arizona and Maine as .08 and approximately

.23, respectively. However, only the difference in Maine is significant.[16] In other words, publicly funded candidates do not receive a benefit from public interaction in Arizona. In Maine, the effect of public interaction for publicly funded candidates is both positive and significant, as they parlay their ability to forgo fund-raising into electoral gains at higher levels than their privately financed counterparts.

In short, while the model results in Maryland confirm expectations of a traditional campaign environment dominated by incumbency and money, those in Arizona and Maine paint quite a different picture. Candidates in both states incur a vote cost due to housekeeping activities. However, in Arizona, only traditional candidates are able to swing votes with public interaction. For whatever reason, publicly funded candidates are unable to increase their vote totals with public interaction tasks. Traditional candidates in Maine face the same problem, as only publicly funded candidates there significantly influence voters with their field activities.

Discussion

Publicly funded candidates in Arizona and Maine generally devote greater time to public interaction during the crucial phases of the election. The key question then becomes, Does it matter? Previous examinations have found that the power of incumbents and money in traditionally funded electoral environments is too strong for challengers to overcome: No matter what they do on the campaign trail, most challengers are destined to lose. Unless they self-fund, challengers must invest substantial time and resources in funding. This necessity presents a substantial time-opportunity cost as challengers find themselves caught in the vicious cycle: To be viable, they must raise funds, but to raise funds, they must be viable. As challengers solve this paradox, incumbents enjoy advantages of funding and name recognition against challengers in all but a handful of cases, sealing the challenger's fate regardless of campaign activity. Such an environment is present in Maryland, where vote totals are unaffected by the time candidates spend interacting with the public. Incumbency, with its advantages of money and name recognition, rules the day. Perhaps in response to these conditions, over 60 percent of respondents from Maryland believe that all state elections there should be publicly funded.

In Arizona and Maine, where full public subsidies are universally available, the picture is more complex. In both states, the effect of public interaction is mediated by candidate participation in public funding; however, while in Maine only publicly funded candidates enjoy a significant relationship between voter interaction and votes, in Arizona the opposite is true. In both states, publicly funded candidates are able to devote significantly more time to voter mobilization efforts, but their efforts lead to higher general-election vote totals only in Maine. If public money is designed to create more efficacious candidates by freeing them from fund-raising, then in Arizona, it has achieved only a partial victory.

There are at least two important ramifications of these findings. First, for publicly funded candidates in Maine, campaigning matters. Candidates enjoy more discretion over how to use valuable campaign time, and so they devote time to crucial voter mobilization tasks. To proponents of clean elections dedicated to restoring a sense of parity on the ledger *and* at the ballot box, this is good news. Among other things, public support for clean elections was predicated on the assumption that incumbents were inherently advantaged and that the time demands of fund-raising were degrading the quality of campaigns. The results here demonstrate that the two issues are not distinct. If they operate within a system characterized by general financial parity, it seems intuitive that traditional incumbent electoral advantage should diminish. Add to this consideration the fact that subsidies require no fund-raising effort in important preelection time periods, and Maine's challengers gain the ability to control their own destiny to a much greater degree.

This trend bears favorably on the future of enhanced electoral competitiveness. It has been noted that electoral competition has become more meaningful in both Maine and Arizona since the implementation of clean elections (Mayer, Werner, and Williams 2006). Clean elections has empowered challengers, allowing them access to sufficient resources to mount effective campaigns. Fund-raising precludes a candidate from devoting time to anything else; if overall campaign time is held constant, an hour spent raising money is unlikely to be made up elsewhere. Consequently, something is lost as candidates jockey for dollars instead of votes. The opportunity cost is recaptured by means of substantially higher amounts of time spent directly engaged in the public solicitation of votes, leading to challengers who are better equipped to shape the election's outcome.[17]

Unfortunately for reformers, Arizona fails to conform to the same happy story. Arizona's publicly funded candidates spend more time in the field than their privately financed counterparts, but do not reap the same benefits. This finding may seem counterintuitive, but there are at least two potential reasons for the model's producing this result. For one, Arizona's legislature is more professionalized, and its elections are more expensive. Elections in Maine occur in small districts where face-to-face campaigning is more likely to offer maximum return. Arizonans, on the other hand, compete in geographically and demographically larger districts, leading them to rely more on mailing and advertising. While publicly funded candidates do devote more time to field activities such as canvassing, it could be that mass campaigning is simply more effective there. Another reason may stem from available data: The Arizona sample is small ($N = 27$), and only five of the respondents included in the regression were traditionally funded candidates. The micronumerosity issue certainly confounds inference, but unfortunately it cannot be overcome with existing data. The best correction for this issue is the gathering of more and better data to clarify the narrative in Arizona.

Second, regardless of the relationship between candidate activities and their vote totals, publicly funded candidates in both Arizona and Maine devote more time to activities expressly intended to mobilize voters. This fact suggests that, when it comes to evaluating public election funding, examinations of macro electoral competitiveness are insufficient. The potential for greater interaction between candidates and the electorate engages the issues of waning participatory inclinations in the electorate and mobilization efforts that are less than all-inclusive. The reality for most American campaigns is that there is not enough time or money to reach every voter in a meaningful way. Public money promises to elevate the resource stature of candidates, equipping them to effectively mobilize supporters inspired to participate in the political process.

Political campaigns are a crucial element of voter education and activation. When campaigns have relatively easy access to the financial resources necessary to communicate with voters, general levels of information about candidates should rise. Moreover, because fewer candidates will be grossly outspent in publicly funded elections, voters should be more likely to trust that their favored candidates have a realistic chance of winning, regardless of that candidate's status as an incumbent or challenger. This belief can be expected to affect political participation: If they feel that their candidate can win, citizens should be more likely to wear buttons, put up signs, or volunteer in some capacity.

Future evaluations of public funding should acknowledge not only the importance of campaign time but also the possibility that success may be found in less readily measurable concepts, such as civic engagement in the electorate. Even if clean elections proposals are not changing victory margins, conclusions of inefficacy are premature. For example, one Arizona candidate running against a strong incumbent said that while he knew he was going to lose, he "gave voters the conversation." In other words, while that candidate would not have bothered to challenge an incumbent if he had to raise his own money, public subsidies allowed him to knock on every door in the district and to send out several targeted mailings. While it seems reasonable to conclude that this activity worked to the incumbent's detriment on election day, the act of presenting voters with a choice may have value in itself. Regardless, political science must move beyond illusory concepts such as competition to account for changing incentives and campaign dynamics, from the perspective of candidates and voters alike.

Appendix: Description of Clean Elections in Arizona and Maine

Passed as a public ballot initiative in 1998, the Citizens' Clean Elections Act (AZ Title 16, Chapter 6, Article 7) was implemented in time for Arizona state elections in 2000. In 2006, the legislation provided participating candidates with a subsidy of $17,918 for the general election and $11,945 for the primary, so long as candidates were able to demonstrate their viability by successfully soliciting at least 210 contributions of exactly five dollars (16-941, 16-946, 16-949, 16-950). During the qualifying phases candidates may privately raise a relatively small amount of seed money, but if they ultimately accept public financing, candidates agree to forgo any additional sources of finance and to spend only the sum of the subsidy (16-941, 16-949). If participants in the program find themselves outspent by traditionally funded opponents, Arizona matches the difference up to three times the subsidy amount (16-952). This provision is also true for independent expenditures made on behalf of opponents. Candidates are required to file reports at monthly intervals (16-941, 16-948), and those who attempt to circumvent any provisions of the legislation are subject to civil penalties or electoral ineligibility (16-941, 16-957).

Public funding in Maine is similar in every regard. The Maine Clean Elections Act (MCEA, Maine Title 21-A, Chapter 14) passed by voter referendum in 1996 and became active during the 2000 election cycle. Like Arizona's law, MCEA provides optional full subsidies for candidates for state office. To qualify in 2006, House candidates solicited fifty contributions of five dollars, after which they received subsidies of $1,504 for the primary and $4,362 for the general election.[18] Senate candidates were required to obtain 150 contributions and received $7,746 and $20,082, respectively. These amounts are equivalent to the average expenditure of candidates in the respective houses for the two previous primary and general elections (Title 21A, Chapter 14, Article 8). Like Arizona, Maine requires stringent financial reporting to ensure compliance and provides matching funds on behalf of participating candidates for expenditures above the subsidy amount made

APPENDIX TABLE 8.1. REPRESENTATIVE CHARACTER OF CANDIDATE SAMPLES, BY STATE (PERCENT)

	Arizona		Maine		Maryland	
	Population	Sample	Population	Sample	Population	Sample
Democrats	34.0	39.7	48.8	52.3	59.3	66.1
Republicans	58.7	52.9	48.5	44.9	35.5	29.8
Challengers	26.3	44.1	40.3	39.2	29.1	43.9
Incumbents	32.0	30.9	30.0	32.0	29.7	27.6
Open seats	41.7	25	29.7	28.8	41.1	28.5
Primary winners	77.4	80.8	93.2	95.4	61.4	62.9
Accepted public money	60.0	67.6	75.1	84.2	N/A	N/A

by opposition campaigns or independent groups. However, Maine matches only up to two times the original subsidy amount, making the program less generous than Arizona's. Aside from this difference, the funding provisions in both states are essentially the same policy designed to provide candidates optional public funds sufficient to mount a viable campaign.

NOTES

Acknowledgments: The author gratefully acknowledges the Government Department at Cornell University for financial support of data collection and Peter Enns, Peter Francia, Paul Herrnson, Michael Jones-Correa, Theodore J. Lowi, and Walter Mebane for insightful comments throughout numerous revisions. In their capacity as discussants or mentors, Allen Carlson, Christopher Larimer, Dean Spiliotes, and Kevin Wagner have provided crucial advice. Especially considering the numerous iterations of this chapter, it should be noted that all mistakes, oversights, and omissions rest with the author alone.

1. Full funding is available for all state elections in two states, and under the *Buckley v. Valeo* (1976) precedent, participation is optional. Here, the focus is on legislative elections. New Mexico opted for similar reforms for its Public Regulation Commission candidates in 2003, and North Carolina implemented full funding for judicial candidates in 2004. Connecticut will begin offering full public subsidies in 2008 state elections, while New Jersey may expand its legislative program beyond a pilot stage. Albuquerque and Portland have recently passed full funding laws for municipal elections, and at least a dozen other cities are considering them.

2. These five states were the only ones with widely available public financing for legislative races in 2004. Data were obtained from the Wisconsin Campaign Finance Project at http://campfin.polisci.wisc.edu/

3. As of the 2006 election, Arizona and Maine were the only two states with available full funding for all legislative candidates.

4. There is no substantive difference between respondent groups that completed the survey online and those that mailed a paper copy. The survey excludes candidates for executive, county, and statewide offices because there was a comparatively small number of such candidates.

5. 124 total responses were received from Maryland (response rate = 24 percent) 69 from Arizona (37.1 percent), and 153 from Maine (39.6 percent).

6. While there are no apparent unnatural abnormalities in the sample data, Maryland and Arizona challengers are slightly overrepresented in the sample.

7. Maryland's House of Delegates had 98 of the 141 members (69.5 percent) caucusing with the majority Democrats. In Arizona's House, 39 of the 60 members were Republicans (65 percent). The upper chambers were also comparable in majority advantage. Maryland Democrats held 32 of the 47 seats (68 percent), while Arizona Republicans occupied 18 of 30 seats (60 percent).

8. Arizona ranks eighteenth, and Maryland is sixteenth.

9. Individuals in Maryland may donate $4,000 to any candidate in a four-year period, and a maximum of $10,000 to all political candidates. Political action committees may contribute up to $6,000 to any candidate within the same four-year period, but have no aggregate limitations.

10. Weakly challenged candidates are those who received more than 85 percent of the vote. In two cases in Maine, the winner was challenged by only a candidate of the Green Independent Party, with the latter candidate receiving more than 20 percent of the vote. In those cases, the GIP candidate was treated as a major party challenger.

11. In Arizona, only 2.9 percent of all nonincumbent legislative candidates can be considered "quality," according to the Arizona Association of Counties 2006 election guide. Fewer than 5 percent of challengers from Maryland during the 2006 general election met the previous office threshold, according to candidate biographies on the University of Maryland's National Center for the Study of Elections Web site. Information on candidates in Maine is more difficult to obtain, but the pattern present in the other two states, combined with Maine's relatively low level of professionalization, is suggestive that challengers in Maine are similarly inexperienced.

12. Candidates were asked to quantify their devotion of time to fund-raising on average throughout the campaign. Many publicly funded candidates factored in the time-consuming process of raising five-dollar qualifying contributions, noting their responses as such. In these cases, fund-raising time is inflated during the primary and general elections, when participating candidates were proscribed from raising money. The shortcoming will be corrected in future research.

13. Samples are treated as independent.

14. Cook-Weisberg tests and Cook's distances indicate no issues with heteroscedasticity or influential observations, respectively. Visual inspection of the residuals also indicates no problems. Mean variance inflation factors range from 1.04 to 2.8. No single term has a variance inflation factor greater than 5.18. As a further robustness check, model results are confirmed with confidence intervals based on a 5,000-sample nonparametric bootstrap. Finally, sign and significance of coefficients remain unchanged when the vote receipt is modeled as a count with a control for total votes cast utilizing a negative binomial model.

15. Traditionally funded candidates are coded 0.

16. Standard errors of the differences in Arizona and Maine are .055 and .071 respectively, yielding t-statistics of 1.45 and 3.24.

17. On this point, a cautionary note is in order. The power of incumbency remains formidable in both Arizona and Maine, and incumbents still win with exceptional regularity. The effect of one weekly hour spent interacting with voters is strikingly similar in the two states, at approximately 0.18 percent, but despite its significance, this effect is likely to alter the outcome of only the closest of elections.

18. Subsidy amounts in Maine are substantially lower than those in Arizona, but they still cover the entire cost of Maine campaigns, which are significantly less expensive than Arizona's.

REFERENCES

Caldeira, Gregory, and Samuel Patterson. 1982. "Bringing Home the Votes: Electoral Outcomes in State Legislative Races." *Political Behavior* 4:33–67.

Cassie, William, and David Breaux. 1998. "Expenditures and Election Results." In *Campaign Finance in State Legislative Elections*, ed. Joel Thompson and Gary Moncrief. Washington, DC: Congressional Quarterly.

Cox, Gary W., and Scott Morgenstern. 1993. "The Increasing Advantage of Incumbency in the U.S. States." *Legislative Studies Quarterly* 18 (4): 495–514.

Donnay, Patrick, and Graham Ramsden. 1995. "Public Financing of Legislative Elections: Lessons from Minnesota." *Legislative Studies Quarterly* 20 (3): 351–364.

Francia, Peter L., and Paul S. Herrnson. 2003. "The Impact of Public Finance Laws on Fundraising in State Legislative Elections." *American Politics Research* 31 (5): 520–539.

Gerber, Alan S. 2004. "Does Campaign Spending Work? Field Experiments Provide Evidence and Suggest New Theory." *American Behavioral Scientist* 47 (5): 541–574.

Gerber, Alan S., and Donald P. Green. 2000. "The Effects of Canvassing, Telephone Calls, and Direct Mail on Voter Turnout: A Field Experiment." *American Political Science Review* 94 (3): 653–663.

Gierzynski, Anthony, and David A. Breaux. 1991. "Money and Votes in State Legislative Elections." *Legislative Studies Quarterly* 16 (2): 203–217.

———. 1993. "Money and the Party Vote in State House Elections." *Legislative Studies Quarterly* 18 (4): 515–533.

Giles, Michael, and Anita Pritchard. 1985. "Campaign Expenditures and Legislative Elections in Florida." *Legislative Studies Quarterly* 10 (1): 71–88.

Goidel, Robert K., and Donald A. Gross. 1996. "Reconsidering the 'Myths and Realities' of Campaign Finance Reform." *Legislative Studies Quarterly* 21 (1): 129–149.

Green, Donald P., Alan S Gerber, and David W Nickerson. 2003. "Getting Out the Vote in Local Elections: Results from Six Door-to-Door Canvassing Experiments." *Journal of Politics* 65 (4): 1083–1096.

Green, Donald, and Jonathan Krasno. 1990. "Rebuttal to Jacobson's 'New Evidence for Old Arguments.'" *American Journal of Political Science* 34 (2): 363–372.

Gross, Donald, and Robert K. Goidel. 2003. *The States of Campaign Finance*. Columbus: Ohio State University Press.

Hillygus, D. Sunshine. 2005. "Campaign Effects and the Dynamics of Turnout Intention in Election 2000." *Journal of Politics* 67 (1): 50–68.

Howell, Susan E. 1982. "Campaign Activities and State Election Outcomes." *Political Behavior* 4 (4): 401–417.

Jones, Ruth, and Thomas Borris. 1985. "Strategic Contributing in Legislative Campaigns: The Case of Minnesota." *Legislative Studies Quarterly* 10 (1): 89–105.

Kramer, Gerald H. 1970. "The Effects of Precinct-Level Canvassing on Voter Behavior." *Public Opinion Quarterly* 34 (4): 560–572.

Kraus, Jeffrey. 2006. "Campaign Finance Reform Reconsidered: New York City's Public Finance Program after Fifteen Years." *The Forum* 3 (4): 1–27. Available at http://www.bepress.com/forum/vol3/iss4/art6/.

Malbin, Michael J., and Thomas L. Gais. 1998. *The Day after Reform: Sobering Campaign Finance Lessons from the American States.* Albany, NY: Rockefeller Institute Press.

Mayer, Kenneth R., Timothy Werner, and Amanda Williams. 2006. "Do Public Funding Programs Enhance Electoral Competition?" In *The Marketplace of Democracy: Electoral Competition and American Politics*, ed. Michael P. McDonald and John Samples. Washington, DC: Brookings Institution Press.

Mayer, Kenneth R., and John M. Wood. 1995. "The Impact of Public Financing on Electoral Competitiveness: Evidence from Wisconsin, 1964–1990." *Legislative Studies Quarterly* 20 (1): 69–88.

Niemi, Richard G., Simon Jackman, and Laura R. Winsky. 1991. "Candidacies and Competitiveness in Multimember Districts." *Legislative Studies Quarterly* 16 (1): 91–109.

Niven, David. 2001. "The Limits of Mobilization: Turnout Evidence from State House Primaries." *Political Behavior* 23 (4): 335–350.

———. 2002. "The Mobilization Calendar: The Time-Dependent Effects of Personal Contact on Turnout." *American Politics Research* 30 (3): 307–322.

Panagopoulos, Costas, and Donald P. Green. 2008. "Field Experiments Testing the Impact of Radio Advertisements on Electoral Competition." *American Journal of Political Science* 52 (1): 156–168.

Parry, Janine, Jay Barth, Martha Kropf, and E. Terrence Jones. 2008. "Mobilizing the Seldom Voter: Campaign Contact and Effects in High-Profile Elections." *Political Behavior* 30 (1): 97–113.

Putnam, Robert D. 1995. "Tuning In, Tuning Out: The Strange Disappearance of Social Capital in America." *PS: Political Science and Politics* 28 (4): 664–683.

Rosenstone, Steven J., and John Mark Hansen. 1993. *Mobilization, Participation, and Democracy in America.* New York: Macmillan.

Schultz, David. 2002. "Special Interest Money in Minnesota State Politics." In *Money, Politics, and Campaign Finance Reform Law in the States*, ed. David Schultz. Durham, NC: Carolina Academic Press.

Squire, Peverill. 2000. "Uncontested Seats in State Legislative Elections." *Legislative Studies Quarterly* 25 (1): 131–146.

Tucker, Harvey, and Ronald E. Weber. 1987. "State Legislative Outcomes: Contextual Effects and Legislative Performance Effects." *Legislative Studies Quarterly* 12:537–553.

U.S. General Accounting Office. 2003. *Report to Congressional Committees. Campaign Finance Reform: Early Experiences of Two States That Offer Full Public Funding for Political Candidates.* Washington, DC: GAO.

Van Dunk, Emily. 1997. "Challenger Quality in State Legislative Elections." *Political Research Quarterly* 50 (4): 793–807.

Wilcox, Clyde. 2001. "Contributing as Political Participation." In *A User's Guide to Campaign Finance Reform*, ed. Gerald C. Lubenow. Lanham, MD: Rowman and Littlefield.

9

◇ ◇ ◇

Does Public Financing of State Election Campaigns Increase Voter Turnout?

Jeffrey Milyo, David M. Primo,
and Matthew L. Jacobsmeier

Proponents of public financing for election campaigns frequently claim that such reforms increase voter participation. This argument not only is offered as a prediction about the effects of reforms but also has been cited as a factual consequence of prior public financing reforms. Despite these assertions, there is little evidence that there exists any such effect on turnout, let alone the dramatic impact claimed by proponents of public financing. This absence of evidence is in part attributable to a lack of attention paid to the question by social scientists. We are aware of only two scholarly investigations of the effects of public financing on voter turnout (Gross and Goidel 2003; Primo and Milyo 2006b). Further, both of these studies examined only voting in gubernatorial elections, and neither of study extended beyond 2000. Therefore, little is known about the turnout effects of either public financing of state legislative campaigns or recent full public financing (i.e., "clean elections") reforms.

In this study, we conduct the first systematic test of the treatment effect of state public financing on voter turnout. We exploit the occurrence of recent campaign finance reforms in the states to estimate the effect on voter turnout from public financing of gubernatorial and state legislative campaigns. The time period that we examine extends from 1990 to 2008, so we are also able to conduct the first evaluation of the effects of "clean elections" reforms in the states on voter turnout. In the next section, we elaborate on the motivation for our analysis. In subsequent sections, we detail our data, methods, and results. We then discuss the implications of our findings.

The Link between Public Financing
and Voter Turnout

The reform community has long argued that public financing will have a dramatic and salutary effect on American democracy. In turn, voluntary participation in elections is widely considered a key indicator of the health of any democracy. It is therefore no surprise that many proponents of public funding for elections see it as an important determinant of voter turnout.

Reformers identify at least two distinct means by which public financing is expected to increase voter turnout: increased confidence in government and increased electoral competition. For example, Warren Rudman, former U.S. senator and honorary cochair of Americans for Campaign Reform, articulates one causal pathway:

> The time has come for our Congress to seriously consider public financing of federal elections. With public financing, the power will be with voters, not special interests. When the cost of financing a campaign is not an intimidating obstacle, more of our most able leaders will run for office. Once elected, they will spend their time and energy attending to the nation's business instead of wasting their time on nonstop fundraising. And when Americans have greater confidence in our democracy, more will participate and more will vote. (Common Cause 2009a)[1]

The second pathway by which public financing increases turnout is captured nicely in the same Web document available from Common Cause:

> While voter turnout is affected by other factors, Clean Elections, by increasing competition and bringing new, fresh faces into the system, encourages people to come out and vote.[2]

Reality Check: Slippery Statistics about Clean Elections

In the wake of the implementation of clean elections reforms in Arizona and Maine, several advocacy groups have issued "studies" of the impact of public financing on elections in these states. Clean elections systems offer candidates the opportunity to receive public monies for campaigns provided that they spend and raise no other funds (beyond an initial set of small contributions to demonstrate support from the voters). This system has been hailed as an elixir that will cure all that ails government. For instance, the Arizona law approved by voters in 1998 promised that it "will improve the integrity of Arizona state government by diminishing the influence of special-interest money, *will encourage citizen participation in the political process*, and will promote freedom of speech under the U.S. and Arizona Constitutions. Campaigns will become more issue-oriented and less negative because there will be no need to challenge the sources of campaign money" (§16-940 of the Citizens Clean Elections Act, A.R.S., Title 16, Chapter 6, Article 2; emphasis added).

Todd Lang, the executive director of the Arizona Citizens Clean Elections Commission, told a reform task force in New Mexico that public confidence and turnout increased in Arizona because of the Arizona reform (New Mexico Governor's Ethics and Campaign Finance Reform Task Force 2006). It is not surprising, then, that in calling for reforms in their own states, reformers elsewhere have pointed to Arizona and Maine as evidence of the good that clean elections can do. Washington Public Campaigns (2009) writes that reform is "not just a pipe dream" in part because Arizona and Maine have "higher turnout." In promoting a possible 2010 initiative, the California Clean Money Campaign (2009) put together a flyer extolling the benefits of clean elections, including the claim that this reform will increase voter turnout just as it did in Arizona. Alaskan legislators, as well as reformers in Marin and San Rafael, California, have also pointed to Arizona turnout as justification for passing similar legislation in their respective locales (Wielechowski and LeDoux 2007; Marin Clean Elections 2009). One representative of the Marin group, after noting in a public meeting that turnout had increased in Arizona, even said, "Coincidence? I don't think so." The group Rhode Islanders for Fair Elections (2009) argues that the Maine and Arizona experiences show that clean elections can lead to "increased voter turnout." As "proof" of success, they write, "Voter turnout increased 23% between 1998 and 2006 in Arizona. In 2004, turnout in Maine hit a record high of 73.75%, in a year that 77% of candidates were publicly financed." Common Cause (2009b), in an issue brief on clean elections, uses similar data to argue that "Clean Money reforms increase voter participation." Specifically, the group writes, "In 2002, Arizona's voter turnout increased 22% over 1998, both gubernatorial election years. In 2004, voter turnout was a full 67% higher than in 1998. Maine's turnout hit a record high of 74% in 2004, in a year that 77% of candidates ran as Clean Election candidates." The paragraph concludes, "Clearly, other factors affect changes in voter turnout as well."

Common Cause is correct that other factors affect changes in voter turnout, and a proper analysis of turnout must account for these factors. We do

TABLE 9.1.   AVERAGE TURNOUT IN ARIZONA, MAINE, AND THE UNITED STATES,
1980–2008 (PERCENT)

	Arizona	Maine	United States
Pre–clean elections			
1980–1998	43	60	47
1990–1998	43	61	45
Post–clean elections, 2000–2008	46	63	51
All elections			
Low	31 (1998)	50 (1986)	38 (1998)
High	56 (2008)	74 (1992)	62 (2008)

Source: Calculated using McDonald data available at http://elections.gmu.edu/voter_turnout.htm.

so in this article. What is remarkable, though, is the misuse of even raw statistics to articulate the case for public financing. There are several ways to show how misleading the preceding figures are. First, in contrasting 1998 and 2004, Common Cause is comparing a presidential election year to a midterm election. As such, this comparison is virtually meaningless, since turnout in presidential election years is virtually always higher than in midterm election years. Second, turnout figures in Maine in 2004 were nearly identical to figures in 1992, and our statistics show that turnout was higher in 1992. This claim, then, is overblown and potentially inaccurate.

What about the other figures? The year-to-year comparisons are misleading because they focus on just two time points. For instance, if one uses the years 1994 and 2006 (i.e., two midterm elections before and after clean elections were implemented), then one can write that turnout in Arizona declined. Neither this claim, nor the claim articulated by Common Cause, is credible without further scrutiny.

When we examine the five elections prior to and after the emergence of clean elections, a clearer picture emerges because we are considering longer periods of time (Table 9.1). Average turnout was 13 percent higher in the United States in the period 2000–2008 compared to 1990–1998, while it was just 8 percent higher in Arizona and 4 percent higher in Maine.[3] Of course, these figures is no way establish that clean elections have led to a decline in turnout, but it is hardly evidence of the "dramatic" increases in turnout heralded by some reformers (Gregg 2009).

Evidence from Scholarly Studies

The quoted statements from reform proponents suggest that public funding may influence voter turnout in two ways: either directly, by altering the public perception of the state political environment in a manner that encourages citizens to participate in elections (i.e., by means of increased trust), or indirectly, by means of increased electoral competitiveness. Yet, despite the prominence of a link to voter turnout in the public debate over campaign finance reform, very little scholarly attention has been paid to this issue. We now briefly review the existing relevant scholarly literature (also see Samples 2004).

Gross and Goidel (2003) devote a chapter of their book on state campaign finance reform to the consequences of such reforms for voter turnout in gubernatorial elections from 1978 to 1998. The authors find a positive association between public funding and turnout, with the presence of public funding for gubernatorial campaigns being associated with about a 3 percent increase in turnout as a percentage of the voting-age population. However, the authors do not control for unobserved state-level confounders (i.e., they do not use a differences-in-differences estimator). This concern is compounded by the fact that Gross and Goidel also do not control for any time trend or year-specific effects, nor do the authors control for the presence of other races that might influence turnout (e.g., a U.S. Senate contest) or any other political institutions that might influence voter turnout (e.g., voter registration laws). In addition, Gross and Goidel fail to consider the potential indirect effects of campaign finance regulations on turnout working through either campaign spending or electoral competition (i.e., no attention is given to structural versus reduced-form models).

The only other scholarly study directly on this topic is Primo and Milyo 2006b, which also examines voter turnout as a percentage of voting-age population in gubernatorial elections. Primo and Milyo estimate the reduced-form effect of public funding on turnout using both aggregate data from state elections and individual-level data from the American National Election Studies. For the post-*Buckley* period (1976–2000) they observe a negative relationship between public financing and turnout in gubernatorial elections, although this result is statistically significant in only their mixed-level analysis, not in their aggregate analysis (and the finding is not robust to including observations from 1950–1975). In contrast to Gross and Goidel (2003), Primo and Milyo control for year and state fixed effects, as well as other political institutions. However, Primo and Milyo do not include controls for the presence of other statewide elections, nor do they check the sensitivity of their results to including controls for the competitiveness of races. Finally, given the time period examined, the authors cannot say much about the effects of clean elections reforms.

One reason for the surprising effect of public funding on turnout in Primo and Milyo 2006b may be that the first link in the causal chain from reform to confidence in government (and from there to higher turnout) is itself negligible or nonexistent. Primo and Milyo 2006a is the only scientific test of the contention that state campaign finance reforms influence citizen perceptions of government, and it reveals that public funding has a perverse effect.[4] In addition, there is limited evidence that public funding increases electoral competition, which in turn should increase voter turnout. For example, in an unpublished study, Stratmann (2009) shows that public financing is associated with more competitive state legislative races, but Primo, Milyo, and Groseclose (2006) fail to find a statistically significant effect of public financing in gubernatorial elections on competitiveness. Given these mixed results, much more work is warranted on the question of whether public funding increases competitiveness.

In sum, there is surprisingly little hard evidence to support the oft-repeated claims of reformers. We now turn to the task of conducting a systematic test of the effect of public financing on turnout, using the most recent data available.

Data and Methods

The dependent variable in our study is voter turnout. As noted earlier, previous authors have measured this as a percentage of voting-age population. However, in this analysis we use a superior measure, turnout as a percentage of the voting-eligible population (McDonald 2002). This measure rules out those individuals who are counted as residents of a state and are of voting age, such as felons who are over eighteen years of age but not permitted to vote. We obtained turnout as a percentage of voting-eligible population (VEP) from Michael McDonald's United States Election Project website (http://elections.gmu.edu/voter_turnout.htm). The VEP-based turnout data is available for November general elections since 1980, although we present results for only the period 1990–2008. This shorter time span is more easily reconciled with a differences-in-differences model, which assumes that unobserved state effects are fixed over time.[5]

The key independent variable in our study is public financing of state gubernatorial or legislative elections. Throughout this analysis, we follow most scholars and political commentators in defining "public financing" to mean that public funds are made available to qualified candidates that voluntarily agree to abide by some aggregate campaign spending ceiling. Because public funding is voluntary, not all candidates will avail themselves of this conditional grant. For this reason, we estimate the impact of state public financing *programs* on voter turnout. That is, we simply classify states according to whether they have a public financing system or not (or a full

TABLE 9.2. PUBLIC FINANCING IN THE STATES, 1990–2008

	1990	1996	2002	2008
Public financing conditioned on expenditure limits				
Gubernatorial elections	7	10	14	14
State legislative elections	3	3	6	7
Full public financing ("clean elections")				
Gubernatorial elections	0	0	3	4
State legislative elections	0	0	2	3

Note: Cell entries indicate the number of states with each type of law.

versus partial public financing system). Table 9.2 lists the number of states with public financing (either partial or full) in six-year intervals; as indicated, the number of states that provide public funding has doubled since 1990. At present, fourteen states now employ public financing in gubernatorial elections, while seven states do so for legislative elections.

Our general model of the potential direct and indirect effects of public financing on state voter turnout may be expressed as

$$V = f[P, C(P), X, Y, Z] \tag{1}$$

where

V is voter turnout measured as a percentage of voting eligible population

P is an indicator for public financing

C is the competitiveness of state elections (which is in turn a function of P)

X is a vector of observable state-level determinants

Y is a vector of year indicators

Z is a vector of state-specific unobserved fixed effects

If we estimate this equation, the coefficient on P may be interpreted as the partial (or direct) effect of public financing on turnout. If instead, we simplify equation (1) by solving out for C, the model becomes

$$V = g(P, X, Y, Z) \tag{2}$$

In this case, the estimated coefficient on P may be interpreted as the total (direct plus indirect) effect on voter turnout.

This simple distinction between the partial and total effects of public financing is complicated by the presence of other statewide elections. For example, the competitiveness of a concurrent Senate election may be thought of as part of X, but it may also serve as a proxy for $C(P)$; we handle this ambiguity by estimating two versions of equation (2). The first includes only controls for the presence of various types of elections (e.g., U.S. Senate), while the second also includes controls for the competitiveness of other statewide elections. Finally, we also estimate equation (1), which includes the competitiveness of gubernatorial elections as a control variable, as well. Of course, we expect the estimated coefficient on this variable to be biased as a result of spurious correlation with omitted variables, but our primary concern here is with the robustness of our estimated coefficient on public financing (i.e., including competitiveness in gubernatorial elections may be understood as including a proxy to control for important unobserved determinants of turnout that might otherwise be spuriously correlated with public financing).

All models are estimated via ordinary least squares, with standard errors adjusted for clustering within state. As indicated by equations (1) and (2), every model includes controls for year and state fixed effects, as well as a set of state-level demographic characteristics. In particular, we control for the percentage of population that is black, the percentage that is of another minority race or mixed race, the percentage with Hispanic ethnicity, the percentage that has not completed high school, the percentage with a college degree, the percentage of persons in poverty, and the percentage of persons over age 65. In addition, we control for the natural logarithm of real per capita income. Every model also includes controls for state variation in political institutions that may influence voter turnout. These include indicators for limits on campaign contributions from individuals or organizations (e.g., PACs), "motor voter" registration laws, universal absentee ballot laws, universal early voting, election day registration (or no voter registration), and vote-by-mail. We also include indicators for states' term limits, the length of gubernatorial terms, and states with ballot initiative elections. Finally, every model also includes controls for the electoral environment. We include indicators for the presence of other elections: state legislative, gubernatorial, and U.S. Senate (year indicators account for presidential election year effects), as well as a control for year-by-year state-specific party tides (measured by the interaction of the year indicators and the Republican share of the major party vote in the most recent presidential election contest in that state).[6]

Results

We present our findings in Table 9.3; each column corresponds to one of the three models described previously. In column 1, we show the estimates for our sparsest model that isolates the direct effect of public financing. Because our dependent variable is voter turnout in every even-year November election, not every observation is coincident with a gubernatorial or regular state legislative election. For this reason, we include indicator variables for whether there is such an election in each state-year. Further, the public financing indicators take the value of 1 in only relevant election years. This means that the indicator for public financing in gubernatorial elections always takes the value 0 in a nongubernatorial election year (and similarly for the indicator for public financing in state legislative elections). The estimates in column 1 indicate that public financing in gubernatorial elections has a positive impact on turnout, although even this modest effect of less than 1 percent is only marginally significant. In contrast, public funding in state legislative elections decreases turnout by a statistically significant 2.7 percent.

While these effects may be surprising, looking across the columns of Table 9.3 shows that these estimates are robust to the inclusion of mea-

TABLE 9.3.   EFFECTS OF PUBLIC FINANCING ON VOTER TURNOUT, 1990-2008 ($N = 500$)

	(1) Percent VEP	(2) Percent VEP	(3) Percent VEP
Gubernatorial public financing	0.77 (1.89)	0.97 (1.73)	0.53 (1.69)
State legislative public financing	-2.74* (1.03)	-2.92† (1.00)	-2.95† (1.03)
Gubernatorial election	1.06 (1.04)	1.12 (1.09)	2.56* (1.17)
State legislative election	3.07 (2.23)	2.08 (2.15)	0.70 (2.15)
Senate election	1.28† (0.36)	2.31† (0.52)	2.31† (0.52)
Presidential vote margin		-13.84† (4.36)	-13.59† (4.12)
Senate vote margin		-4.56† (1.33)	-4.54† (1.30)
Gubernatorial vote margin			-7.55† (1.84)
Year and state indicators	Yes	Yes	Yes
Demographic controls	Yes	Yes	Yes
Other political controls	Yes	Yes	Yes
R^2	0.92	0.93	0.93

Note: Standard errors in parentheses are adjusted for clustering at the state level. Voter turnout is the highest total vote in even years for any statewide election (including federal races) as a percentage of voting eligible population. Demographic controls include race, ethnicity, educational attainment, poverty status, and log per capita income. Political controls include indicators for campaign contribution limits, voter registration laws, convenience voting, term limitations, and ballot initiatives. All models also control for year indicators interacted with share of the Republican vote by state in the most recent presidential election in order to control for partisan tides in turnout.

VEP, voting eligible population.

*$p < 0.05$; $^\dagger p < 0.01$.

sures of competitiveness as controls. This observation implies two important results. First, the direct effect of public financing on turnout is negative for legislative elections and insignificant for gubernatorial elections. Second, the indirect effect working through competitiveness is essentially zero. We discuss the meaning of this result in our conclusion.

Before moving on, several other observations arise from the results in Table 9.3. All three of our models explain nearly all the variation in voter turnout. This result mitigates any concern that our findings suffer from any important omitted variable bias. Also, the indicator variables for the presence of a statewide election are positive and significant in the full model. Further, the coefficients on winning margin are all negative and statistically significant. The signs on these control variables are all in the expected direction and thus corroborate our other findings.

Of course, not all public financing systems are the same. The recent wave of clean elections reforms that started in Arizona and Maine has been touted as superior to earlier-vintage partial financing systems, such as that employed in Wisconsin. In Table 9.4, we check whether there is any important difference between these systems for voter turnout. For each of our three models, we estimate separate coefficients for full and partial public funding in each type of election. The estimated impact of full public financing on voter turnout is negative in both types of elections (and significantly so in legislative elections). However, we cannot reject the null hypothesis that full and partial public financing have the same effect in legislative elections, nor can we reject the null that full and partial public financing have the same effect in gubernatorial elections. In other words, Clean elections really are not very different in terms of their impact on voter turnout.

We have also estimated these same models using voter turnout measured as a percentage of voting-age population. Doing so produces almost

TABLE 9.4.   ARE "CLEAN ELECTIONS" DIFFERENT? (NOT REALLY)

	(1) VEP (percent)	(2) VEP (percent)	(3) VEP (percent)
Gubernatorial *full* public financing	−1.05 (1.18)	−0.67 (1.02)	−1.41 (1.17)
State legislative *full* public financing	−2.26* (0.68)	−2.51* (0.68)	−2.42* (0.71)
Gubernatorial *partial* public financing	1.22 (2.18)	1.37 (1.98)	1.00 (1.93)
State legislative *partial* public financing	−3.01 (2.59)	−3.03 (2.58)	−3.23 (2.53)
R^2	.92	.93	.93

Note: Standard errors in parentheses are adjusted for clustering at the state level. Voter turnout is the highest total for any statewide or federal office as a percentage of voting-eligible population. The control variables included in each model are identical to those listed in Table 9.3.

*$p < .01$.

no change in our key estimates. Similarly, we have examined elections going back to 1980 (the McDonald data are missing one observation for Louisiana in 1982). This procedure does not substantively alter the qualitative findings presented here, although our estimated standard errors are somewhat larger.[7] Finally, we have also estimated the effects of voter turnout in all gubernatorial elections since 1980 or 1990 (i.e., including odd-year elections and omitting nongubernatorial election state-year observations). This alternative approach yields estimated coefficients on public financing between –1 percent and –2 percent, albeit still not statistically significant at conventional levels.

Discussion

This study presents the first systematic within-state estimates of the effects of state legislative public financing on voter turnout, as well as the first such estimates of the effects of clean elections reforms on voter turnout. In both cases, the estimated effect of these reforms on turnout is negative, although only the perverse effect of state legislative financing is statistically significant. These findings contrast with earlier work. However, Primo and Milyo (2006b) examine only data up to 2000, while Gross and Goidel (2003) do not control for state-specific fixed effects. Further, we have implemented a number of improvements in our empirical analysis, including using turnout measured by voting-eligible population and controlling for a broader array of political institutions that also influence turnout. Given these modifications, we are confident in stating that the most recent and best available evidence simply does not support the frequent claim that public financing will lead to higher voter turnout. In fact, for legislative elections, just the opposite is true.

Our analysis does give rise to an intriguing puzzle: We observe that the indirect effect of public financing working through competitiveness is essentially zero, even though previous studies have found that public funding tends to increase electoral competitiveness. We suspect that the explanation for this seeming inconsistency lies in the fact that the acceptance of public funding requires candidates to accept campaign expenditure limits. Therefore, not all competitive races are alike. A privately funded competitive election is typically associated by a deluge of campaign spending, while a competitive publicly financed election is not. We speculate that the reason that competitive races are positively associated with voter turnout is largely because of the increased campaign advertising typically associated with such races. We look forward to investigating this possibility further in future work.

NOTES

1. Similarly, Senator Arlen Spector (D-PA) announced: "I am joining Senator Durbin in introducing legislation in the Senate to provide for public financing because I believe it will be a significant step in improving public confidence in the election process" (Public Campaign 2009).

2. Another example of this argument has been made by Heartland Democracy (2009): "Clean Elections increase competition and bring new candidates into the system, which encourages people to come out and vote."

3. For arguments using similar calculations, see Hayward 2006 and Smith 2009.

4. Regarding the link between campaign finance reform and confidence in government, also see Persily and Lammie 2004; for related findings on the relationship between campaign *spending* (or advertising) and confidence in government, see Coleman and Manna 2000; Primo 2002; and Freedman, Franz, and Goldstein 2004.

5. Nevertheless, our findings are not sensitive to substituting the voting-age-population-based measure of turnout for the VEP-based measure, nor does extending the time period examined back to 1980 have any substantive impact on our findings.

6. State demographic data is taken from the U.S. Census Web site (some 2008 values are imputed from earlier years using simple straight-line estimation). Data on state political institutions are culled from a variety of public sources, including the *Book of the States*, *Campaign Finance Law*, the National Conference of State Legislatures, and Rigby and Springer 2009. Data on election outcomes is taken from *America Votes* and the *Almanac of American Politics*.

7. The only difference worthy of note is that the statistical significance of the estimated coefficient on public funding in legislative election falls to $p < .10$ in columns 1 and 3 of Table 9.3.

REFERENCES

California Clean Money Campaign. 2009. "California Fair Elections Act Flyer." Available at http://www.caclean.org/content/pdf/cfea_flyer.pdf (accessed August 14, 2009).

Coleman, John J., and Paul F. Manna. 2000. "Congressional Campaign Spending and the Quality of Democracy." *Journal of Politics* 62 (3): 757–789.

Common Cause. 2009a. "The Benefits of Clean Elections Reform." Available at http://www.commoncause.org/atf/cf/%7BFB3C17E2-CDD1-4DF6-92BE-BD4429893665%7D/CLEAN%20ELECTIONS%20BENEFITS.PDF (accessed August 14, 2009).

———. 2009b. "What Elected Officials Say about Public Financing." Available at http://www.commoncause.org/site/pp.asp?c=dkLNK1MQIwG&b=4773903 (accessed August 14, 2009).

Freedman, Paul, Michael Franz, and Kenneth Goldstein. 2004. "Campaign Advertising and Democratic Citizenship." *American Journal of Political Science* 48 (4): 723–741.

Gregg, Katherine. 2009. "Advocates Call for Public Financing of Assembly Campaigns." Projo Politics Blog, February 3. Available at http://politicsblog.projo.com/2009/02/embargoed-until.html (accessed August 14, 2009).

Gross, Donald A., and Robert K. Goidel. 2003. *The States of Campaign Finance Reform*. Columbus: Ohio State University Press.

Hayward, Allison R. 2006. "Campaign Promises: A Six-Year Review of Arizona's Experiment with Taxpayer-Financed Campaigns." Policy Report No. 209, Goldwater Institute.

Heartland Democracy. 2009. "Clean Elections." Available at http://www.heartlanddemocracy. org/cleanelections.html (accessed August 14, 2009).

Marin Clean Elections. 2009. Various Web pages. Available at http://www.marincleanelections. org (accessed August 16, 2009).

McDonald, Michael P. 2002. "The Turnout Rate among Eligible Voters for U.S. States, 1980–2000." *State Politics and Policy Quarterly* 2 (2): 199–212.

New Mexico Governor's Ethics and Campaign Finance Reform Task Force. 2006. Approved Minutes of the Third Meeting. June 28 and 29.

Persily, Nathaniel, and Kelli Lammie 2004. "Perceptions of Corruption and Campaign Finance: When Public Opinion Constitutes Constitutional Law." *University of Pennsylvania Law Review* 153: 119–180.

Primo, David M. 2002. "Campaign Finance and Public Opinion: Reformers versus Reality." *Independent Review* 7 (2): 207–219.

Primo, David M., and Jeffrey Milyo. 2006a. "Campaign Finance Laws and Political Efficacy: Evidence from the States." *Election Law Journal* 5 (1): 23–39.

———. 2006b. "The Effects of Campaign Finance Laws on Turnout: 1950–2000." Manuscript. University of Rochester and University of Missouri, February.

Primo, David M., Jeffrey Milyo, and Tim Groseclose. 2006. "State Campaign Finance Reform, Competitiveness, and Party Advantage in Gubernatorial Elections." In *The Marketplace of Democracy: Electoral Competition and American Politics*, ed. Michael P. McDonald and John Samples. Washington, DC: Brookings Institution Press, 268–285.

Public Campaign. 2009. "Quotes from Federal Elected Officials." Available at http://www. publicampaign.org/node/39241 (accessed August 14, 2009).

Rhode Islanders for Fair Elections. 2009. "Fair Elections in Rhode Island." Available at http://www.fairelectionsri.org/issue.php (accessed August 14, 2009).

Rigby, Elizabeth, and Melanie J. Springer. 2009. "Does Electoral Reform Increase (or Decrease) Political Equality?" Manuscript. Washington University, St Louis.

Samples, John. 2004. "Three Myths about Voter Turnout in the United States." *Policy Analysis*, no. 524. Washington, DC: Cato Institute.

Smith, Bradley. 2009. "Prepared Testimony." Committee on House Administration Hearing on H.R. 1826 and the Public Financing of Congressional Campaigns." July 30.

State of Arizona. 2009. "Citizens Clean Elections Act." Arizona Revised Statutes (A.R.S.). Title 16, Chapter 6.

Stratmann, Thomas. 2009. "The Effect of Public Financing on the Competitiveness of Elections." Manuscript. George Mason University.

Washington Public Campaigns. 2009. "Why Public Financing of Campaigns?" Available at http://www.washclean.org/Library/Why-Public-Financing08.pdf (accessed August 14, 2009).

Wielechowski, Bill, and Gabrielle LeDoux. 2007. "Clean Elections Bill Introduced." Press release dated May 15.

10

◇ ◇ ◇

Public Financing, Attitudes toward Government and Politics, and Efficacy

Michael G. Miller and Costas Panagopoulos

The strength of democracy can often be gauged by citizens' attitudes and relationship toward their government, elected officials, and the political process. Positive evaluations of government are generally viewed as a desirable feature of democratic governance. In the United States, however, scholars have detected sharp declines in overall levels of public trust or confidence in government since the 1950s (Alford 2001). Americans' political efficacy—the belief that one can influence the political process— has similarly declined over the same period, resulting in lower levels of political participation (Rosenstone and Hansen 1993). Concerns about deteriorating confidence in public figures, institutions, and processes, together with the potential implications of these developments, have ignited spirited intellectual and policy debates. Some analysts contend that reforming the system of campaign financing in the United States would improve Americans' perceptions about the political process. Public financing of elections is often touted as a policy antidote for anemic levels of trust in government and political efficacy.

Proponents of "clean" or "fair" elections programs routinely assert that these initiatives will enhance public perceptions about government and political efficacy. A recent federal proposal for public funding of elections, the Fair Elections Now Act (H.R. 1826), introduced by Rep. John Larson (D-CT) in 2009, explicitly lists seven ways in which the reform would result in the "enhancement of democracy." Among these, the sponsors claim the bill would "restore public confidence in the integrity and fairness of the electoral and legislative processes" and increase "the public's confidence in the accountability of Members to the constituents who elect them." Advocates argue public funding programs would reduce the appearance of corruption or the influence of moneyed interests in the electoral process, thereby strengthening perceptions of government and elected officials.

Despite the fact that reformers frequently conjure up the purported link between public financing and attitudes toward government, surprisingly few systematic assessments of this relationship exist. A recent study that similarly laments this void in the extant scholarly literature and seeks to shed light on this question finds no evidence that campaign finance regulations influence political efficacy (Primo and Milyo 2006). In fact, the authors find that public financing, in particular, may actually exert a negative impact on efficacy levels (Primo and Milyo 2006). This initial finding is compelling and, in some ways, surprising and counterintuitive. Additional empirical investigation is warranted to confirm, contextualize, or update this preliminary conclusion.

In this chapter, we analyze available survey data to reconsider the impact of public financing of elections on attitudes toward government and political efficacy. First, we outline our analytical procedures, arguing that we advance refinements that represent improvements over previous approaches. Following our description of the empirical protocols, we present the results of our analyses and a discussion about their implications. By way of conclusion, we end with a brief summary of the findings and suggestions for subsequent research.

Data and Methodology

Our study focuses on examining the relationship between public funding and mass efficacy in Arizona and Maine, which first implemented full funding systems in the 2000 elections. In those states, candidates may qualify for full public funding by raising a relatively small amount of money from a fixed number of individual contributors. Once they successfully fulfill this requirement, clean elections candidates receive public subsidies sufficient to wage a credible campaign. In return, participating candidates agree to raise no further funding from private sources and to abide by spending limits equal to their subsidy amounts. Because public funding fully supports participating candidates in Arizona and Maine, we anticipate that the capacity of funding programs to affect public sentiment toward government will be most observable in those states. Arizona and Maine therefore seem to be logical places in which to search for a more trusting or efficacious electorate.

We employ survey data from the 2004 National Rolling Cross-Section of the National Annenberg Election Survey (NAES) to advance our analyses. We opt for NAES data because the sample size is sufficiently large to allow for meaningful comparison of the fully funded states of Arizona and Maine with others. The data set was compiled using telephone interviews conducted between October 2003 and November 2004, and contains over 81,000 completed interviews, including 1,455 from Arizona and 553 from Maine. The NAES is a broad survey that included a number of questions designed to measure respondent confidence and trust in government institutions, as well as individual political efficacy.

The NAES data set includes direct measures of confidence in state-level elected officials as well as large samples from individual states. Moreover, the data from 2004 were collected in the third cycle of fully funded state elections in both Arizona and Maine. Taken together these features facilitate the isolation of public funding effects on public opinion of state officials specifically. Given that statewide public funding programs affect elections for these individuals most directly, it is reasonable to expect to find more evidence of an impact for state-level officials compared, for example, to federal officials. Thus we believe that the NAES data allow for an improvement over previous studies in this area (e.g., Primo and Milyo 2006).

We examine respondent attitudes in the fully funded states on several fronts, including trust in government and elected officials as well as confidence in both the legislative and executive branches and state and local institutions. A complete list of the questions we employ to construct our dependent variables can be found in the Appendix; in all cases, the variables are constructed from ordinal data. Accordingly, to determine whether enhanced trust, confidence, or efficacy is related to the presence of full public election funding, we fit a number of fixed-effects ordered logit models. The ordinal data from the political efficacy section (Section M, Subsection B) of the NAES are generally coded from 1 to 4, with higher numbers reflecting more negative responses. For example, on the question "How much trust do you have in the honesty of elected officials in Washington?" the response "a great deal" is coded as 1 while "none" is coded as 4. To aid in interpretation of the models that we describe, we invert the coding of those variables so that higher values reflect more trust and confidence.

In order to determine whether the presence of full public funding is associated with higher levels of confidence, trust, and efficacy, we construct a dichotomous indicator of respondent residency in Arizona or Maine, which we include in the models as an independent variable. To control for other factors that likely influence responses, we also include measures of respondent gender, age, income, personal ideology, employment level, race, citizenship, church attendance, military service, marital and voter registration status, voting history, attention to politics, and the urbanity of the respondent's community. Because we recognize that local or state events or other factors could also affect political attitudes, we fix effects by state.[1]

The variables above are operationalized as follows: We include dummy variables coded 1 if the respondent was male, white, a U.S. citizen, a current or former member of the military, or married (or living as married). We also include separate dichotomous indicators of whether the respondent voted in the previous presidential election, was registered to vote in the 2004 election, was employed full-time or part-time, and attended at least one weekly religious service. We preserve the original coding of the respondent's age in years.

Respondent education, household income, personal political ideology, urbanity, and orientation to politics are all operationalized as ordinal predictors. Education is coded as a nine-category predictor; the referent category is less than an eighth-grade education, and higher values reflect higher education levels. The income variable contains six categories ranging from less than $10,000 to more than $150,000. For urbanity, we code rural as 0, suburban as 1, and urban as 2. Ideology adopts the five-point scale from the NAES question; "very conservative" is the referent category, and higher levels indicate more liberal respondents. We capture how closely respondents report that they "follow what is going on in government and public affairs" on a four-category predictor ranging from "hardly at all" to "most times."

Finally, because we believe that personal ideology in particular is an important determinant of political trust and confidence, we include a multiplicative interaction term to account for the possibility that personal ideology mediates the relationship between public funding and the dependent variables. The coefficients of the interaction component terms, in this case the treatment dummy and the ordinal measure of ideology, reflect the expected effect of those variables when the other equals zero. The interaction term reflects the difference in slope that occurs when public funding is available. If public funding leads to higher levels of trust, for example, we would expect this coefficient to be significant and positive.

Results

Table 10.1 contains the coefficients and standard errors returned by the ordered logit models run on the dependent variables constructed from the questions asking respondents about the extent to which they agree with the following three statements: "Sometimes politics seems so complicated that a

TABLE 10.1.   ESTIMATING THE IMPACT OF FULL PUBLIC FUNDING OF ELECTIONS
             ON POLITICAL EFFICACY (NAES 2004)

	Politics Too Complicated	Have No Say	Candidates Keep Promises
Fully funded state	0.027	−0.356	−2.519*
	(0.225)	(0.409)	(1.114)
Full funding × Ideology	0.052	0.051	0.228
	(0.061)	(0.119)	(0.226)
Ideology	−0.005	0.072*	−0.221*
	(0.010)	(0.018)	(0.040)
Registered voter	−0.078*	−0.187*	0.506*
	(0.033)	(0.058)	(0.164)
Voted 2000	−0.148*	−0.342*	0.042
	(0.031)	(0.058)	(0.120)
Male	−0.392*	0.029	−0.081
	(0.021)	(0.039)	(0.083)
Age	0.015*	0.013*	−0.009*
	(0.001)	(0.001)	(0.003)
Income	−0.101*	−0.056*	−0.010
	(0.006)	(0.011)	(0.022)
Education	−0.185*	−0.096*	0.043*
	(0.005)	(0.009)	(0.019)
Employed full-time	0.066*	−0.007	−0.047
	(0.024)	(0.045)	(0.099)
Employed part-time	0.009	−0.045	0.042
	(0.032)	(0.060)	(0.125)
White	−0.037	−0.144*	0.381*
	(0.028)	(0.052)	(0.108)
Citizen	0.105	0.271*	−0.211
	(0.062)	(0.116)	(0.244)
Church attendance	0.057*	−0.313*	0.157*
	(0.020)	(0.037)	(0.079)
Veteran	−0.044	−0.205*	−0.128
	(0.029)	(0.054)	(0.118)
Married	0.169*	−0.006	0.062
	(0.021)	(0.038)	(0.083)
Urban	−0.099*	−0.020	−0.017
	(0.014)	(0.025)	(0.054)
Follow politics	−0.575*	−0.292*	0.313*
	(0.012)	(0.021)	(0.049)
N	40,271	11,568	2,861
Log likelihood	−51,501	−15,554	−3,191
Pseudo R squared	0.08	0.04	0.03

*Statistical significance at the $p < .05$ level using two-tailed tests.

person like me cannot understand what is going on"; "People like me have no say over what the government does"; and "Candidates try to keep their campaign promises while in office."[2]

Several coefficients are significant in all three models reported in Table 10.1. First, respondents who were registered to vote were less likely to believe that politics is too complicated or that they have no say in government, and they were more likely to believe that candidates try to keep their promises. The same pattern exists for respondents with higher levels of education and those who follow politics closely. The opposite relationship is apparent with age in all three models; older respondents tend to believe that politics is too complicated and that they have no say, and were also less likely to trust that candidates keep campaign promises. Respondents who attended at least one weekly religious service were more likely both to view politics as too complicated to understand and also to trust that candidates try to keep campaign promises.

Certain variables were significant in only one or two of the models reported in Table 10.1. Specifically, respondents who voted in 2000 as well as those with higher incomes were less likely to either view government as too complicated or to believe that they have no say over government affairs. Men were less likely than women to view politics as too complicated to understand, but the opposite is true for those who were employed full-time. Whites were less likely to feel that they have no say and more likely to trust that candidates will keep promises. Contrary to the intuitive expectation, citizens were more likely to believe that they have no say. The opposite is true of veterans. Respondents in more urban areas were less likely to view government as too complicated.

Finally, in both the "have no say" and "keep promises" questions, personal ideology is a significant predictor. Because it is a component variable in an interaction, the ideology coefficient is interpreted as the effect of being increasingly liberal in states for which no public election funding is present. As the positive coefficients indicate, more liberal respondents in the traditionally financed states are also more likely to have low levels of political efficacy and to have less faith that candidates will keep their promises. Neither the interaction term nor the treatment dummy variable achieves significance in either model, leaving little reason to believe that the presence of public funding mediates the relationship between ideology and these factors. In other words, it is reasonable to conclude that more liberal respondents in the publicly funded states would have similar feelings of low efficacy and distrust. In short, the presence of full public funding does not seem to affect the way in which respondents answer the questions presented in Table 10.1.[3]

Table 10.2 contains coefficients and standard errors for the dependent variable constructed from responses to the following question: "How much of the time do you think you can trust the federal government to do what is right?" In addition, we report in Table 10.2 the results of models of respondent confidence in the president and the U.S. Congress, as well as in state and local government. Of the covariates we report in Table 10.2, several are significant in a number of models. Specifically, those who follow politics more closely trust the federal government to a greater degree and also report more confidence in the president, Congress, and their local government officials. The same is true for respondents who attend church at least once a week. Older respondents were less likely to trust the federal government or to report confidence in the president or Congress, but they were more likely to trust their local elected officials. Whites exhibited higher levels of trust as well as greater confidence in the president and Congress, while the opposite is true of U.S. citizens. Men were less likely to trust Congress or state officials than women, but registered voters reported higher levels of confidence in state officials. Those with higher income report more confidence in the president, while those with more education were less confident in both the president and Congress. Respondents with full-time jobs were less likely to trust the government, but the opposite is true of respondents in more urban areas.

Personal ideology is a significant predictor of respondent attitude toward the federal government; liberals were less likely to trust the government in Washington and were also less likely to report confidence in the president or Congress. Given the political atmosphere in 2004, this finding is not surprising. However, as in the models reported in Table 10.1, the interaction term does not achieve significance in any model, indicating that the presence of public election funding does not affect respondent trust or confidence in government.[4]

Conclusion

Overall, and consistent with previous work (Primo and Milyo 2006), we find no association between the presence of full public election funding and trust, confidence, or political efficacy in the mass electorate. Using data from the 2004 National Annenberg Election Study, we cannot conclude that there exist linkages between public funding and increased positive feelings toward government, nor can we demonstrate that persistent negative feelings among the electorate led to the referendum passage of clean elections laws in Arizona and Maine.

TABLE 10.2. ESTIMATING THE IMPACT OF FULL PUBLIC FUNDING OF ELECTIONS
ON ATTITUDES TOWARD GOVERNMENT AND ELECTED OFFICIALS
(NAES 2004)

	Trust Federal Government	Confidence in Federal Executive	Confidence in U.S. Congress	Confidence in State Officials	Confidence in Local Officials
Fully funded state	0.947	−0.788	−0.182	1.082	1.922
	(0.583)	(0.556)	(0.531)	(1.020)	(1.015)
Full funding × Ideology	−0.178	0.002	−0.023	−0.049	−0.048
	(0.177)	(0.121)	(0.124)	(0.232)	(0.227)
Ideology	−0.213*	−0.650*	−0.128*	−0.016	0.0001
	(0.026)	(0.021)	(0.020)	(0.038)	(0.038)
Registered Voter	0.048	0.069	−0.022	0.257*	0.005
	(0.082)	(0.060)	(0.061)	(0.125)	(0.122)
Voted 2000	0.099	0.021	−0.004	−0.103	−0.001
	(0.081)	(0.061)	(0.062)	(0.123)	(0.119)
Male	0.086	−0.066	−0.150*	−0.193*	−0.049
	(0.054)	(0.041)	(0.042)	(0.081)	(0.080)
Age	−0.011*	−0.011*	−0.009*	−0.001	0.010*
	(0.002)	(0.001)	(0.001)	(0.003)	(0.003)
Income	0.027	0.066*	0.019	0.006	0.031
	(0.015)	(0.011)	(0.012)	(0.022)	(0.022)
Education	−0.005	−0.047*	−0.024*	−0.008	0.034
	(0.012)	(0.009)	(0.010)	(0.019)	(0.018)
Employed full-time	−0.128*	0.020	−0.048	−0.147	−0.128
	(0.062)	(0.048)	(0.049)	(0.096)	(0.094)
Employed part-time	−0.066	−0.006	−0.080	−0.057	0.001
	(0.084)	(0.064)	(0.065)	(0.125)	(0.122)
White	0.447*	0.633*	0.181*	0.109	0.167
	(0.073)	(0.055)	(0.056)	(0.111)	(0.109)
Citizen	−0.871*	−0.491*	−0.734*	0.0003	−0.457
	(0.150)	(0.119)	(0.128)	(0.249)	(0.244)
Church attendance	0.136*	0.329*	0.230*	0.101	0.172*
	(0.051)	(0.040)	(0.040)	(0.078)	(0.077)
Veteran	0.043	0.047	−0.103	−0.051	−0.209
	(0.075)	(0.058)	(0.059)	(0.113)	(0.112)
Married	0.102	0.010	−0.034	0.118	0.062
	(0.054)	(0.041)	(0.042)	(0.080)	(0.079)
Urban	0.071*	−0.016	0.016	−0.049	−0.004
	(0.034)	(0.027)	(0.028)	(0.053)	(0.052)
Follow Politics	0.219*	0.102*	0.086*	0.088	0.128*
	(0.030)	(0.023)	(0.023)	(0.045)	(0.044)
N	7,901	11,406	11,374	3,188	3,108
Log likelihood	−6,648	−12,212	−11,442	−3,288	−3,481
Pseudo R squared	0.03	0.07	0.01	0.03	0.02

*Statistical significance at the $p < .05$ level using two-tailed tests.

One possible explanation for the failure to detect public funding effects on attitudes toward government and efficacy levels is the general lack of public awareness about the existence of these programs. The public tends to pay little attention to changes in campaign finance law generally (Primo 2002). For instance, Woolley and Vercellotti (2007) report that in New Jersey, which has been running full-funding pilot programs in some legislative districts since 2005, approximately 80 percent of respondents in eligible districts are unaware of the program's existence despite a focused public policy experiment that garnered substantial news coverage. In other words, it is unreasonable to expect that mass knowledge *itself* of the fact that elections are publicly funded causes higher trust, efficacy, and confidence.

That is not to say that a linkage is impossible. It is reasonable to expect that less observable, indirect conditions may provide cues to the electorate that will lead to higher levels of confidence. For instance, if candidate behavior is altered in the manner Miller suggests elsewhere in this volume, fully funded candidates may parlay a greater capacity for direct mobilization into more intimate relationships with citizens. Still, even the inclusion of additional interactions in the models we report yields no evidence that education or general political interest mediates the relationship between public funding and the dependent variables (see note 1). Taken together, it remains possible that the null finding reflects an improvement over negative attitudes that existed prior to implementation of full funding in the states, but our data do not allow us to analyze trends over time. Future analysis should track efficacy and trust in the fully funded states before and after passage.

Appendix: Questions

NAES Variable	Question Topic	Question Wording
cMB01	Trust government (Wording 1)	Thinking about the federal government in Washington, how much of the time do you think you can trust the federal government to do what is right—always, most of the time, or some of the time?
cMB02	Trust government (Wording 2)	Thinking about the federal government in Washington, how much of the time do you think you can trust the federal government to do what is right—always, most of the time, some of the time, or never?
cMB05	Confidence in executive branch	Please tell me how much confidence you have in the executive branch of the federal government; this includes the office of the president and all the federal agencies and departments—do you have a great deal, a fair amount, not too much, or none at all?

NAES Variable	Question Topic	Question Wording
cMB06	Confidence in legislative branch	Please tell me how much confidence you have in the legislative branch of the federal government, that is, the U.S. Congress—do you have a great deal, a fair amount, not too much, or none at all?
cMB08	Confidence in state elected officials	Please tell me how much confidence you have in elected officials in your state—do you have a great deal, a fair amount, not too much, or none at all?
cMB09	Confidence in local government	Please tell me how much confidence you have in the government of the city or town where you live—do you have a great deal, a fair amount, not too much, or none at all?
cMB10	Politics too complicated	Do you agree or disagree that sometimes politics seems so complicated that a person like me cannot really understand what is going on?
cMB11	People like me have no say in government	Do you agree or disagree that people like me have no say over what the government does?
cMB15	Candidates try to keep promises	How often do you think candidates try to keep their campaign promises once they are in office—always, most of the time, some of the time, rarely, or never?

NOTES

1. We note we obtain substantively similar results when we exclude state fixed effects. Data available upon request.

2. Sample sizes differ across models because of the length of the survey window for the dependent variables of interest, which is considerably longer for some questions. For example, the "trust government" question was asked between October 2003 and September 2004, whereas "confidence in state and local government" questions were asked only between September and December 2003.

3. Note that we also estimated alternative specifications that excluded the interaction terms but found no substantive differences in terms of the impact of public funding. For simplicity, we report only the models that incorporate the interactions. Data available upon request.

4. Note that neither restricting the analysis to citizens alone nor interacting public funding with political interest or education levels changes the substantive (null) results. Data available from the authors upon request.

REFERENCES

Alford, John R. 2001. "We're All in This Together: The Decline of Trust in Government, 1958–1996." In *What Is It about Government that Americans Dislike?* ed. John R. Hibbing and Elizabeth Theiss-Morse. Cambridge, UK: Cambridge University Press, 28–46.

Primo, David. 2002. "Public Opinion and Campaign Finance." *Independent Review* 7 (2): 207–219.

Primo, David, and Jeffrey Milyo. 2006. "Campaign Finance Laws and Political Efficacy: Evidence from the States." *Election Law Journal* 5 (1): 23–39.

Rosenstone, S. J., and M. J. Hansen. 1993. *Mobilization, Participation and Democracy in America*. New York: Macmillan.

Woolley, Peter, and Tim Vercellotti. 2007. "Public Attitudes toward the Clean Elections Initiative." Available at http://eagletonpoll.rutgers.edu/polls/CE_FinalReport_11_07.pdf (accessed August 15, 2009).

Conclusion

The Future of Public Financing in American Elections

Costas Panagopoulos

The integrity of the electoral process is of paramount importance in democratic polities. In the United States, reformers remain vigilant to ensure that imperfections in the political arena are speedily rectified to avoid compromising democracy. In recent decades, advocates have promoted the adoption of public financing measures in pursuit of this goal. In an era of swelling campaign spending and incumbent dominance, public-funding-for-elections policies are designed to reduce the potential for corruption, heighten candidate responsiveness and electoral competition, and enhance citizens' relationships with government, among other objectives.

The selections included in this volume highlight the complexities associated with proposals for publicly financed campaigns. In Part I, the authors showcase the breadth of options available to reformers and demonstrate the considerable variation that exists across states and municipalities that have adopted public funding programs. It is also clear that efforts are on the mount in jurisdictions across the nation, including in the U.S. Congress, to promote clean elections proposals aggressively. In Chapter 4, Weissman and Hassan (with assistance from Santucci) demonstrate that the public generally favors such reforms, but Americans are apprehensive about financing such initiatives using tax dollars and are reluctant to contribute directly to support public funding programs. Despite the growing number of jurisdictions with clean elections programs, these reservations on the part of the public have the capacity to impede further progress on this score. With programs now in place for long periods in certain states, proponents of public funding programs will be compelled to demonstrate that the initiatives are achieving their objectives.

The selections in Part II speak directly to this question. Authors ask, and empirically assess, whether public funding programs actually influence levels of electoral competition, candidate behavior, or citizen attitudes and political activity. Overall, the evidence does not necessarily point clearly in a single direction. Empirical support for the notion that public financing boosts electoral competition is mixed. Voter attitudes and behavior do not appear to be influenced much by public funding programs, and there are even indications that the impact of public financing of campaigns is perverse. Nevertheless, candidates appear to be responsive to public financing programs, and in Chapter 8 Miller shows that public funding enables candidates to devote more time to voter mobilization and direct interactions with constituents. Even as clear evidence that public funding is effective across the board is elusive, some of the effects described by the authors have the potential to enhance democratic responsiveness and representation.

The chapters in this volume suggest that there may be shortcomings associated with the effectiveness of public financing programs along some dimensions, but that there are also hopeful prospects. If anything, the preceding chapters may help to temper claims advanced by both critics and supporters of publicly financed campaign proposals. Perhaps a more constructive view would enable the public to revise its expectations about what public funding has the capacity to achieve. Moreover, the failure of public funding programs to attain certain objectives may inspire the introduction and adoption of refined policies that integrate elements that are most successful. Or the policies may simply need more time to bear fruit. In many respects, public financing programs remain ongoing policy experiments that require intensive scrutiny, evaluation, and assessment. Rigorous scholarly inquiry is necessary to monitor changes and developments. The current volume is compiled in this spirit.

Contributors

Conor Dowling, Ph.D., is a postdoctoral fellow at the Institution for Social and Policy Studies at Yale University.

R. Sam Garrett, Ph.D., is a senior researcher with the Congressional Research Service.

Ruth A. Hassan is a researcher at the Campaign Finance Institute.

Matthew L. Jacobsmeier, Ph.D., is an assistant professor of political science at the University of New Orleans.

Jeffrey Kraus, Ph.D., is a professor of political science and provost at Wagner College.

Michael Malbin, Ph.D., is a professor of political science at the State University of New York at Albany and the director of the Campaign Finance Institute.

Michael G. Miller, Ph.D., is an assistant professor of political science at the University of Illinois at Springfield.

Jeffrey Milyo, Ph.D., is a professor of economics and the Middlebush Chair in the Social Sciences at the University of Missouri.

Costas Panagopoulos, Ph.D., is an assistant professor of political science and the director of the Center for Electoral Politics and Democracy at Fordham University.

David M. Primo, Ph.D., is an associate professor of political science at the University of Rochester.

Robert M. Stern, Ph.D., is the president of the Center for Governmental Studies.

Stephen R. Weissman, Ph.D., is a researcher at the Campaign Finance Institute.

Index

Note: Page numbers followed by t *refer to tables.*

Aggregate large donors, 56–57
Aggregate small donors, 53, 54t
Allen, Sen. James, 23
Americans for Campaign Reform, 38, 226
Analysis Group survey on public campaign financing, 130–131, 132t, 136–137
Arizona: public attitudes in, 239–246, 242t; public campaign financing in, 63, 66–67, 69, 71, 73n5, 206, 220, 226–227; state legislative election campaigns in, 207–208, 208t, 209–220, 210t, 211t, 213t, 215t, 221t; voter turnout in, 228, 228t
Attitudes. *See* Public attitudes toward government; Public attitudes toward public financing

Barron, Charles, 161
Bauer, Gary, 41
Bipartisan Campaign Reform Act (BCRA), 13, 14, 16–17, 31, 46
Bloc grants for full public financing, 68–70
Bloomberg, Michael, 156, 170
Boren, Sen. David, 26, 29
Broadcast communications, 20; congressional-level study of, 180–182; federally funded vouchers for, 27; mayoral-level studies of, 179–180; in New York City Council campaigns, 158–159
Brown, Jerry, 41
Buchanan, Patrick, 41, 42

Buckley v. Valeo, 16, 25, 37, 40, 64, 151, 229
Bundlers, 12, 56, 59; in New York City elections, 154–157, 167–169, 171n14
Bush, Pres. George H. W.: 1980 campaign of, 41, 42; S. 3 veto by, 30
Bush, Pres. George W., 2, 53–55; refusal of public funds by, 4, 37, 46, 47; 2000 campaign of, 42, 44

California Clean Money Campaign, 227
Campaign Finance Institute, 5, 6
Candidate-centered campaign, 11–12
Cannon, Sen. Howard, 23–24
Capehart, Sen. Homer, 20
Carter, Pres. James Earl, 25–26; 1976 campaign of, 41, 43, 45–46
CBS News survey on public campaign financing, 136, 136t
CBS/*New York Times* polls on public campaign financing, 135t, 136, 137, 137t, 139t
Center for Governmental Studies, 6
Chapel Hill, North Carolina, public campaign financing in, 62, 63
Citizens' attitudes. *See* Public attitudes toward government; Public attitudes toward public financing
Citizens' Clean Elections Act, 220, 226–227
Citizens United v. Federal Election Commission, 15

Clinton, Pres. William, 31, 42, 44, 176
Clinton, Sen. Hillary, 47–49, 48t, 50t, 51–54, 54t
Collins, Sen. Susan, 60
Common Cause, 226–228
Competition, 176–183; in gubernatorial elections (*see* Gubernatorial elections); incumbency and, 177–178; mayoral-level studies of, 179–180; New York City Campaign Finance Act and, 150–152, 162–166, 164t, 168–169; observational studies of, 178; public financing and, 40–42; randomized field experiments on, 178–182; in state legislative elections, 206–208, 218, 235 (*see also* State legislative elections)
Confidence in government, 24–25, 226, 227, 229, 238–246, 245t
Congressional campaign financing, 16–32; Federal Election Campaign Act regulations on, 16–17; 1956 public financing legislation and, 16, 18–21; 1960s public financing legislation and, 20–21; 1970s public financing legislation and, 17t, 21–26; 1980s public financing legislation and, 26; 1990s public financing legislation and, 17t–18t, 26–31; self-financing and, 16; 2007–2008 public financing legislation and, 31–32; winning-campaign spending and, 14, 15t
Congressional elections (2006), Spanish-language radio advertisements in, 180–182
Congressional elections (2008), spending for, 14–15, 15t
Congressional elections (2010), spending for, 15
Connecticut, public campaign financing in, 63, 69, 71
Contribution limits: in Bipartisan Campaign Reform Act, 13–14, 14t, 40, 46, 56; in New York City Campaign Finance Act, 147, 149–150, 153–154; in state public campaign financing, 72, 96t–102t
Coordinated expenditures, 11, 57, 157
Corporations, 2, 15, 137, 150, 155, 167, 167t, 171n11
Corruption: risk for, 20; risk of, 12; Sen. Kennedy on, 22–23; Sen. Mondale on, 23
Crotty, Jane, 156

Dean, Gov. Howard, 42, 48, 48t, 54t; Internet use by, 46; refusal of public funds by, 4, 37, 44
Democracy, 21, 59–60
Dinkins, David, 155, 157, 158
Dole, Sen. Robert, 1996 campaign of, 43–44

Domenici, Sen. Pete, 25
Durbin, Sen. Richard, 31, 60

Edwards, Sen. John, 42, 48t, 50t, 51, 54t
Eristoff, Andrew S., 156

Fair Elections Now Act, 31, 32, 238–239
Federal Election Campaign Act (FECA), 13–14, 14t, 16–17, 19, 21, 23–24, 40
Feingold, Sen. Russell, 2, 13–14, 60
Ferrer, Fernando, mayoral campaign of, 155, 156, 160
First Amendment, 16, 30, 37, 39, 157
Fisher, Kenneth, 169
501(c), 2, 15
527 group, 2, 15
Florida, public campaign financing in, 71
Forbes, Steve, 3–4, 43
Ford, Gerald R., 1976 campaign of, 45–46
Front-loading, 42–45, 46
"Functional equivalency," 52–57
Fund-raising, 1–2

Gallup polls, on public campaign financing, 125–127, 126t, 134–137, 135t
Garamendi, Lt. Gov. John, 2
Gejdenson, Rep. Sam, 29, 31
Gillibrand, Rep. Kirsten, 2
Giuliani, Rudy: mayoral campaign of, 154, 157, 158; presidential campaign of, 48, 48t, 49, 50t, 54t
Goldin, Harrison J., 148, 153–154
Goldwater, Sen. Barry, 23
Greenberg, Quinlan, Rossner Research poll: on public campaign financing, 131, 132, 134t; on taxpayer checkoff, 139–140, 141t–142t
Gubernatorial elections, 184–204; ballot access laws in, 192–194, 198, 199t, 200; candidate entry in, 185–189, 194–196, 195t, 196t, 197t; candidate typology in, 184, 188–190, 191t; decision-making calculus for, 185–187; economic factors in, 194; experienced vs. amateur candidates for, 188–190, 191t, 196–200, 197t, 199t; incumbency and, 187, 189; incumbent-party challengers in, 194, 195t, 197t, 199, 199t, 201; occupied-seat, 194–195, 195t, 197–198; open-seat, 187–189, 196–198, 196t, 197t; out-party challengers in, 194, 195t, 196t, 199t; party endorsements in, 193, 195t, 197, 197t; petition requirements in, 200, 201; state-specific funding for, 191–194, 191t; term limits and, 193,

195t, 198; voter turnout in, 229–230, 233–235, 233t, 234t

Hart, Gary, 1984 campaign of, 41
Housekeeping index, 209–210, 215–217, 215t
H.R. 3 (1993), 18t, 30–31
H.R. 1614 (2008), 31
H.R. 1826 (2010), 31, 32
H.R. 2817 (2008), 31
H.R. 3750 (1991), 17t, 29
H.R. 5400 (1990), 17t, 28
H.R. 6116 (2010), 31, 32
H.R. 11104 (1973), 17t, 21
Huckabee, Mike, 48, 48t, 50t, 54t

Ideology, 15, 241, 242t, 243, 244
Incumbency: campaign finance reform and, 177–178; in gubernatorial elections, 187, 189; in New York City elections, 159–160, 164, 168–169; in state legislative elections, 212, 215–216, 215t, 217, 222n17
Independent expenditures: New York City public campaign financing and, 157; state public campaign financing and, 71–72, 103t–105t
Intermediaries, 147, 154–157, 167, 168, 171n14
Internet: Barack Obama's use of, 40, 49, 51, 52, 55, 59; Howard Dean's use of, 46; John Kerry's use of, 46
Iowa caucus, 41, 43, 45

Jackson, Jesse, 41, 42
Joint fund-raising committees, 56–57

Kennedy, Sen. Edward, 21–23
Kerrey, Sen. Bob, 38–40
Kerry, Sen. John, 42, 47, 48, 54t; Internet use by, 46; refusal of public funds by, 4, 37, 44
Koch, Mayor Edward I., 148, 153–154, 158, 171n16

Lang, Todd, 227
Large contributions: in New York City elections, 149–150, 153–155, 154t, 157; in 2008 presidential primary, 49–52, 50t, 54t, 56–57
Larson, Rep. John, 31, 238
Lauder, Ronald, mayoral campaign of, 155–156
Leichter, Franz, 148–149, 170n3
Lobbyists, 63, 137, 149, 154, 168, 205
Local municipality public campaign financing, 62–73, 106t–120t. See also New York City Campaign Finance Act
Los Angeles Times survey, on public campaign financing, 131, 133t

Maine: public attitudes in, 239–246, 242t; public campaign financing in, 63, 69, 71, 206, 220–221; state legislative election campaigns in, 207–220, 208t, 210t, 211t, 213t, 215t, 221t; voter turnout in, 228, 228t
Maine Clean Elections Act, 220–221, 227
Marin Clean Elections, 227
Mark-Viverito, Melissa, 157
Maryland: campaign finance regulation in, 210; state legislative election campaigns in, 209–220, 210t, 211t, 215t
Massachusetts, public campaign financing in, 63–64, 73n3
McCain, Sen. John, 16–17; acceptance of public funds by, 4, 7n, 37; federal campaign finance legislation of, 2, 13–14; 2000 campaign of, 42, 44; 2008 campaign of, 47–49, 48t, 50t, 52, 53, 54t, 55–57
McConnell, Sen. Mitch, 27–28
Mellman Group surveys on public campaign financing, 127–130, 128t–130t
Messinger, Ruth, 158, 160
Miami-Dade County, Florida, public campaign financing in, 63
Michigan, public campaign financing in, 71
Millard, Charles, 160
Miller, Gifford, mayoral campaign of, 155
Minnesota, public campaign financing in, 62, 64, 66, 70–71, 74n10
Mitchell, Sen. George, 27
Mondale, Vice Pres. Walter, 23, 41

National Rolling Cross-Section of the National Annenberg Election Survey (NAES), 240, 246–247
NBC/Wall Street Journal poll on public campaign financing, 137, 138t
Nebraska, public campaign financing in, 67
Nelson, Michael, 161
Neuberger, Sen. Richard, 16, 18–23, 32
New Hampshire Primary, 41, 43, 45
New Jersey, public campaign financing in, 62, 64
New Mexico, public campaign financing in, 63, 69, 71
New York City Campaign Finance Act, 6, 147–175; Board membership and, 149, 169, 170n6, 172n28; candidate qualification for, 151; competition and, 150–152, 162–166, 164t, 165t, 168–169; contribution limits of, 149–150, 153–154; election results and, 153–166; expenditure limits of, 150, 150t, 158–162, 159t, 160t, 161, 168;

New York City Campaign Finance Act (*cont.*)
five-to-one match of, 151, 152; four-to-one
match of, 151–152, 171n10; government-con-
nected business contributions and, 167, 167t;
intermediary fund raising and, 154–157,
167, 171n14; one-to-one match of, 151; passage of, 148–149; prohibition of corporate
contributions and, 155, 167, 167t, 171n11;
public disclosure requirement of, 152–153;
self-financed campaigns and, 156, 166, 169,
170; six-to-one match of, 59, 69, 152, 171n10;
two-to-one match of, 151, 166
New York City Council elections: campaign
expenditures for, 158–162, 159t, 160t; competitive campaigns for, 162–166, 164t, 165t;
debates for, 166; incumbency and, 159–160,
164; independent expenditures for, 157; one-
sided campaigns and, 160–162; self-financed
campaigns for, 156, 166, 169; term limits
and, 163–164; voter guides for, 166
Nixon, Pres. Richard M., 21, 40, 126
North Carolina, public campaign financing in,
62, 69, 71

Obama, Pres. Barack: Internet use by, 40, 49,
51, 52, 59; joint fund-raising for, 57; prenomination fund-raising by, 45, 47–49, 48t,
50t, 51–56, 54t; refusal of public funds by,
4, 37, 124
Obey, Rep. David, 31

Palma, Annabel, 157
Party committees, contribution limits for, 14t
Patients' bill of rights, polling on, 142
Patterson, Gov. David, 2
Paul, Ron, 48, 48t, 49, 50t, 54t
Personal ideology, 241, 242t, 243, 244
Political action committee (PAC), 2, 12; contri-
butions from, 14t, 15, 26, 29, 30; in Mary-
land, 210; polling on, 131, 137; vote buying
and, 149; voter turnout and, 232
Political efficacy, public perceptions of, 6, 219,
238–248, 242t
Political parties, 11–12; individual contributions through, 23, 157; joint fund-raising
committees of, 57; public funds for, 18–19;
unlimited spending by, 39
Polling. *See at* Public attitudes
Portland, Oregon, public campaign financing in, 63
Presidential campaign public financing, 3–4;
competition and, 40–42; front-loading and,
42–45; general election, 37; goals of, 40–46;
1971 legislation and, 21; 1960s legislation

and, 20–21; opting out of, 3–4, 37–40,
42–45; prenomination, 36–37, 40, 42–45;
small donor participation and, 45–46; spending limits and, 42–45; Theodore Roosevelt's
proposal for, 11–12; 2008 collapse of, 37–39
Presidential election (2008), 47–57; joint fund-
raising committees in, 56–57; large contributions to, 49–52, 50t, 54t; prenomination
fund-raising for, 47–56, 48t, 50t, 54t; refusal
of public financing for, 3–4, 37–40; small
contributions to, 49–56, 50t, 54t, 59
Presidential Election Campaign Fund, 125, 131,
139–140
Presidential election primaries, 42–45, 47–56,
48t, 50t, 54t
Public attitudes toward government, 238–248,
242t, 245t; in Arizona, 239–246, 242t, 245t;
on confidence in government, 240, 244,
245t; in Maine, 239–246, 242t, 245t; personal ideology and, 241, 242t, 243, 244;
socioeconomic factors and, 241, 242t, 243;
on trust in, 240, 244, 245t
Public attitudes toward public financing, 3,
124–143, 238–248; Analysis Group survey for, 130–131, 132t, 136–137; CBS News
survey for, 136, 136t; CBS/*New York Times*
polls for, 135t, 136, 137, 137t, 139t; Gallup polls for, 125–127, 126t, 134–137, 139t;
Greenberg, Quinlan, Rossner Research polls
for, 131, 132, 134t, 139–140, 141t–142t; *Los
Angeles Times* survey for, 131, 133t; Mellman Group surveys for, 127–130, 128t, 129t,
130t; NBC/*Wall Street Journal* poll for, 137,
138t; negative-findings polls (1993–2008),
133–139, 135t, 136t; polling design and,
124–125, 140, 142; positive-findings polls
(1993–2008), 125–133, 126t, 128t–130t,
132t, 133t; *USA Today* polls for, 135, 135t,
137, 139t
Public campaign financing, 2–3; advocates of,
3, 12, 15–16, 176–177, 226, 238–239; in
congressional elections, 16–32 (*see also* Congressional campaign financing); functional
equivalence of, 52–57; future of, 249–250;
in gubernatorial elections, 184–204 (*see also*
Gubernatorial elections); in local municipality elections, 62–73, 106t–110t, 111t–116t,
117t–120t; in 1956, 20; in 1990s, 27–30; in
1974, 24–25; opponents of, 12–13, 177; in
presidential elections, 3–4 (*see also* Presidential campaign public financing); public attitudes toward (*see* Public attitudes toward
public financing); in state elections, 62–73,
184–224 (*see also* Gubernatorial elections;

State legislative elections; State public campaign financing); in 2008, 38–39; voter turnout and, 226–232 (*see also* Voter turnout)

Radio. *See* Broadcast communications
Reagan, Pres. Ronald, 41–43
Repeat contributions, 55–56
Revenue Act (1971), 22
Rhode Island, public campaign financing in, 71
Rhode Islanders for Fair Elections, 227
Robertson, Pat, 41
Romney, Mitt, 48, 48t, 49, 50t, 54t
Roosevelt, Pres. Theodore, 11–12, 16, 18, 19
Roper Center for Public Opinion Research, 142–143
Rose, Rep. Charles, 29–30
Rudman, Sen. Warren, 226

S. 3 (1991), 17t, 28–29
S. 3 (1992), 18t, 30–31
S. 3 (1993), 18t, 30–31
S. 137 (1990), 17t, 26–27
S. 372 (1973), 22, 24
S. 752 (2010), 31, 32
S. 1285 (2008), 31
S. 3044 (1974), 17t, 23–25
S. 3242 (1956), 16, 18–21
S.Amdt. 651 (1973), 17t, 21–22
Self-financing: for congressional campaigns, 16; for New York City campaigns, 155–156, 166
Service Employees International Union Local 1199, 157
Simpson, Sen. Alan, 29
Small contributions, 41, 45–46, 59, 60; definitions of, 49, 53; Internet-based, 46, 49; for matching-funds financing, 29, 68–69; in 2008 presidential primary, 49–56, 50t, 54t
Smith, Bradley, 38
Soft money, 26, 34, 131
Spanish-language radio advertisements, 180–182
Special interests, 125, 127, 136, 155, 226
Specter, Sen. Arlen, 60
Spending limits: *Buckley v. Valeo* on, 16, 25, 37, 40; in New York City Campaign Finance Act, 150, 150t, 157–162, 159t, 160t, 166; opting out and, 42–45; polling on, 127, 129, 129t, 137–138, 138t, 142; ranges of, 57–60; Rep. Rose on, 29–30; Sen. Kerrey on, 38–39; Sen. Mitchell on, 27; in state public campaign financing, 70–72
State legislative elections, 205–224; in Arizona, 207–220, 208t, 210t, 211t, 213t, 215t, 221t; candidate time allocation in, 210–214, 211t,

213t, 215t, 216–218; challenger-incumbent spending gap in, 207–208, 208t; challenger vs. incumbent in, 212, 215–217, 215t; competition and, 206–208; contributions to, 210, 210t; face-to-face campaigning in, 207; in Maine, 207–220, 208t, 210t, 211t, 213t, 215t, 221t; in Maryland, 209–220, 210t, 211t, 215t; non–publicly funded candidates in, 214–215; voter turnout in, 230–235, 233t, 234t
State public campaign financing, 3, 62–73; bloc grant funds allocation for, 69–70; candidate qualification for, 67–68, 90t–95t; contribution limits for, 72, 96t–102t; eligibility for, 64–65, 65t; funds allocation for, 68–70, 75t–89t; funds sources for, 65–67, 75t–89t; general fund for, 65–66; for gubernatorial elections (*see* Gubernatorial elections); independent expenditures and, 71–72, 103t–105t; for legislative elections (*see* State legislative elections); matching funds allocation for, 68–69; opponent spending and, 71, 103t–105t; partial vs. full, 63–64, 67–70; spending ceilings for, 67, 70–72, 90t–95t; voter turnout and, 225–237 (*see also* Voter turnout)
Stein, Andrew, 148, 156
Stevenson, Sen. Adlai, 23, 24
Stringer, Scott, 157
Swift, Rep. Al, 28

Tax add-ons, 66
Tax checkoff: federal, 3, 22, 66; polling on, 139–143, 140t–142t; state, 66, 75t–90t
Thomas, Rep. Bill, 30
Thompson, William, Jr., 156
Tierney, Rep. John, 31
Trust in government, 240, 244, 245t
Tsongas, Paul, 42
Tucson, Arizona, public campaign financing in, 62
Turnout. *See* Voter turnout

Ullman, Rep. Albert, 21
Unions, 2, 15, 26, 52, 156, 157
USA Today polls on public campaign financing, 135, 135t, 137, 139t

Vallone, Peter, 160
Vermont, public campaign financing in, 68, 71
Voter turnout, 3, 6, 225–237; in Arizona, 228, 228t; in gubernatorial elections, 229–230, 233–235, 233t, 234t; in Maine, 228, 228t; models of, 231–235, 233t, 234t; New York City Campaign Finance Act and, 147, 160, 169, 179;

4

Voter turnout (*cont.*)
  public financing and, 226–232; in state
  legislative elections, 230–236, 233t, 234t
  (*see also* State legislative elections); by voting-age population, 229, 234–235; by voting-eligible population, 230, 233–235, 233t,
  234t

Watergate, 21–26, 129
Weiner, Anthony, mayoral campaign of, 155
Wertheimer, Fred, 59–60
Whitehead, John, 161
Wisconsin, public campaign financing in, 57,
  65, 65t, 66, 71, 187, 192
Working Families Party, 157